Teaching with Hacker Handbooks

Topics, Strategies, and Lesson Plans

D1487418

Marcy Carbajal Van Horn
formerly of St. Edward's University

Jonathan S. Cullick
Northern Kentucky University

Sara McCurry
Shasta College

With contributions from

Elizabeth Canfield
Virginia Commonwealth University

Dànielle Nicole DeVoss
Michigan State University

Nancy Sommers
Harvard University

Terry Myers Zawacki
George Mason University

Bedford / St. Martin's
Boston ◆ New York

Manufactured in the United States of America.

8 7 6 5 4 3
f e d c b a

For information, write: Bedford/St. Martin's, 75 Arlington Street, Boston, MA 02116 (617-399-4000)

ISBN 978-1-4576-1829-1

Foreword

Dear Colleagues:

As the lead author of the current editions of Hacker/Sommers handbooks, I have traveled around the United States, talking with students and teachers at colleges and universities. It is a pleasure to watch instructors in action and to meet so many dedicated teachers who develop innovative ways to integrate Hacker/Sommers handbooks into their courses. At every school I visit, we discuss the best practices for teaching academic writing, effective approaches for meeting the needs of today's students, and time-saving methods for reading and responding to student writing. Teachers seek practical solutions to real classroom challenges and are eager to learn from one another.

Teaching with Hacker Handbooks, written by Marcy Carbajal Van Horn, formerly of St. Edward's University; Jonathan S. Cullick of Northern Kentucky University; and Sara McCurry of Shasta College, with contributions from experienced teachers of academic writing, provides a wealth of ideas for integrating the lessons of Hacker/Sommers handbooks into your classroom. We've chosen these lessons in response to specific classroom needs — designing effective assignments, working with multilingual writers, responding to student writers, for example — and because we know that the more students rely on their handbook and learn from its lessons, the more effective they become as writers. Teaching with Hacker Handbooks offers strategies, examples, and lesson plans to ensure that the handbook becomes a used and useful reference, both for students and instructors.

Teaching is a collaborative enterprise, and we've designed Teaching with Hacker Handbooks so that instructors can learn from their fellow practitioners. I would certainly have benefited from such a resource during my first year teaching composition, when I was learning each lesson along with my students, sometimes (but not always) one step ahead. This second edition was developed with feedback from colleagues who have used it in teacher training workshops and to enrich their own teaching practices. I know that the wisdom and practical knowledge this second edition offers will appeal to both novice and veteran teachers looking to put Hacker/Sommers handbooks to work in their classrooms.

With all good wishes,
Nancy Sommers

Introduction to *Teaching with Hacker Handbooks*

Teaching with Hacker Handbooks *contains much of the information I learned in bits and pieces, through trial and error, and from speaking in the hallways with senior faculty between classes or at professional development activities. . . . [The book]* presents everything you need to know before you start your first class.

— Denise Coulter, Atlantic Cape Community College

At the beginning of each term, instructors of college-level writing courses accept a daunting task: to ensure that students can successfully produce college-level writing during and after the course. We do this by addressing global issues such as critical thinking, argument, research, revision, citation, and logic — and more local concerns such as grammar, punctuation, and sentence style. Those of us who love this profession know that its challenges are outweighed by its rewards, but we also have learned (sometimes the hard way) that to succeed in meeting all the objectives of a writing course in the time available, we need excellent, accessible resources for our students and for ourselves. *Teaching with Hacker Handbooks* supports both new and seasoned composition instructors who are striving to help their students get the most out of their handbook and their course.

The Role of the Handbook in the Course

If you have already taught composition courses, you will be familiar with some of the common questions students ask: "When is it okay to use *I* in my writing?" "How can I revise choppy sentences?" "How do I cite an article I found on a Web site?" It is gratifying when students ask these questions because it shows that they care about their academic writing and genuinely want to improve their work. What happens, then, when our students go home and begin to work on their papers? In a perfect world, they will turn to a reliable handbook, such as any of those in the Hacker/Sommers franchise, for help. They will take responsibility for their choices as writers and view seeking out reliable answers to their questions as an integral part of their writing process. But many students are unfamiliar with references for writers. They need assignments and class activities to connect their handbook to their work in the course and their growth as writers. Without a reliable handbook, they may make uninformed guesses or turn to less authoritative online resources for help. Worse still, they may not pursue their questions at all.

Assigning a Hacker/Sommers handbook will benefit your students in many ways. Integrating it into your daily lesson plans puts students in a position to discover that familiarity with their handbook helps them improve and refine their writing. It also helps new college writers navigate the trickier aspects of documentation or grammar. The more opportunities students have to use the handbook on a regular basis in class, the better the chances that they will use the handbook on their own, building a habit of self-reliance. Additionally, a handbook helps create a common language about writing in the course. For example, many of us have taught thesis statements using a variety of terms such as *assertion, theme, central idea,* or *claim.* As instructors, we can readily accommodate fluctuating terminology from class to class or institution to institution because we are firmly grounded in the basic concept of thesis construction. For our students, however, such variations in terminology can be confusing or frustrating. The handbook can provide a common vocabulary, helping your students to understand your comments on the writing process in general and on their writing in particular, to have meaningful discussions with each other about their writing during peer reviews, and to apply commentary confidently as they revise their papers. Incorporating a handbook and teaching from it throughout the course can empower your students to take ownership of their writing both in and beyond the classroom.

The Role of the Handbook in the Writing Program

In addition to fostering students' sense of responsibility for and engagement in their own work, integrating one of the Hacker/Sommers handbooks in your course offers several other benefits. For example, the handbook directly supports individual institutions' course and program outcomes. The following chart demonstrates how specific sections in one Hacker/Sommers handbook, *A Writer's Reference,* Seventh Edition, can easily be linked to course objectives for a first-year composition course.

Sample objectives from English 1A	Find it in *A Writer's Reference*
Critically read, analyze, and evaluate a variety of nonfiction texts for their rhetorical and technical merit, with consideration of the principles of unity, coherence, tone, persona, purpose, methods, and the effects on a target audience.	Read actively: Annotate the text (A1-a) Guidelines for active reading (p. 68) Evaluating arguments (A3)
Write clear, well-developed academic essays using a variety of rhetorical strategies, which may include textual analysis, comparison/contrast, causal analysis, and argument.	Analyze to demonstrate your critical thinking (A1-d) Sample student essay: analysis of an article (A1-e) Guidelines for analyzing a text (p. 77) Constructing reasonable arguments (A2)
Write sentences of varying structure in order to emphasize meaning, relationship, and importance of ideas.	Sentence emphasis (S6) Sentence variety (S7)

→ Sample objectives from English 1A	Find it in *A Writer's Reference*
Organize paragraphs into a logical sequence, developing the central idea of the essay to a logical conclusion.	Draft a working thesis (C1-c) Sketch a plan (C1-d) Writing paragraphs (C4)
Find, analyze, interpret, and evaluate outside sources, including print and electronic media.	Conducting research (R1) Evaluating sources (R2)
Integrate the ideas of others through paraphrase, summary, and quotation into papers that express the writer's own voice, position, or analysis.	Citing sources; avoiding plagiarism (MLA-2) Managing information; avoiding plagiarism (R3)
Use current MLA guidelines to document sources.	Documenting sources (MLA-4) Manuscript format; sample paper (MLA-5)
Revise, proofread, and edit your essays for public presentation so they exhibit no major errors in English grammar, usage, or punctuation.	Revising (C3) Glossary of usage (W1) Punctuation and mechanics (P)

The content of the Hacker/Sommers handbooks is also consistent with the recent work of the Council of Writing Program Administrators, whose 2011 *Framework for Success in Postsecondary Writing*[1] identifies key habits and practices that should be encouraged in college writing courses. The "habits of mind" discussed in the *Framework* (curiosity, engagement, responsibility, and others) are developed through a variety of classroom experiences such as exploring rhetorical situations, learning flexible strategies to aid in the writing process, practicing critical and analytical thinking skills, and becoming familiar with conventions of style and research. You, your colleagues, and your program administrators will find that you can easily link specific content in your Hacker/Sommers handbook to the *Framework*'s objectives.

In addition to meeting course and program objectives, a handbook also helps build common expectations among students, instructors, and writing centers, improving the odds that conversations about student writing will be consistent from one instructor or tutor to the next. If assigned campus-wide, the handbook can give students a familiar set of rules and practices as they navigate the diverse writing tasks and genres expected across disciplines. When paired with professional development workshops for all faculty who assign writing across the college or university, workshops in which participants develop ways to integrate the handbook into their specific courses, the handbook can support institutional goals related to developing skillful communicators. *Teaching with Hacker Handbooks* can help writing program administrators and coordinators integrate a handbook into the school's curricula by providing immediate course-building support to new instructors in their programs and by offering a consistent point of reference for group discussions of course practices, particularly in programs or departments that have adopted one handbook in common.

[1] The *Framework* is a collaborative effort by the Council of Writing Program Administrators, the National Council of Teachers of English, and the National Writing Project.

Features of *Teaching with Hacker Handbooks*

Teaching with Hacker Handbooks includes advice on planning effective courses, strategies for tying the handbook to assignments and class activities, and an extensive collection of samples from college instructors in various teaching situations across the country. These resources will allow you to help your students get the most out of class time and class materials while building critical skills for college-level writing in composition and beyond.

Best practices for improving your course. Part I of *Teaching with Hacker Handbooks* ("Topics") offers proven advice for building or enhancing your own composition or writing-intensive course. Developed with input from seasoned instructors, the topics in Part I provide class-tested methods and models designed to engage students:

- Planning your course and designing your syllabus
- Engaging students in class discussion
- Designing effective assignments
- Responding to student writing
- Working with multilingual writers (teaching ESL)
- Addressing writing in the disciplines

These topics contain cross-references to the lesson modules in Part II so that you can easily locate additional resources on the topic, including lesson plans and specific assignments.

Practical strategies for common classroom goals. Part II presents lesson modules covering essential topics in writing instruction, such as crafting successful thesis statements, avoiding plagiarism, and analyzing multimodal texts. Packed with advice and practices from the composition community, each module is presented in a sequenced format that will help you make the most of your time.

- The **Challenges** section briefly introduces some of the teaching and learning challenges you and your students may encounter when you cover the topic in class.

- The **Strategies** portion of the module describes techniques and activities you can use to address the challenges in various situations. It also includes a step-by-step sample lesson that thoroughly illustrates — with models, prompts, and handouts — how to carry out one or more of the suggested activities in class.

- The **Resources** grid at the end of each module directs you to the sections, exercises, and ancillaries from all of the Hacker/Sommers handbooks that reinforce the lesson. You can quickly scan the grid to find the sections and pages that will best serve you and your students.

Together, the modules offer effective practices that will help your students use their handbooks as tools to improve their writing.

Model syllabi, assignments, and rubrics, ready to tailor. Part III of *Teaching with Hacker Handbooks* includes sample syllabi, assignments, and rubrics to which you can refer as you build your own course. These selections, which represent a variety of course types and teaching approaches, show how other instructors have integrated the handbooks into their teaching. With contributions from writing instructors in programs across the country, this collection of authentic materials can inspire you with fresh ideas, whether you are a new or veteran composition instructor.

Online community at hackerhandbooks.com

Online, **hackerhandbooks.com** connects you to the community of instructors who use Hacker/Sommers handbooks and the composition professionals who have helped create them. Here, you'll find assistance in choosing the best handbook for your course objectives as well as tools to help you use that handbook effectively throughout your course. In addition to a comparative chart that helps you decide which handbook is right for you, hackerhandbooks.com offers links to the online resources available for each handbook. You can also browse available instructor resources; in the specific handbook links under "Browse Instructor Resources," you'll find many exercises (complete with answer keys), PowerPoint presentations, and diagnostic tests, all ready to download. Additionally, you can keep in touch with Nancy Sommers, lead author of the current editions of Hacker handbooks, by subscribing to her teaching journal "Between the Drafts," where she shares conversations with peers across the country and offers teaching tips, encouragement, and notices of upcoming workshops.

From hackerhandbooks.com, you can also access *Teaching with Hacker Handbooks* online, where you can download the complete manual and explore supplemental resources such as a scavenger hunt to help familiarize students with use of the handbook and a complete online module, "Integrating Multimodality into Your Teaching." The resources at hackerhandbooks.com act as a portable library of instructional and reference materials for your handbook and an effective way to keep up with the latest news in composition.

Contents

Topics

Part I presents topics you might consider prior to starting your course.

Notes

Topic 1
Planning your course and designing your syllabus

Before you begin teaching the course, you must do some planning. The advice in this topic can help you design an effectively sequenced schedule for a process-based writing course.

Gathering information

Preparing a new course can be both daunting and exciting for novice and veteran instructors alike. It may be tempting to begin your preparations by immediately writing specific assignments and working on a course schedule, but before you jump into the particulars, you should learn as much as you can about key factors that will shape your course. You should identify the goals of the course and the needs of your student population and analyze the environment in which you'll be teaching. These considerations can help you establish clear guidelines and an effective structure for your course.

Identify your course outcomes.   Be sure to consult your department's outcomes statement when planning your course. Your department liaison should be able to provide this information for you. If the department isn't able to furnish you with official course outcomes, you can find the information you need by reviewing the syllabi of other instructors and by asking questions such as the following:

- When students exit a course at this level, what skills are they expected to have acquired? What practices are they expected to have demonstrated?

- Does this class require specific types of assignments, such as in-class timed writing or long-term research papers?

- How does your course serve the school? Is it a prerequisite for other courses?

Learn about your students.   Once you've identified the course outcomes, learn as much as possible about your student population. Even though you will not have met your students at this stage in the planning process, you can anticipate trends and patterns by asking your department chair or other instructors, or by performing

Questions to ask about your incoming students

Experience

- Will your classes be filled with traditionally aged college students, who likely have some prior knowledge of common rhetorical essay forms, argumentation strategies, and citation conventions?

- Will you have any nontraditional students who are returning to school after years in the workforce or at home?

- Do many students at your school typically come from high schools that don't require much writing? If many of your students are local, you may want to find out what kind of writing is expected in the K–12 system in your state.

- Are many of your students coming out of developmental courses that might require no more than paragraph-length writing?

- Have all the students in your class followed your school's typical writing course sequence, or have some taken other writing-intensive courses outside of your department?

- Are any honors students enrolled in your course?

- Will you have a large number of multilingual writers who will need help with language development as well as writing skills? What additional services (tutors or writing labs, for example) does your school provide for such students?

Goals

- What are your students' majors?

- Are all the students following the same degree track (AS, AA, BS, BA, and so on)?

- In general, how many writing-intensive courses will students take after they complete your course?

Workload, time management, and special considerations

- What is your ratio of part-time to full-time students?

- Do students at your school typically have part-time or full-time responsibilities (either in or outside the home) in addition to their college work? How are these commitments likely to affect their participation in your course?

- Will you have student athletes who may miss classes for games or other events? If so, what is your school's policy for accommodating athletes?

- Are any students registered with the disabilities service office at your school? If so, what accommodations will they require?

a quick search on your school's Web site. (Many school Web sites include student statistics.) Knowing this information will help you tailor your assignments to meet your students' general needs and build in enough steps to scaffold your assignments effectively.

Consider your teaching and learning environment. Once you've established course goals and given some thought to your students' backgrounds and needs, consider the environment in which you will teach and your students will learn. Whether you teach face to face or online, for example, will guide some of the decisions you make in planning the course. Some course environments afford you the opportunity to interact personally with students on a regular basis and therefore make certain activities possible, whereas others lend themselves well to asynchronous communication, such as discussion posts. Considering the limitations and opportunities posed by your course environment is an essential step in constructing an effective course plan.

Planning for a face-to-face, hybrid, or fully online teaching environment

Face-to-face teaching and learning

If you and your students will spend class time together regularly and in a fairly traditional classroom, it will be helpful to address the following as you plan your course:

- What is the layout of the room? Are desks, tables, and chairs movable or stationary? Will the possible seating arrangements accommodate your planned lectures? Pairs activities? Small group sessions?

- What presentation capabilities will you have? Chalkboard or white board? Laptop and projector? These considerations will affect how you cover certain material and how you and your students present certain lessons in the course.

- What other technology is available? If you will have regular access to a computer lab that has a computer station for each student, you can schedule dates into the syllabus for peer review or revising electronically during class time. This allows for on-the-spot conferences during the writing process. It may also facilitate collaborative writing activities and hands-on research.

- How will you facilitate and measure participation and engagement? Will you arrange the desks in a circle or some other configuration to encourage interaction? What, in addition to contributions in class discussion, will count as participation? Attendance? Feedback on a peer's paper? Questions asked in or out of class? Trips to the writing center? What activities will you plan for the purpose of engaging student writers in conversations with their peers about ideas, drafts, revisions, or other course materials?

- What opportunities exist for others to teach the class? Will you have a library orientation? Will you have any guest speakers? Do you want to supplement instruction related to argument writing with a live debate? How often will students be assigned to present material to the class?

→

→

Hybrid or fully online teaching and learning

In a hybrid environment, your class will meet face-to-face periodically, but much of the course content and many of its activities will be available and completed online. A fully online teaching and learning situation involves no face-to-face class sessions. Some fully online courses allow for face-to-face office hours. If your class will be conducted primarily or fully online, it will be helpful to address the following as you plan your course:

- How will you incorporate discussion into the course? A class blog? A discussion forum through a course management system (CMS)?

- How will you and your students share and respond to writing?

- What activities can students do collaboratively? How are they to collaborate?

- How will you deliver instruction or lectures? Will you use video? Podcasts? PowerPoint, Prezi, or other presentation technology?

- How will you facilitate and measure participation and engagement? You can set up collaborative assignments that enhance the sense of community in your online course. By familiarizing yourself with your CMS, you should be able to find a tool that allows your students to provide peer feedback on each other's drafts as well.

- How will you encourage students to work with the handbook? Whether your handbook is in print or e-book format, you can use page or section references to direct students to help from within assignments or feedback on their writing.

- What other resources can you provide links to from your online course space? Direct students to companion resources for the handbook, library materials and databases, major newspapers, and Web sites containing material related to your discussion topics.

Establishing a schedule for your writing course

Each instructor has a different method for establishing a course schedule. Some instructors like to work organically, assigning projects inspired by current events or the students' own experiences. Other instructors approach their tasks systematically, planning assignments for the entire semester before the first day of class. If you are new to teaching, a detailed plan might work best; once you have the scaffolding for your course, you can always adapt it as necessary depending on the needs and interests of your students.

Determine the number and types of assignments.   Many process-based writing courses for first- and second-year students include four to six major writing assignments per semester, sometimes with additional informal writing tasks. The number and types of assignments you can offer will depend, in part, on program requirements. If your department has a common or suggested syllabus, one or more assignments may already be specified for you. The writing you assign will also depend on your students and how much support they may need with each one. It may be necessary to provide more scaffolding and a variety of low-stakes exercises for less prepared writers. If you expect that you will have to accommodate a wide range of skill levels, consider planning a few challenging assignment variations for more advanced students.

If you will be teaching a nontraditional or other specific population (for instance, second-career students, multilingual writers, developmental writers, or students with disabilities), include assignments that accommodate their needs and guide them toward achieving the course goals. Better yet, think about assignments that might draw on their particular talents and experiences.

Establish benchmarks for achievement.   Consider creating a rubric, a grid that matches assignment features with descriptions of various levels of achievement. Doing so helps you to establish benchmarks for your course. Describe the standard features of an A or excellent project, a B or above-average project, and so on. Include a list of the features you plan to assess, such as development, organization, expression and style, and sentence-level control. If discussion and peer review will contribute to the grade, clarify those expectations as well.

Although not all projects will fit neatly into these grade categories, rubrics can provide a general structure that will help both you and your students. If you choose, you can include a general rubric as part of the syllabus so that students are aware of your grading standards from the beginning of the course. You can use assignment-specific versions of this rubric when you assess student work.

For a sample rubric and additional discussion, see "Work with rubrics" in Topic 4 (p. 40).

Set due dates at regular intervals over the semester.   Distributing major assignments throughout the course benefits students and instructors. Students will have sufficient time for planning, drafting, and revising, and you will have enough time to evaluate writing and offer feedback before the next draft or final piece is due. If you are teaching more than one course, and particularly if you are teaching a full load, try to stagger the due dates for your major writing assignments among your sections to avoid receiving a daunting number of essays all at once.

Build in enough time for writing, review, and revision.   When planning the course, begin with a simple timeline that maps the number of class periods you'll have with your students and the number of assignments you'll give. For each assignment, reserve a minimum of three class sessions for planning and review:

- At least one class session for explaining the assignment, previewing models, and brainstorming ideas
- At least one session for reviewing preliminary drafts with both peer feedback and your feedback on the draft
- One session (or a partial session) at the time papers are returned, or shortly after, for students to ask questions about your comments and begin to apply your feedback

If possible, consider adding days for students to plan or draft the essay in class, perform self-assessments, review citation conventions, and conduct research. In addition, give yourself sufficient time to grade and return assignments before students begin the next paper. (One week is typically a realistic turnaround time, although if you are teaching more than one course, you may find that you will have more than one section's worth of essays to grade at a time.) Sprinkle in additional skill-building activities on other days: preparing for assignments with reading and discussion, reviewing sentence-level issues and working on exercises, and generating ideas with in-class or informal writing assignments.

Here's a sample assignment schedule for a class that meets three times a week:

	Monday	Wednesday	Friday
Week 1	As a class, discuss one or two selections students read for homework. The readings will provide a foundation for an essay.	Introduce the assignment and preview model essays.	Conduct a brainstorm activity to generate ideas.
Week 2	Initial planning assignment due for peer review and class feedback.	**Draft 1 due.** Lead students through a self-assessment and revision workshop.	Present model introductions and conclusions from the handbook followed by revision work-shop on student drafts.
Week 3	**Draft 2 due.** Conduct a peer review workshop.	Review a sentence-level topic from the handbook (such as commas) and conduct an editing workshop.	**Final draft due.** Final proofreading workshop. Reflective writing in class.

Determining assignment sequences

When you design assignments for your course, create opportunities for students to build on skills they have previously practiced. Begin with an assignment that requires the fewest new skills. Then, with each subsequent assignment, increase the challenge by requiring the use of one or two new skills that you've covered in class.

In a first-semester writing course, for example, you could begin with a relatively simple essay assignment that focuses on the basics of purpose (crafting a thesis), organization (planning topic sentences), and development (writing effective paragraphs). The next essay might require students to add one new focus to the previous three: the integration of one source. The third essay could build on the first two assignments by requiring the use of two sources cited in MLA style. Continue scaffolding the assignments in manageable steps. See the sample assignment sequence for a beginning-level writing course.

Sample assignment sequence for a first-year college writing course

Assignment 1: Personal narrative. Focusing on three basic features: purpose (thesis statement), organization (topic sentences and appropriate transitions), and development (coherent paragraphs with the use of concrete details).

Assignment 2: Summary and analysis of a text. Quoting, paraphrasing, and using signal phrases, along with basics from Assignment 1.

Assignment 3: Critical response. Using quotations, paraphrases, signal phrases, and citations to agree/disagree with a text.

Assignment 4: Position paper. Using evidence from texts to support a position. Require two texts so that students learn to refer to more than one author and practice synthesizing sources.

Assignment 5: Research paper (multiple sources). Locating, evaluating, integrating, and citing sources.

Striking a balance between rhetorical topics and sentence skills

Novice writers typically need help with learning to analyze texts, construct arguments, structure their thoughts, and develop an academic voice — common rhetorical topics covered in first-year writing. Often they also need help with recognizing sentence-level errors in their work and using resources (such as the handbook) to find answers to their questions. Finding the time to address all of these needs in class is challenging. You may struggle to balance your coverage of global issues (rhetorical topics such as critical thinking, analysis, and research) with local issues (such as using correct grammar and punctuation).

To ensure that students devote enough attention to both global and local writing issues, build a series of workshop days (time for students to work on their own writing with a partner or peer group) into the course calendar. For each writing assignment, schedule at least one workshop during the drafting stage to address global rhetorical issues and at least one workshop during the revision stage to address sentence skill issues. Let the needs of your students and the demands of the assignment determine the topics you cover in each workshop. Ask students to prepare for these workshop sessions by bringing drafts of their papers. Structure each session so that students have time to write, review, or otherwise engage with their own work in class.

Conduct a workshop on rhetorical (global) issues during the drafting stage.
Early in the writing process, conduct at least one workshop in which students consider rhetorical strategies. For instance, if your students are working on an essay with an argumentative purpose, you can begin the workshop by discussing the

argumentation strategies outlined in the handbook or reader. Review any sample thesis statements or outlines that the handbook or reader provides, and ask students to compare their work to the models. Give the students an opportunity to share their ideas and receive feedback, either from the whole class or from a few peers.

Conduct a workshop on sentence-level (local) issues during the revision stage.   Later in the writing process, after students have drafted their papers, guide them through one or more revision and editing workshops focused on local issues. For example, you might begin an editing workshop by discussing the sections in the handbook that cover comma usage. Review a few flawed sentences (either from the handbook exercises or from students' own papers) and work together to correct them by applying tips from the handbook. Then give students an opportunity to check their own work for similar errors and to receive feedback from you or from a few peers. See the sample workshop series for additional ideas.

Sample workshop series for an argument essay assignment

Day 1 (global issues)   Discuss the assigned reading homework, a persuasive essay; assign a position paper on a related topic. Have students brainstorm possible positions or topics with their peers.

Day 2 (global issues)   Students bring initial topics and thesis statements to class. Review model thesis statements from the handbook and lead students through a peer review of their thesis statements. Have students discuss whether their own thesis statements are debatable. Encourage them to revise their thesis statements, seeking feedback from you or from peers as necessary.

Day 3 (global issues)   Students bring skeletal drafts or outlines to class. Review the content and organization of model papers. Define ethical, emotional, and logical appeals, and look for examples of these appeals in the models. Ask students to exchange their work with peers to evaluate their own appeals. Encourage them to revise the content of their skeletal drafts or outlines in class.

Day 4 (local issues)   Students bring complete drafts to class. Discuss the sections in the handbook that cover coherent paragraphs and cohesive elements (transitions). Ask students to revise for coherence in class, exchanging papers with peers for additional feedback. (Students having trouble with coherence may find that they need to return to global revision and reconsider the overall structure of their essays.)

Day 5 (local issues)   Students bring revised drafts to class. Present (or assign a few students to present) the handbook section on run-on sentences, and answer any questions students may have about the practice exercises. Ask students to exchange papers to identify run-on sentences in their peers' work. Once students have identified errors, have them return papers to the owners for editing.

Day 6 (local issues)   Students bring final drafts to class. Present (or assign a few students to present) the section on commas from the handbook, and review a few of the practice exercises. Ask students to do final proofreading for commas before they submit their papers for grading.

Integrating the handbook

As teachers of writing, we teach skills, but we also teach academic habits. For instance, we teach students to think about different sides of an argument, and we teach them to value jotting down notes before they write. Teaching students to rely on a handbook is another such academic habit. During the semester, reinforce the practice of consulting the handbook to answer different kinds of writing questions — those related to rhetorical topics (thesis, argument, evidence), to grammar topics (fragments, subject-verb agreement), and to research topics (integrating sources, MLA citation).

The more students use the handbook under your guidance, the more comfortable they will become with using it on their own. If possible, take time to show students how to navigate the text to find specific advice. Doing so will help them understand why they have been asked to purchase the book and how the book can help them beyond a single assignment or the composition course. Consider using a scavenger hunt as a pairs activity that asks students to locate specific content in the handbook. And build references to the handbook directly into your syllabus and your assignments. If the course covers finding and using sources for research, for example, the syllabus or assignment sheet should list the sections in the handbook that cover those topics.

As you plan your course, find advice and models in the handbook to use for in-class activities or to assign for homework reading. Your students will likely be surprised to learn that the handbook offers more than grammar and citation.

See **hackerhandbooks .com/teaching** for a sample scavenger hunt.

Designing a syllabus

A syllabus describes the course for your students. It introduces your students to the course and explains how the course will work. It serves as a reference for students throughout the semester when they have questions about course requirements and policies.

A syllabus is also a contract between you and your students. It should include key information for successfully completing the course. It should inform students about required texts, assignments, and course policies, for example, without providing so much material that students get lost. Your department or program might have a standard syllabus, a model syllabus, or a set of guidelines that you are required to use. If your school does not have these resources, use the information below as a guide.

See Part III of this collection and visit **hackerhandbooks .com/teaching** for a variety of sample syllabi.

Sections of a syllabus

Critical components

- Course information: number, section, title, meeting times, location, term/ year, name of school
- Instructor contact information: name, office location and hours, phone number, e-mail address
- Textbooks: titles, authors, edition number, ISBN, where to purchase
- Course goals: key questions and learning objectives to be addressed in the course

- Grading method: grade scale, how each assignment will be weighted, how the final course grade will be computed
- Attendance policy
- Late and makeup work policy
- Academic integrity or plagiarism policy: a description of the forms academic dishonesty can take with a mention of the consequences
- Class schedule: a list of readings and assignments, or directions for finding the class schedule if it is posted online
- Any other sections mandated by your department or school

Additional components

- Required materials in addition to textbooks
- Descriptions of major assignments
- Formatting directions for papers
- Grading rubric
- Other grading policies: incompletes, appealing grades
- Classroom conduct: Are laptop computers allowed? Should cell phones be turned off?
- Writing center or writing lab information
- Services for students with disabilities
- Services for multilingual students

Presenting the syllabus

Early in the semester, take time to go over the syllabus with your class. Point out the course objectives and how the assignments relate to those objectives. Explain any key terms that will make the formal descriptions in the syllabus more meaningful to students. Cover important policies, especially those that relate to academic honesty and attendance. Give multiple opportunities for students to ask questions.

Students will adhere to course policies more when they understand the purposes of those policies. Explain how the policies will help students be successful. For example, you could explain that the attendance policy is necessary because a writing course is a workshop in which active participation is crucial. If you have a policy limiting late assignments, you could explain that a student falling behind in assignments can become overwhelmed; thus, students will benefit from meeting deadlines.

Refer to the syllabus throughout the semester to help your students adhere to the general guidelines and the course schedule. If possible, post a copy online for easy reference.

Sample Syllabus

The following sample syllabus shows one instructor's use of *The Bedford Handbook* in a twelve-week introductory composition course for traditional students. Note the course information that the instructor provides, the sequence of assignments, and the use of the handbook throughout the term.

ENG 101: College Composition 1

Meeting times:	Tu and Th, 9:00–10:30 a.m.
Instructor:	Professor Warren
Phone:	(xxx) xxx-xxxx
E-mail:	warren@yourcollege.edu
Office:	Roberts Hall, Room 214
Office hours:	M, W, F, 8:00–10:00 a.m.

Course description

Welcome to College Composition 1! This course will prepare you to be a successful writer in your college courses. You will learn how to plan, organize, draft, and revise the most common kinds of writing you will do as a college student—essays that analyze and argue positions. You will learn how to research and use sources in your writing. You will learn how to edit your own writing. I hope this course will help you feel more confident and prepared in all the writing you do.

Course outcomes

By the end of this semester, you will be able to
- develop and organize a college-level academic essay
- revise and edit your own work
- find, use, and document sources in a research paper
- collaborate effectively with other writers and give useful feedback

The syllabus defines course outcomes and shows students what is expected of them and what they can expect from the course.

Textbooks (available in the college bookstore)

The Bedford Reader, Eleventh Edition (Kennedy, Kennedy, and Aaron)
The Bedford Handbook, Ninth Edition (Hacker/Sommers)

Assignments and grade distribution

Assignment 1 (all drafts): 10%
Assignment 2 (all drafts): 10%
Assignment 3 (all drafts): 20%
Assignment 4 (all drafts): 20%
Assignment 5 (all drafts): 30%
Homework and participation: 10%
A=90–100%, B=80–89%, C=70–79%, D=60–69%, F=59% or less

Attendance policy

Because this is a workshop class, your participation is important and determines your ability to succeed. You are expected to attend every class. If you must be absent, please obtain notes or missed work from a classmate. You are allowed two absences without penalty; each additional absence will reduce your final grade. Regardless of the reason for your absence, you are responsible for any information you miss.

Grading, attendance, and makeup policies are clearly established to guide and protect students and instructors.

Late and makeup assignment policy

In general, no late assignments are accepted, and no makeup credit is granted. If you have an emergency situation, please contact me (by e-mail or phone) within twenty-four hours of the missed class session to determine whether alternative arrangements can be made. Expect to provide official documentation to prove your need to be absent. Except in pre-approved situations, assignments missed due to absence or lateness may not be made up or accepted late. Do not wait until the last moment to complete or print an assignment; give yourself plenty of time to deal with unexpected problems such as computer malfunctions. You are responsible for submitting your assignments on time, so I urge you to submit them to me personally in class and keep electronic copies.

Academic honesty

The work you will do in this course is subject to the Student Honor Code. Academic dishonesty includes (1) submitting under your own name work that someone else wrote, even work you have rewritten, including any material from the Internet; (2) plagiarism—quoting, paraphrasing, or borrowing ideas without giving full documentation of the source; (3) allowing someone else to write part of an assignment for you; (4) receiving any unauthorized assistance on assignments; (5) submitting the same work in two courses without both instructors' approval. Academic dishonesty—whether intentional or accidental—may result in a failing grade for the course and possibly action by the Dean of Students.

The academic integrity statement makes students aware of the consequences of plagiarism, including accidental plagiarism.

Special services

The Writing Lab (Penn Center, Room 224) offers free services to all students. I encourage you to take your drafts to the lab for additional feedback.

If you are a student with a disability, please register with the Disability Service Office (Penn Center, Room 132) to be eligible for academic accommodations.

The syllabus points out services for students with special needs.

Important dates

Last day to add/drop this course: September 15
Last day to withdraw with a W on your transcript: November 4

Computers, cells, courtesy

Please do not use a laptop computer in this class as it inevitably leads to checking e-mail, surfing the Internet, and doing unrelated work, which is distracting to the rest of us. Completely turn off pagers and cell phones. Practice good classroom manners: no texting or doing work unrelated to the class.

Submission of assignments

All of these assignments leading up to a final writing project (drafts, revisions, research notes, etc.) must be submitted on schedule throughout the unit. Neglect of these directions can result in a significant grade reduction or even a failing grade for the essay.

Important note

By remaining enrolled in this section, you agree to this syllabus. I may have to correct or make adjustments to this syllabus as the needs of the entire class dictate.

ENG 101 Course Schedule

Week 1

Tu Introduction to the course
- Review syllabus

Th Diagnostic essay (in class)
- Preview the table of contents in both textbooks

The instructor previews the handbook with the students early in the term to familiarize them with its contents.

Week 2

Tu Editing workshop: Sentence boundaries; edit diagnostic essay
- Handbook: Fragments (19) and run-ons (20)
- **Edited essay due at the end of class**

Th Active reading; prepare for Assignment 1
- Reader: Chapter 1
- Handbook: Annotating texts (4a); being an active reader (55a)

Week 3

Tu Planning and drafting; thesis statements
- Handbook: Planning (1a–1d) and drafting (1e–1g); thesis statements (5c)

Th Revision workshop: Paragraphing; concrete details
- Handbook: Paragraphs (3)
- **Draft 1 due in class for the workshop**

Week 4

Tu Editing workshop: Strong verbs
- Handbook: Active verbs (8); shifts (13); subject-verb agreement (21)
- **Draft 2 due in class for the workshop**

Th Preview analysis assignment
- Handbook: Writing about texts (4)
- **Assignment 1 final draft due**

The instructor integrates the handbook at all stages of the writing process: planning, drafting, revising, and editing.

Week 5

Tu Discuss reading; prepare for assignment
- Reader: Chapters 3 and 5
- Handbook: Review model essay (4e)

Th Revision workshop: Integrating sources
- Handbook: Integrating sources (52)
- **Draft 1 due in class for the workshop**

The instructor reserves several sessions for the planning and review of each assignment.

Week 6

Tu Editing workshop: Focus on punctuation
- Handbook: Commas (32 and 33); quotation marks (37)
- **Draft 2 due in class for the workshop**

Th Argument and persuasion
- Reader: Chapter 6
- **Assignment 2 final draft due**

→

Week 7

Tu Argumentation
  • Handbook: Reading and writing arguments (6)

Th Discuss reading; prepare for assignment
  • Handbook: Review model essay (6k)

The instructor uses the handbook and model papers to introduce rhetorical strategies.

Week 8

Tu Revision workshop: Focus on argumentation
  • Handbook: Supporting claims (6h); countering opposing arguments (6i)
  • **Draft 1 due in class for the workshop**

Th Editing workshop: Focus on word choice
  • Handbook: Wordy sentences (16); appropriate language (17); exact words (18)
  • **Draft 2 due in class for the workshop**

Due dates for final drafts are distributed evenly over the semester so that students have sufficient time to engage in the writing process and the instructor has sufficient time to assess papers.

Week 9

Tu Preview research assignment
  • Reader: Chapter 11
  • Handbook: Sample research paper (57b)
  • **Assignment 3 final draft due**

Th Choosing research topics
  • Handbook: Conducting research (50)

Week 10

Tu Evaluating sources
  • Handbook: Evaluating sources (52)
  • **Tentative thesis due**

Th Research: Visit the library to learn about databases and to find at least one source
  • Bring your handbook to the library; refer to the Citation at a glance on pages 612–613

Students are encouraged to use their handbooks both in and outside of class.

Week 11

Tu Planning workshop: Structure
  • Handbook: Review outlines (1d)
  • **Outline due in class for the workshop**

Th Revision workshop: Focus on support and avoiding plagiarism
  • Bring research materials to class
  • Handbook: Managing information and avoiding plagiarism (51 and 54)
  • **Draft 1 due in class for the workshop**

Week 12

Tu Editing workshop: Focus on citations
  *   Handbook: Review integrating sources in MLA papers (52)
  *   **Draft 2 due in class for the workshop**

Th Editing workshop: Focus on final edits
  *   Handbook: Review commas (32) and quotation marks (37)
  *   **Assignment 4 final draft due**

Topic 2
Engaging students and leading discussions

Years ago a popular movie, *Ferris Bueller's Day Off*, featured a classroom scene of an economics teacher lecturing at length in a monotone. Occasionally, he would pause to ask an uninspiring question addressed to no one in particular. As the students sat bored and unengaged, he would ask, "Anyone? Anyone?" Then, he would answer his own question and continue lecturing, oblivious to his students and their needs.

As students or as teachers, we have all been in this situation. It can be uncomfortable at best and excruciating at worst. Anyone who teaches can relate to the experience of a class discussion that does not work. But over time we develop ways of engaging students and fostering fruitful class discussion.

Understanding resistance to class discussion

One of the first steps toward building healthy class discussion is understanding why students are sometimes reluctant to participate. If you are teaching a required writing course, some students may start off feeling uninspired. They didn't choose to take the course, so they may resist engaging with the material or with classmates. Some students may feel insecure. They worry about being wrong or challenged with disagreement in front of their peers. Still others may simply feel that they have nothing to contribute, especially if the topic of discussion is new and unfamiliar. Students coming directly out of high school into the college classroom may view group discussions as an obligation rather than an opportunity or may feel that active participation in discussion may make them look like a "teacher's pet."

Fortunately, all of these obstacles can be overcome. You can take steps to engage your students and raise their interest. You can offer them a sense of security that enables them to speak up. You can even help them discover that they have something to say.

Think again about that classroom scene in *Ferris Bueller's Day Off*. What could the teacher have done differently to engage his students? Rather than restricting himself to lecture, he could have involved students in a writing exercise or small group exercise to explore causes and effects. Or rather than asking students to recall specific facts, which forces students to risk being wrong in front of everyone, he could have asked questions that allow for a variety of responses. He could have invited students to share their thoughts in response to the assigned reading or class discussion topic, or he could have presented perspectives that students could agree or disagree with. Rather than trying another approach, this instructor merely answers his own question when his students refuse to respond. Ferris Bueller's teacher needs to create a positive classroom environment so that his students feel safe rather than closed off, and he needs to set goals for the activity so his students have a reason to engage.

Setting the tone: Helping students feel comfortable contributing

Generating active discussion requires creating favorable conditions for discussion. Think of your classroom as a learning environment with consistent expectations and guidelines.

Determine your role in discussion. Do you see yourself as an active participant in the classroom discussion? A mediator? A mentor? As an instructor, your role in discussion may closely align with one of these approaches or blend them as necessary given the flow and objectives of the conversation. If you teach online, spend some time deciding how (and how frequently) you will respond to students' posts in the discussion forums. Rather than encouraging student activity, too many instructor comments in the forums (especially if they contain corrections on students' posts) may make students feel judged and therefore reticent about further participation. On the other hand, if an instructor is completely absent from the forums, students may feel that they do not have to work very hard. One option is to comment lightly in the forums and send a follow-up e-mail to the whole class that respectfully highlights and addresses specific points raised in a particular discussion.

Establish clear guidelines for students' participation in discussion. In a face-to-face classroom, remind everyone that when one student has the floor, the rest of the class should listen closely before responding. In an online classroom, encourage students to read peers' posts carefully and thoroughly before posting a comment of their own. Establish practices that generate respect. Teach your students several response-starters, and consider giving them extra credit for using them. Some possibilities are "I hear what you're saying, but I have a different perspective" or "I like what [So-and-so] is saying, and I want to add to that." It may even be fun to ask students to work together to make a list of extra-credit response-starters. Make sure to let students know that disparaging remarks about peers' comments will require a private conversation with you. You may also remind students to monitor the frequency of their contributions to the discussion; nothing is more agonizing than a twenty-minute "class discussion" that takes place solely between the instructor and one (admittedly enthusiastic) student. Encourage students to participate by explaining that more voices often reveal varying perspectives, leading to more engaging discussions. In an online course, let students know your expected word count for initial and follow-up posts as well as any deadlines for posting. Consider developing a rubric specifically for your discussion forums that evaluates posting length, content, frequency, timeliness, and any other important criteria, and sharing it with your students.

Create a community of learners. Make everyone feel welcome. On the first day of class, conduct an activity that gives everyone a chance to learn each other's names. For example, you can put students in pairs and give them a few minutes to learn something about each other. Then each student introduces his or her partner to the whole class. To make students in an online course feel welcome, assign a "Meet & Greet" forum in which you ask students to introduce themselves and perhaps answer a few basic questions — their field of study, type of work (you may want to caution students not to divulge their specific workplace), hobbies, interests, and one or two unique life experiences. To create community online, it's important to respond to every student's original post in this forum. In discussions, model the use of class members' names on a regular basis.

Treat every student with respect. Despite our best intentions, a student might feel disrespected if their statements in class are corrected, questioned, or challenged. Sometimes we must correct, question, or challenge a student's statement, and find respectful ways to do so. Saying the equivalent of "That answer is wrong" leaves the student with no incentive to respond. Here are some alternatives that can keep the conversation going:

> "Thanks for your response, but let me ask you to reconsider one point."
> "I'm going to ask you to support your point a little more."
> "Interesting comment. Thank you. Now, can anyone add to that or offer a different viewpoint?"

It always helps to get "thank you" in there somewhere, so that students know you appreciate their contributions.

Remember that treating students with respect includes giving them time to respond to a question you pose or to comment on a peer's statement. In a face-to-face classroom, adopt a five-second rule, even if it means silently counting to five before answering your own question or responding to an especially provocative student comment. You want to encourage students to jump into the discussion, and purposely creating a bit of silence can do just that. Think back to Bueller's teacher, who often allows just a half-second to pass before talking again. In an online discussion, you may prompt other students with simple posts such as "Other thoughts, class?" or "What else can we say about this?"

Avoid humor directed at students. Students can misunderstand even well-intentioned humor. Because you are the authority figure, a humorous statement on your part might be taken seriously. If it is directed to a student, it could be taken as ridicule, and when students fear ridicule, they will not speak up in class. Never allow sarcasm. If a student in your class speaks to other students disrespectfully or ridicules what they say, you must address this behavior or it will dampen discussion. For discussion to occur, the classroom must be a safe environment for everyone to speak up and offer ideas. Humor can be especially tricky in online courses, where, for example, a humorous remark followed by a winking emoticon may be misread by a student who is insecure about his or her performance in the class. If there is the potential for a student to misread your humorous statement, rewrite it.

Establishing goals: Helping students feel motivated to participate

First, ask yourself whether discussion is the best strategy for the lesson. If your goal is for students to efficiently take in information, lecture and readings might be more fruitful than discussion. If you want students to personally explore a topic, reflective writing might be the best course. When your purpose is to invite a variety of perspectives, discussion is the tool to use. Think of discussion as a collective brainstorming tool, which is best used when you need to tap into the experiences and thoughts of the group.

Once you've settled on discussion, ask yourself, "What do I want my students to get out of this discussion?" Setting a goal does not mean having a predetermined conclusion in mind. Discussion is unpredictable; you never know what unique idea might be introduced. That is what makes it invigorating. Discussion works best when the lesson has room for flexibility and less of a need for definite closure. For example, if the goal of a discussion is to invite the students to observe characteristics of a writer's style, you could prepare questions that point out specific features of the text for students to evaluate. Setting a goal and sharing it with students helps them understand that there's a reason for them to participate.

Be clear about the direction for the discussion but flexible enough to allow the conversation to take its own shape. Have a few questions already written in your lesson plan. You may even want to share some of them with students ahead of time so that they can prepare some ideas for the discussion. At the same time, if the students become talkative on an issue, it may be fruitful to allow the conversation to continue. You do not need to go through all of the questions. You can even hold a couple of questions in reserve to use when the conversation hits a pause, reaches a stopping point, or goes off on a tangent. If the conversation is too rigid, students may not feel welcome to freely share their ideas. Flexibility gives students the feeling that they're not just answering questions — they're helping to shape the conversation.

Posing questions that encourage conversation

Yes/no questions come naturally to us, but they often evoke limited responses. If students think there is only one right answer, they may feel they're being "tested," and only the confident ones will answer. Most will want to avoid the risk of embarrassment. Questions that can be settled with a one-word answer also tend to be uninspiring. Try to ask questions that invite students to share their own ideas about something. For example, rather than asking, "Does the writer include evidence to support her claim?" you could ask, "What evidence does the writer use to support her claim? Does that evidence seem weak or strong to you? Why?" If you teach online, consider what forum structure (a single discussion thread or multiple threads, for example) will be most appropriate for the questions you are posing and will encourage the liveliest conversation. Questions are the fuel of discussion. Keeping the following tips in mind can help you develop questions that get the conversation started:

- **Phrasing.** Ask only one question at a time, and phrase the question simply and directly. If you present too many questions or they're unclear, students may feel too confused to offer a response.

- **Waiting.** Wait for a response. "Wait time" is the time that elapses between the asking of a question and the response. An instructor who feels uncomfortable with silence in the classroom might keep talking after posing a question, even to the extent of answering the question. After posing a question, pause for at least five seconds before speaking again so that there's an opportunity for discussion to begin.

- **Prompting.** Prompting means providing clues for a response, but use prompting sparingly because it suggests you are looking for one correct answer.
- **Clarifying.** Ask students if the question makes sense; if necessary, rephrase it.

Keeping conversations going

How you receive student responses is just as important as the questions you ask to elicit those responses. Keeping in mind the tips below can help you encourage students to build on their own responses and those of their peers.

- **Listening.** When you are leading a discussion, it is easy to keep thinking about what you are going to do or say next rather than what students are saying. Pay attention and maintain eye contact with the student who is responding. Do not interrupt; allow him or her to complete the response. Make sure everyone can hear; if necessary, ask the student to repeat the response.
- **Being flexible.** Allowing a student's response to take the conversation in a slightly different direction can be fruitful. If you are too focused on what you intend to say next, the conversation may feel disjointed or forced, and students won't get the sense that their contributions are valued. If a student gets far off topic, acknowledge the idea but gently steer back to the main topic.
- **Positioning.** Avoid letting the discussion turn into a conversation between you and the student who is talking. In a face-to-face class, if you position yourself near the student, it could make others in the classroom feel closed off from the discussion. By standing at a distance, you can open the classroom space, which invites everyone. Judicious use of movement to various sections of the classroom can also help keep students engaged (but avoid pacing and do not use uncomfortable proximity to a student as a method of redirecting his or her attention).
- **Summarizing.** To ensure the class understands the response, summarize (or ask another student to summarize) what a student has said. This technique of "saying back" also lets contributors know that they've been heard and understood.
- **Redirecting.** Redirect attention to other students. Rather than always responding to a student yourself, you could involve other students in the discussion. Ask for agreement or disagreement. By doing this you will let your students know that everyone's participation is welcomed and valued.
- **Following up.** Asking students extension questions gives them an opportunity to explain an answer further with more information or examples. "What statement in the text illustrates the tone you are observing?" You can also continue the conversation by asking students to clarify: "When you use the word *government* in that context, what specifically are you referring to — federal, state, local?" Justification questions prompt students to support a claim with reasons or evidence. "What current factors lead you to make that prediction about the new law?"

Preparing students for discussion

Asking clear, thought-provoking questions and helping students build on each other's responses are key to starting a healthy discussion and keeping it going. Before your conversation even begins, however, you may want to engage students in low-stakes activities that give them an opportunity to develop ideas on the topic to be discussed.

Many students will feel more confident about contributing if they've had a chance to try out some thoughts on their own or with a small group before sharing them with the whole class.

Freewriting can help pave the way for discussion. We're used to thinking of it as a way to generate ideas for a paper, but it can also help students prepare for a conversation with the class. Try asking students to brainstorm about the discussion topic in writing. You can offer a general prompt, such as *What did you like most about the reading? What new discovery did you make? What did the writer say that surprised you? Do you agree or disagree with the writer, and why?* You could pose a more focused prompt suitable for the specific reading.

Before the students begin writing, remind them that this is a freewrite; it will not be submitted for a grade. Tell them that whatever they write will be private, but they will be asked to share some part of their writing with others. Providing this heads-up information at the outset respects the students' ownership of their own writing and encourages them to invest in the writing activity even though it is low-stakes, ungraded writing.

At the conclusion of the freewrite, ask the students to review what they have written and select one point they feel might be their best. Let them know that they will be asked to share this point with others. This gives them the sense of security that comes from knowing that they will control how their freewrite will be made public. Students who came to class thinking they had nothing to say will discover that they do have something to contribute.

Sharing ideas

When it's time to share ideas, giving students opportunities to be active can encourage them to engage in the conversation.

- **Working in groups.** Put students into small groups (four to a group works well for a face-to-face class; six per group is effective in an online setting). Each member will share ideas with the group. Then the group will agree on ideas to share with the whole class. Small groups give students a low-pressure environment in which to actively participate in discussion. Students who are uncomfortable talking in front of the whole class will probably feel more comfortable sharing ideas with only two or three peers. If you want the whole class to benefit from these small group discussions, you can ask each group to assign a spokesperson to share the small group's ideas with everyone. The spokesperson approach gives shy students an opportunity to experience the class's reactions to their ideas in the comfort of anonymity. If they see the class engaging with their ideas, they might be more likely to share with the whole class themselves in the future. If you're teaching online, most course management systems allow small group interaction. A slightly larger (five- or six-person) group may be more effective online for generating discussion, especially in asynchronous courses where students may not access the class every day. Small group discussions online should have clear guidelines and objectives listed as part of the assignment, and they will generally require specific due dates, particularly if you are using them as initial steps toward a full-class discussion.
- **Posting.** Have students or groups use tape to post their written individual or group responses on the walls of the classroom. Everyone gets up, walks around,

and views all of the responses (like a "gallery" of freewriting). You can have each group report their ideas to the whole class by writing on the board or the classroom computer or by projecting their response with a document camera (if available). These strategies have the benefit of allowing quieter students to participate without requiring them to speak. It is another technique that gives those students an opportunity to experience other students' reactions to their ideas, which encourages them to participate more.

- **Moving.** To respond to a text that requires readers to take a position, you could designate different areas of the classroom with different positions. One corner could be the "agree" corner, another the "disagree" corner. Ask the students to get up and stand in the area that best reflects their reaction to the reading. This strategy has everyone physically moving and literally taking a stand, and it allows everyone to see where everyone else stands. Once all the students are in their corners you can ask, "Why did you choose that position?" You can redirect to others by asking, "Those of you taking the opposite stance, how would you respond to their argument?" This kinetic strategy followed by questions rarely fails to get discussion going. If you are teaching online, create and post a document that students can add to. Create a continuum of agreement for pro/con prompts, and ask students to place themselves on the continuum. Or create a class web (or cluster diagram) and ask students to add ideas as satellites of a couple of main ideas that you start the document off with.

Turning discussion into writing

You may want to ask students to follow up on class discussions with reflective writing. Reflection can help students develop and refine their brewing ideas about a topic. This strategy may also reinforce the value of discussion for students who may find writing about a topic easier after discussing it with a peer group or the whole class.

Note: A small minority of students have deep fears about speaking in class. Regardless of what strategies you employ, they are going to remain quiet. They are also going to experience every class period with anxiety, especially if they feel the additional pressure of being graded on participation. Because many instructors want to acknowledge and reward students for their participation, these students are placed at a disadvantage.

There is a compromise solution. Rather than using a participation grade, you could build an "engagement grade" into the course. Students would have an option of participating actively in discussion or keeping a journal to document their overall engagement with the course. If you are teaching a hybrid or fully online class, you could also provide students the option of keeping an online journal or a blog. They could use the journal to express their thoughts and show that they have been thinking actively about the course material.

Topic 3
Designing effective assignments

The quality of student writing can sometimes reflect the quality of the assignment. Clear, meaningful assignments often lead to insightful responses and student investment. Vague or confusing assignments may frustrate students or distract them from the course's objectives, thwarting growth and achievement. The advice in this topic will help you craft assignments that provide guidance and support for your students.

Determining the objectives of an assignment

Each assignment is an opportunity for students to show what they have learned and to move toward the designated outcomes for your course. Before creating an assignment, consider your students' experience level and which of the course objectives they are prepared to fulfill. The assignment outcomes should mirror one or more of these course objectives.

Remember that students probably will not be prepared to fulfill all the objectives from the start of the term but instead will need to build skills slowly through a sequence of assignments. Consider the chart on setting assignment objectives (p. 28), which shows the correlation between course objectives and two assignments in a first-year course. The first assignment, a beginning analytical essay, requires students to focus on a few basic course objectives: showing reading comprehension, writing thesis statements and topic sentences, developing paragraphs, and using the writing process. The second assignment, a final research project that is the fifth assignment in the course, shifts to more advanced course objectives. These objectives, which include evaluating sources, using citation conventions, and writing a research paper, can be accomplished only after students have developed a solid foundation in basic essay writing.

> **In this topic:**
>
> Determining the objectives of an assignment 27
>
> Choosing a topic and crafting an assignment 29
>
> Creating a sequence of steps within an assignment and integrating the handbook 30
>
> Providing explicit instructions 31

For more information on the order of assignments, see "Determining assignment sequences" in Topic 1 (p. 8).

Setting assignment objectives that help students accomplish course objectives

THE COURSE Student objectives for a first-year course	THE ASSIGNMENTS Student objectives for a beginning analytical essay (Assignment 1)	
Read and show comprehension of college-level texts	Write a thesis in response to an analytical prompt	Basic skills
Formulate effective thesis statements for analytical essays	Develop the essay with paragraphs that use topic sentences to support the thesis	
Develop essays with paragraphs that support the thesis; write paragraphs that include details and concrete evidence to support generalizations (topic sentences)	Use evidence from the source text to support the thesis and topic sentences	Intermediate skills
Use the writing process to draft, revise, and edit materials	Draft, revise, and edit the paper	
	Student objectives for a research project (Assignment 5)	
Formulate an effective thesis for at least one argumentative research essay	Articulate a clear position that can be backed by research	Advanced skills
Learn to conduct research and evaluate sources	Integrate at least five credible sources in the paper	
	Draft, revise, and edit the paper	
Show skill in using MLA style for page formatting, in-text citations, and a list of works cited	Format the paper in MLA style; include in-text citations and a list of works cited	

Choosing a topic and crafting an assignment

After spending some time with your students either in face-to-face or online discussions, you will be the best judge of which topics will engage their interests and help them achieve course objectives. However, if you are just starting the semester, you may want to consult your course reader for inspiration or ask seasoned instructors in your department for sample assignments. If your department requires a diagnostic essay as a first assignment, you may need to find out if one or more required prompts already exist.

Once you have determined the objectives for an assignment and chosen the topic, you will be prepared to draft the wording of the overview, the first part of the assignment. The overview typically takes the form of questions, specific prompts, or open-ended prompts.

*For sample assignments, see Part III of this collection and visit **hackerhandbooks .com/teaching**.*

Sample assignment overviews

Questions
Write a well-focused one-to-two-page essay on the following question:

In the article "Surfing's Up and Grades Are Down," Rene Sanchez examines the effects that computers have on college students' education and lives. **What are some of the <u>negative effects</u> that computers can have on students' academic success, according to the author? Support your answer with specific details from the text.**

Specific prompts
Develop a two-to-three-page essay on the following prompt:

In "Weasel Words," William Lutz shows how advertisers use different types of misleading words to encourage people to buy their products. **Explain how "weasel words" used in advertising distort the truth, according to Lutz.**

Open-ended prompts
Write a six-to-eight-page research paper about a topic related to your major or intended career. **The thesis of your paper should argue for a change in a specific approach or policy.** Use at least five credible sources to support your thesis. Format your paper using MLA style conventions.

Novice writers working on beginning-level assignments often benefit from narrow, straightforward questions or prompts that help them focus their thoughts. Advanced writers who have had practice articulating thesis statements and developing ideas in cohesive essays can often handle more open-ended projects.

As you draft the assignment overview, make the goals and outcomes explicit. Doing so will help you create an assignment within the students' skill range and avoid setting goals that students are not yet equipped to meet. Specifically, include key terms relevant to your course or subject, directives (such as *discuss, explain, analyze, argue, trace, compare, contrast*, and *synthesize*), and other guidelines (such as *support your response with at least three examples from the text*) that clarify the purpose of the assignment. In class or online (in video, audio, or text presentation), take time to explain the key terms and directives to your students, who might not fully understand what words such as *trace* or *synthesize* entail.

Creating a sequence of steps within an assignment and integrating the handbook

When you design the steps of an assignment, split the larger tasks into manageable chunks and set a due date for each step. If you are teaching an online or hybrid class, consider using your learning management system's course calendar to remind your students of these dates; also list them on your assignment overview. Provide several checkpoints — especially for research projects and longer analysis papers — so that students can receive guidance from you, their peers, or a writing center consultant long before their final drafts are due. Encourage online students to share their thesis statements or first drafts with you and consider setting up groups within your online course so that students receive peer feedback during the writing process as well. Dividing assignments into smaller steps will help students avoid both procrastination and plagiarism. It will also allow you to direct students to specific help in their handbook for each assignment element (see the example assignment on pp. 32–33 for sample handbook cross-references).

For a sample lesson, see Module 11, "Teaching students to avoid plagiarism."

The objectives you have already established for the project will help you determine the specific steps to assign. Depending on the assignment outcomes and your students' needs, you can set due dates for individual student tasks such as a project topic, a tentative thesis, an outline, a list of sources, and multiple drafts. The following chart provides a sample sequence of lesson steps and student tasks leading to a final research project.

Sequencing the steps of an assignment

Lesson steps	Student tasks
1. Discuss the handbook's coverage of choosing a topic and review the sample research paper.	Develop a list of three to five possible topics. Exchange feedback in a peer review session.
2. Discuss thesis statements. Practice with the handbook's print or online thesis exercises.	Settle on a topic and write a tentative thesis. Submit the thesis to the instructor for preliminary approval.
3. Discuss the handbook sections on conducting research and evaluating sources.	Find at least five sources. Bring them to class for a source-evaluation workshop.
4. Review the handbook's coverage of end citations and complete related exercises in class.	Create a list of end citations for your sources. Submit it to the instructor for feedback.
5. Review sample outlines in the handbook and discuss tips on organizing information.	Create a tentative outline. Receive feedback in a peer review session.

6. Review the handbook section on making global revisions.	Bring your first draft to class for a peer review session. Focus on global issues.
7. Discuss the handbook sections on integrating sources, avoiding plagiarism, and revising sentences.	Bring your second draft to class for a peer review session. Focus on in-text citations and sentence-level editing.
8. Ask students to share specific editing challenges. Review topics and discuss corresponding print or online handbook exercises.	Proofread your final draft and submit it for evaluation.

Providing explicit instructions

After you have drafted the assignment overview and determined the individual tasks your students will undertake, create explicit instructions for students to follow. To provide thorough support, include the following:

- An overview of the assignment (the question or prompt, including the specific objectives of the assignment)

- A brief explanation of the purpose of the assignment, showing how it relates to the outcomes of the course

- A list of the required tasks and their due dates (for online courses, consider using your learning management system's course calendar to convey these dates)

- Specific formatting and submission requirements, if any

- Evaluation guidelines (such as a list of the specific features of a successful paper or a copy of the rubric you will use to assess the work)

- A list of extra tips or resources, such as relevant sections of the handbook, to which students can refer during the writing process (provide links to resources for online or hybrid courses)

For additional help, see the sample assignment handout on page 32.

ENG 101

Assignment 2: Text Analysis Essay

(Note: TBH = *The Bedford Handbook*)

Overview

In standard written English, write a two-to-three-page academic essay using MLA conventions for formatting, in-text citations, and a works cited list. Your essay should respond directly to the following prompt and must include properly cited **direct quotations** and **paraphrases** (see TBH 54b).

Prompt: In "The Roots of War," Barbara Ehrenreich compares war to "an infectious disease." How are war and disease alike, according to Ehrenreich? Is this an appropriate, reasonable metaphor?

The overview clarifies the objectives of the assignment.

Purpose

The purpose of this assignment is to give you practice using MLA conventions for formatting, quoting, paraphrasing, and documenting sources. This assignment builds on the basic essay-writing skills you learned in Assignment 1.

The purpose section points out the relevance of the assignment.

Due dates for assignment tasks

9/23: Tentative thesis statement and rough outline (see 1c and 53b in TBH)
9/25: List of possible sources: must include citation information
9/27: Preliminary draft (#1): must include *at least* a thesis statement and body paragraphs
10/4: Revised draft (#2): must include the introduction, body, and conclusion
10/9: Final draft (#3)

The sequence of steps reinforces writing as a process and helps students avoid plagiarism. References to the handbook provide students with extra support.

Formatting instructions

Use MLA conventions for formatting, in-text citations, and a works cited list. Do not use a title page.

Evaluation guidelines

Excellent (A grade) papers will display the following characteristics:
- A thesis that clearly states your position on the topic (see TBH section 1c and chapter 53)
- Body paragraphs that support the thesis effectively (see TBH chapter 3)
- Fluidly integrated in-text citations for both direct quotations and paraphrases (see TBH chapter 55)
- An organizational pattern that advances the thesis and suits your purpose and audience (see TBH 3c)
- Carefully crafted sentences in standard academic English (see TBH Part III)
- An accurate works cited list and page formatting in MLA style (see TBH chapters 56 and 57)

Evaluation guidelines provide a simple rubric and tie standards for achievement to handbook content.

Extra help

- Review the information on integrating sources and avoiding plagiarism (see 51 and 52 in TBH).
- If you have any specific questions about your draft, stop by my office (Johnston Hall, 156-B) during my office hours or visit the Writing Center in LeCrone Hall, Room 204.

Additional tips point students to sections in the handbook and resources on campus that can help them produce successful drafts.

Topic 4
Responding to student writers

It's not *in* class but *after* class that many writing instructors begin their most demanding work — that of responding to and evaluating student papers. Your feedback is key to your students' growth as critical thinkers and effective communicators, but you have only so much time to evaluate their work. The advice in this topic can help you provide useful feedback without overextending yourself.

Understanding the purposes of responding

Many instructors, particularly those who are just starting their careers, may feel overwhelmed by the task of responding to student writers. In outcome-driven, skill-oriented programs, in particular, some instructors may feel responsible for addressing all of their students' errors with every assignment. It may be helpful to pause and reflect on the purpose of responding, which — ultimately — is to empower students to become stronger communicators. Your role as a writing instructor is not to point out every flaw in a student's paper or to edit every mistake; rather, your role is to establish (with the student's input) manageable targets for learning and growth. Keep the following points in mind as you comment on your students' drafts.

Write to the student, not to the paper. If you keep in mind that you are responding to a writer — a human being who is working toward becoming stronger and more skillful — and not just to a piece of writing — with its likely variety of successes and flaws, large and small — you can focus your feedback on the manageable steps that the writer can take to improve a specific draft in a specific time period.

Provide students with specific tools. Teacher responses help students build skills. Written or recorded audio responses on student papers and oral feedback provided during teacher-student conferences (including phone or video calls for online courses) are perhaps the most beneficial when they provide specific, targeted advice that students can understand and apply immediately (in the same paper) or shortly thereafter (in a future draft or assignment). (See the sample comment on student writing on p. 36.)

> **In this topic:**
>
> Understanding the purposes of responding 35
>
> Providing useful feedback 36
>
> Building fluency and rhetorical awareness 38
>
> Managing the paper load 39
>
> Encouraging students to reflect on their own work 42

Animal rights activists are often portrayed as menacing. Many times, I have noticed that their coverage of stories involving animal rights groups focuses on the activists' harsh accusations or damages to property, rather than the plight of the animals they want to protect.

Whose coverage? See 23d in the handbook. Also, jotting down "pronoun reference 23d" on your editing log might prompt you to check for this error in your next draft.

Create a scaffold for future growth. It is difficult, particularly when working with novice writers, to look beyond numerous surface errors and structural flaws. Remember that writing development is slow and recursive and that you can help students learn to review their own work and introduce them to tools for revision. You can't provide your students with all the skills they will ever need as academic writers. You will best serve your students by crafting specific feedback that is sensitive to their individual abilities and needs at given stages of their development as writers.

Answer students' questions. Perhaps the most important purpose of teacher response is to provide students with answers to their own questions. Students can suggest questions about their work in cover letters or reflection journals. You also may be able to gather student questions by looking through drafts where changes are tracked electronically or editing is marked by hand. When students start the conversation and let you know when or where they would most appreciate your advice, they will be interested in and better able to apply your feedback.

Providing useful feedback

As you read over your students' drafts, keep in mind that each response is a chance for you to teach and for your students to learn. It isn't your responsibility (and some would say not your right) to copyedit a student's draft. Limit your responses to carefully chosen chunks of information that the student can digest and advice that the student will have an opportunity to follow. The following suggestions can help you focus your responses effectively.

Comment on the rhetorical situation — not just on form. To help your students become better communicators, try to vary the focus of your feedback. Resist the temptation to focus in early drafts on errors in form, such as grammatical mistakes and formatting flaws, though many students need help with these issues. First address global issues such as content, organization, and the general clarity of ideas. The questions on the following page can help you assess global issues in your students' papers.

Addressing global issues in students' papers

- Does the content meet the general requirements or scope of the assignment?
- Does the thesis or argument respond to the prompt and suit the genre?
- Does the paper provide sufficient detail to support the thesis?
- Is the organization logical? Does the organizational pattern advance the writer's purpose and thesis?

Offer direction and praise on a few key points. Students benefit from feedback in manageable portions that they can apply soon after they receive your comments. When providing focused direction for your students, try to praise one or two specific features of the paper and identify one or two specific areas in need of improvement. You can do this with notes in the margins or at the end of the paper. Audio commenting, which allows you to convey enthusiasm, genuine interest, and sincerity with your tone of voice, can be particularly effective for this type of feedback.

Positive comments are particularly important because they can affirm students' efforts to establish their voices as writers. Affirmation builds students' confidence and their ability to recognize strengths in their own work and that of their peers, and it guides students to use similar successful patterns in comparable writing situations. Comments that suggest revisions make students aware that they need to try different strategies in the future if they wish to communicate clearly and effectively. The following sample comments are useful models for identifying strengths as well as areas in need of improvement.

Sample comments

Sample comments on strengths

- Your introduction is strong because you present readers with a clear debate and include a thesis that anchors the rest of the essay.
- Your thesis statement works well because it responds clearly and effectively to the assignment.
- You include excellent details in your paper. Your description of the shooting accident in the third paragraph vividly supports your main idea about gun control.

Sample comments on areas in need of improvement

- Your second body paragraph would be stronger if you added a specific example of the misunderstandings between the two characters.
- Your argument begins strong but doesn't seem fully developed. To make your argument more convincing, try adding a third supporting point.
- You repeat the same information in these three sentences. Focus your reader's attention by omitting the first two.

Building fluency and rhetorical awareness

Avoid vague language and jargon.   Comments that are either vague or too technically detailed can thwart your efforts to help your students learn and may even frustrate students because, quite simply, they will not understand what you are trying to teach them. Try to avoid using vague generalities (such as *good work*) and jargon or cryptic abbreviations (such as *awk*). If you decide to use codes or abbreviations, be sure to define them for your students (see the sample comments on p. 37). When responding to student writers, provide specific praise or concrete suggestions for improvement.

See suggestions for identifying errors with handbook codes under "Managing the paper load" on page 39.

Think of yourself as part of the writer's audience, rather than the grader. Many students enter writing classes with the preconception that they will "receive" good grades if their instructor "likes" their work. To them, instructor comments often seem to reflect arbitrary opinions instead of the observations of a trained reader. Try to build students' rhetorical awareness by writing comments from a typical reader's perspective rather than a purely personal standpoint.

Compare the two sets of comments in the following box on positioning yourself as a reader. Each set attempts to provide the same advice from a different perspective. The first two comments, written in the first person, may lead students to think that they are writing for one person only — you — and may dissuade them from transferring lessons to other writing situations. The second two comments, written in a more general voice, can build audience awareness because they remind students to write for a community of readers.

Encouraging students' audience awareness

Avoid presenting yourself as the only reader.

- Next time, I'd like to see more specific details from the source text.

- I liked your conclusion. It left me with a sense of urgency about the problem of global climate change.

Position yourself as one of many readers.

- Next time try to include more specific details from the source text so that readers will be more convinced by your argument.

- Your conclusion is strong because you leave readers with a sense of urgency about the problem of global climate change.

When correcting surface errors, begin with those that most interfere with communication.   Sometimes you may be able to comment on all of your students' errors because your students already have solid control over standard written English and make only a few mistakes. With many students, however, marking all the errors is not the best way to offer help. When you are working with less experienced students, avoid peppering their papers with your comments. Doing so leaves little time for other class preparation and often discourages students, who may feel overwhelmed by the number of comments they must address. Instead, focus on only those errors — or patterns of error — that interfere with the writer's communication. If you feel the need

See "Managing the paper load" on page 39.

to let students know that their papers require significant editing, point out this fact in an end comment rather than through a legion of marks.

Establish goals for the next draft or assignment.   In your concluding comments, present one or two realistic targets that are based on the specific feedback you've provided throughout the paper. For example, if you have suggested that the essay would have been stronger with more details, advise the student to focus on developing supporting points in the drafting stage of the next assignment. If the sentences are missing commas after introductory elements, require the student to edit the next paper specifically for this error. Ask students to evaluate their own progress toward these goals in a cover letter accompanying future assignments.

See the sample cover letter under "Encouraging students to reflect on their own work" on page 42.

Managing the paper load

Responding to student writers is a time-consuming process. Even though providing feedback will never be as quick and easy as sending bubbled forms through a Scantron, the following strategies can help you provide thoughtful, constructive comments in a relatively short time.

Limit the amount of commenting you do.   Be selective when you comment on student papers. Your role as an instructor and a coach is not to edit your students' work but to provide useful feedback that will encourage their growth. *Resist the urge to copyedit.*

- **Do an initial reading without commenting**. Read through the paper once before providing any feedback. Try to identify patterns or major features that warrant advice. Then read the paper a second time, limiting your comments to advice about those features that you identified the first time through.

- **Identify patterns of error — not all errors.** If a paper contains frequent errors of the same type, don't feel pressured to point out each occurrence. The number of marks may overwhelm both you and the student and may, in the end, thwart your effort to help the student improve sentence-level control. Instead, identify one or two examples of the most prominent errors and allow the student to find the remaining errors of the same type. Such a practice will save you time and will provide the student with a valuable skill-building exercise. If some students resist this method and look to you to correct all errors for them, explain your process and help them understand that they will learn best if they focus on a limited number of grammatical forms at one time and make their own revisions.

- **Mark errors with the symbols or rule labels used in the handbook.** The rules and patterns explained in Hacker handbooks are accompanied by letter-number codes: for example, the rule "Balance parallel ideas in a series" is S1-a in *A Writer's Reference* and 9a in *Rules for Writers*. To make error identification simple and direct, point to specific handbook rules in your comments. You can key your marks in several ways: (1) identify the error with the letter-number code of the relevant handbook section, (2) use the standard revision symbols in the chart at the end of the handbook, or (3) provide students with a key that matches sections of the handbook to your own revision symbols. (See the box "Keying editing symbols to the handbook.") Whichever method you choose, be sure to alert students to the key you are using so that they can interpret the

See sample comments on page 37.

codes. Give students some time to look over your feedback in class and to ask questions about your shorthand.

Keying editing symbols to the handbook

Using letter-number codes from the handbook

The code 32b, written above the error, points the student to the rule "Use a comma after an introductory clause or phrase."

Even though Paulson's article provides an interesting perspective $\overset{32b}{it}$ fails to address solutions to the problem.

Using revision symbols*

The shorthand symbol *frag* lets the student know that the sentence is a fragment in need of revision.

Which the researcher should have used first. *frag*

*If you use symbols, be sure to point students to the list of revision symbols at the end of the handbook, or provide students with your own key. See p. 37 for sample comments.

See also the sample rubric below.

Work with rubrics. Rubrics are scoring instruments that match assignment requirements with descriptions of various levels of achievement and help establish benchmarks for your course. Holistic rubrics provide broad, general descriptions for each score or grade category. Analytical rubrics provide descriptions of particular features (such as purpose, content, organization, and sentence-level clarity) at each score or grade category, as shown in the box "Sample analytical rubric." The explanations in the rubric help clarify and create shortcuts for written feedback on student work. The best rubrics are specific to particular writing situations.

Sample analytical rubric

Feature	Excellent	Fair	Needs Improvement
Thesis/main idea	Focused, compelling, and sophisticated; provides specific direction for the reader	Focused; provides sufficient direction for the reader	Provides very little or no direction for the reader
Content and support used	Consistent use of relevant, specific examples and details from the text to create a compelling essay	Some use of relevant, specific examples and details from the text to create a compelling essay	Consistently vague or general use of examples from the text

Organization	Excellent use of paragraphs in a logical order; effective use of transitions between paragraphs and ideas	Good use of paragraphs; transitions between paragraphs and ideas may be weak; no ideas out of place	Random use of paragraphs to chunk ideas together; ideas may be out of place
Written expression	Lively, sophisticated language and sentence structures	Clear language with good control over sentence boundaries and variety	Unclear language choices; needs significant sentence-level revision

Ask students to determine areas for feedback.   In a cover letter accompanying their final drafts, students can identify one or two key features that they would like you to assess. You can provide more extensive written or audio commentary on these features while using the rubric criteria to give students feedback on other features of the assignment.

Hold student conferences.   Inexperienced writers may need more assistance than you can reasonably provide in written or audio comments. Rather than making copious remarks for students to digest on their own, meet with them during your office hours to discuss the assignment. If you teach online and you have students who cannot attend office hours or who live outside of the area, you can conference with them through chat, video, or phone call.

Meeting with each of your students for individual conferences during regularly scheduled class time can sometimes be the best use of your time and theirs. These conference periods can serve a variety of goals: You can identify repetitive surface-level errors, check for the basic requirements of the assignment, or help the student sort out the organization of the paper. If your class is new to research writing, you can spend a few minutes with each student discussing how to integrate sources. Require students to take notes during these meetings, and briefly check their comprehension by asking them to summarize the discussion for you at the end of the session. These measures help students feel prepared to write effective essays and can shorten the time you spend commenting on final drafts.

Use a portfolio system.   Not every draft or essay students write needs to be formally graded. You can assign several essays and ask students to submit them in portfolios, collections of student-chosen writing samples. Portfolios provide students the opportunity to evaluate their own writing and to submit for assessment the pieces that they feel reflect their strongest work.

Although this system may vary depending on the course and your department's or school's requirements, most portfolio-keeping methods follow similar guidelines: The instructor asks students to collect all of their work (prewriting notes, early drafts, revisions, and final drafts) in a folder or binder. At established points during the term (at the midpoint and the end of the semester, for example), the instructor requires students to select a few of their best pieces, revise them, and turn them in for assessment. The instructor can then formally assess — with a rubric and written comments — the pieces that students have identified as their best work. The entire portfolio may receive a holistic grade based on the number and general quality of the entries, but the instructor does not need to comment on each piece of writing in the portfolio.

Encouraging students to reflect on their own work

All the time and energy you spend responding to student writers will not benefit students unless they themselves participate in the review and revision of their work. To encourage their investment in their writing and the feedback process, involve your students in activities that train them to evaluate their own work both during and after the writing process.

See the workshop ideas under "Striking a balance between rhetorical topics and sentence skills" in Topic 1 (p. 9).

Provide checkpoints within the writing process.   In-class writing workshops and student self-assessments can help students learn to revise and identify errors *before* they submit their papers. These intermediate steps allow students to reflect on their writing process and submit their best work.

- **In-class writing workshops**. After students have written preliminary drafts, conduct an in-class writing workshop during which students can evaluate their own work and others'. Workshops are often most productive when you structure each session with specific steps or points for review rather than merely asking students to exchange papers and comment on what they see. For instance, you might guide students through a structured self-assessment (see the next bullet point). You might also model the revision process with a sample paper while students check for the same features or flaws in their own work. (Annotated sample student papers are available on your handbook's Web site.) To maximize their opportunity for reflection and application, let students do most of the talking. Allow them to critique the sample piece, read their own work aloud, and offer advice to other students in the class. If you're teaching online, most learning management systems offer the ability to divide students into groups, a useful option for creating online workshop groups.

- **Structured self-assessments**. Less experienced writers often benefit from structured self-assessments that guide them to check each key feature of their drafts. These self-assessments can be presented as checklists with simple yes/ no questions (*Does your essay introduce the source text in the first paragraph? Does your paper include a works cited page?*) or as lists of simple directives with questions (*Underline your thesis statement. Does it respond to the assignment prompt?*). You can walk students through a structured self-assessment during a workshop session, or you can require students to attach assessment forms to interim or final drafts.

Provide students with opportunities to reflect after they complete their final drafts.   Activities that encourage students to reflect on finished assignments establish a sense of continuity in the course and, more important, stress to students that each assignment is an opportunity to learn and grow. You can create activities that will focus on both sentence-level and rhetorical issues.

- **Editing journals.** To help students reflect on and learn from the surface-level errors in their papers, require them to keep editing journals throughout the semester. In these journals, students can copy flawed sentences from their writing and then correct the sentences by applying a principle from the handbook. (See the sample editing journal entry.) This activity helps students become better editors of their own work as well as learn to use the handbook on their own.

See Module 13, "Teaching grammar and punctuation," for a complete discussion of this activity and a sample handout.

Sample editing journal entry

Original sentence:

> Sedaris thinks that the things he did in his childhood was worthless compared to the things his friends was able to do.

Edited sentence:

> Sedaris thinks that the things he did in his childhood <u>were</u> worthless compared to the things his friends <u>were</u> able to do.

Rule applied:

> 21a: Standard subject-verb combinations

- **Reflective self-assessments and cover letters.** To encourage students to think about rhetorical issues and the overall effectiveness of their work, ask them to complete open-ended, reflective self-assessments. Reflective self-assessments often work best when they are assigned at the end of the writing process (as cover letters submitted with final drafts) or after several assignments have been completed (as cover letters on portfolios of work). In these self-assessments, students can reflect on the revision process, express triumphs and frustrations, identify the specific areas with which they would like help, and establish goals for future assignments. See the sample cover letter on page 44.

Sample cover letter

Directions from the instructor: Insert a page break at the top of your final draft. On the blank page, type a brief cover letter to me that describes how you feel about this paper. Describe (1) what you think the strengths of this paper are, (2) which parts troubled you most and why, (3) why you did or did not incorporate your peer reviewers' suggestions, and (4) which parts or features of your essay you would like me to focus on in my assessment comments.

Student cover letter

Dear Professor Moore,

I think the strongest part of my paper is the introduction. I worked hard to think of a creative opening, and I like how it turned out. I also think that the thesis statement asserts my position clearly. I felt pretty confident when I was analyzing the advertisement, and I think my thesis does a good job of stating what the company's message is.

I like thinking about images and their messages, so I didn't have too much trouble with this assignment overall. I did have some trouble with the organization of my main points, though. I wasn't sure whether I should start with my analysis of the colors used in the ad or whether I should start with the paragraph about the image of the globe. My peer reviewers seemed to think that it was OK as is, so I left it in the original order.

The peer reviews were helpful. They gave me good advice about the page format and works cited list, which I have fixed for the final draft. One reviewer thought I should change the hook in my intro, but the other reviewers thought it was strong. Since these reviewers liked it and I did too, I decided to keep it. You can let me know if you disagree.

Again, I feel that I did a pretty good job on this assignment, so I don't have too many questions. I would like you to comment on the organization and let me know if you think the essay would be stronger if the points were switched around. I'd also like to know how I could improve the conclusion. I don't think the conclusion was as effective as the introduction, and I wish I could have made it better. I'd appreciate your suggestions. Thank you for taking the time to review my paper.

Sincerely,

Oscar Salamon

Topic 5
Working with multilingual writers (teaching ESL)

Multilingual writers are enrolling in colleges across the United States in higher numbers than ever. While the increase in diversity will undoubtedly bring a welcome richness to your classroom, it may also pose instructional challenges that you may not feel prepared to handle.

As you work with multilingual writers, keep in mind that the skills they are learning take time and focus to build. Although there are few quick fixes, the advice in this topic can help you begin to address the needs of these students in your classroom.

Understanding your students' linguistic and educational backgrounds

Important to the advice in this topic is the distinction between *fluency*, or the natural use of language with appropriate levels of formality, and *accuracy*, or grammatical control over language. Some students may be highly fluent users of English with low levels of grammatical accuracy, and some students may produce technically accurate forms that sound mechanical or contextually inappropriate. Each student, depending on educational experience and linguistic exposure, will fall at a different place along the fluency and accuracy spectrums.

When you help individual students create a plan for improvement, consider these starting points and all the variables that contribute to the students' learning needs. Conduct an informal needs assessment by finding answers to questions, like the ones that follow, about your students' linguistic and educational backgrounds. You can often discover the answers by holding brief, casual conferences with your students. Asking them what they like or don't like to read in their native language can lead to important clues about their native-language literacy levels. Or you can ask them to write about their educational experiences in the diagnostic essays you assign at the beginning of the term.

What cultural and educational contexts are most familiar to my students?
Knowing your students' experiences with various educational contexts will help you predict the types of coaching they will need throughout the term. Some students have

spent many years in the US educational system. These students will probably be very familiar with the types of tasks you will assign and the classroom behaviors you will expect. They may be aware of typical expectations for collaborative activities, such as class discussions and peer reviews, and they may already be familiar with some academic genres, such as argument essays.

Students who are new to the US educational system, however, may need extra assistance in understanding expectations for classroom behavior and academic genres. The writing styles they prefer may seem ornate, illogical, or mechanical to you, and they may not be comfortable with actively engaging in discussion or group work. These students may need structured guidance for practices that other students have already internalized.

How did my students initially learn English — aurally or through formal English as a foreign language (EFL) education?
Your students' original exposure to English will affect the types of rhetorical and grammatical patterns they initially produce in college writing assignments. Students who learned English primarily through conversation (whether through casual contact or secondary-level English immersion programs) often have a solid sense of style, idiom, and cadence, but they may make local errors, particularly with subtle word endings and sounds (confusing *being* and *been* or leaving off the final *-d* in a past participle or past-tense verb, for example). Typically, these students will benefit most from literacy activities that help them connect the patterns they have heard with the written forms they will be expected to produce.

Some ideas for promoting sentence-level accuracy are described in Module 13 and under "Addressing surface-level writing issues" on page 48.

Students who learned English as a foreign language in a traditional classroom setting often need fluency practice, or help learning what "sounds right" in an academic context. These students often enter college writing classes with rule-based grammatical knowledge, but they may have trouble with more contextual aspects of language: semantic boundaries (understanding the meaning of *tall* versus the meaning of *high*, for example), levels of formality, and rhetorical expectations. These writers tend to benefit less from decontextualized exercise sets and more from activities involving authentic material in context. Such activities help them learn not just how to form a particular linguistic pattern but also when and how to use it appropriately.

See "Building fluency and rhetorical awareness" and "Addressing surface-level writing issues" on page 48 for activities that provide fluency practice. See also Module 13.

What are my students' native-language literacy levels?
Learning about your students' native-language literacy levels can give you a sense of how quickly your students will be able to respond to writing instruction. Students who are highly literate in their native languages may enter your class with metalinguistic awareness — an understanding of how language works — and they often develop their English writing skills at a rapid pace. Students who don't have strong native-language skills may need extra time to develop as writers because they are building two skills — both English fluency and literacy in general — at once. For students in the second group, try creating activities that will build reading skills, even if your class focus is on writing. Remind these students to be patient with their own progress and to seek additional support, if possible, at your school's reading and writing labs.

How much time do my students spend speaking and hearing English every day?
The answer to this question, like the answer to the previous one, lets you and your students know how quickly they might build English fluency. Some students may use English in class, at work, and at home with their siblings, spouses,

or roommates. Others may listen to English only at school and may spend the rest of their time using their native languages. Naturally, the more exposure students have to comprehensible, contextualized language, the more opportunities they will have to build fluency. Remind students that their growth as writers depends on their exposure to English in all of its forms — both written and spoken — in contexts of varying levels of formality.

Promoting open classroom communication and helping students understand academic expectations

Throughout the semester, you may need to define expectations that your native English-speaking students take for granted. This is especially true if you are working with international students who have not been exposed to the academic culture of the United States or if you are working with first-generation college students. Open, friendly, and consistent communication can build the trust that is critical to the growth of these students.

Be as clear as possible with all of your students; provide models and explicit instructions.   Being direct and open with students from the start can help develop appropriate classroom behaviors and can avoid miscommunication and frustration. Try not to assume that your students "should know better." Realize that some students may need instructions for classroom behaviors and procedures, such as speaking in class or working in groups, or basic formatting principles, for example where to staple a document or place their names on assignments. Provide key guidelines in writing and discuss them with the class. Be explicit when encouraging students to ask for clarification outside of class as well. For some students, contacting an instructor may seem inappropriate.

As you cover some of the model papers in your handbook or reader, be sure to point out rhetorical forms as well as formatting tips that may help your students understand your expectations. In addition, help ease the transition to the US classroom by pointing students to the ESL coverage in your handbook, which provides both linguistic and general academic help. Your handbook may include a directory of ESL boxes in the ESL menu near the end. You might also refer to section E1, "Understanding college-level expectations," in *Resources for Multilingual Writers and ESL*, a Hacker Handbooks Supplement.

See section E1, "Understanding college-level expectations," in Resources for Multilingual Writers and ESL.

Invite students to your office for conferences.   If your course context and schedule allow, leave time for extra office hours to meet with those multilingual students who would benefit from one-on-one attention. Extend an invitation to stop by for individual help, which you may not have time to provide during class.

Students may assume that they are disturbing your work or that they are inconveniencing you if they contact you or visit during your office hours. International students from some cultures will not come to your office unless you take the initiative to set an appointment with them. To make students comfortable with seeking individual help, clarify your policies at the beginning of the term, and point them to the guidelines offered in section E1-e of *Resources for Multilingual Writers and ESL*.

For more advice on holding student conferences, see "Managing the paper load" in Topic 4 (p. 39).

Building fluency and rhetorical awareness

Students who write with language that seems stilted, mechanical, or illogical often just need more exposure to English. Many of these students can progress if they are given multiple models and repeated contact with standard linguistic and rhetorical patterns. To help students build fluency and rhetorical awareness, you might need to offer activities beyond the exercise sets in your handbook. The following classroom practices can help.

Engage all four linguistic modalities — even in classes designed to focus only on writing.   Create opportunities in class for your students to *listen*, *speak*, *read*, and *write* in English. Try reading aloud to your students, guiding them through a choral reading (of a poem, for instance) or assigning dictation or text-reconstruction activities in addition to the customary reading and writing tasks.

If possible, increase your students' exposure to English by assigning tasks that will allow them to use the language outside of the classroom. For example, you might ask students to attend a talk on campus or see a play at a local theater to help them build receptive language skills.

Offer "extensive" reading and writing practice.   "Intensive" practice focuses on grammar exercises and finely edited essays. "Extensive" practice typically favors *quantity* over precision and provides multilingual students much-needed repetition with high-frequency forms. Extensive practice helps students work on general comprehension and fluency — the ability to understand and use English without translating from their native languages (the source of many transfer errors). As you design your syllabus, try to build in some extensive activities, such as keeping a journal or reading the newspaper, that allow students to strengthen their skills.

For a list of extensive language activities, see the chart in section E2 in Resources for Multilingual Writers and ESL.

Assign practice writing that will not be graded.   You might ask students to write responses to the discussion questions at the end of a textbook reading. If the reading addresses the subject of a formal essay they will write later in the term, such ungraded assignments give students the chance to grapple with the vocabulary and rhetorical patterns they will need to know when they write for a grade.

Create opportunities for self-assessment and reflection.   To lead students toward mastery of particular concepts or rhetorical patterns, build writing assign-ments in multiple steps that require reflection. For example, provide checklists for students to use at various stages of the writing process, assign editing logs, ask students to keep journals about their writing experiences, or ask them to submit final drafts with cover letters in which they reflect on the strengths of their papers and the challenges they faced while writing. Such reflection activities will both reinforce class topics and help students build confidence as writers.

Addressing surface-level writing issues

Assigning intensive practice — having students complete exercises and identify and correct errors in their own writing — is a good starting point for helping students address surface-level issues. But most multilingual writers will need additional practice to become effective editors. Offer print or electronic exercises that require students to fill in the blank or edit problem sentences as a first step toward mastering grammatical patterns. These exercises can help your students begin to recognize errors in other writers' work and to become comfortable with some of the grammatical terminology you use in class. Such exercises, however, should not be presented as a sole remedy or a quick fix. Once students become more comfortable with the grammatical patterns they encounter in the exercises, create opportunities for them to extend the practice to their own writing. This section presents a few strategies you can use to heighten your students' awareness of and control over English linguistic patterns.

Create awareness-raising activities.   Draw students' attention to specific language patterns with activities, such as those listed below, that focus on building linguistic awareness and receptive knowledge or on listening and reading comprehension.

- **Self-editing with attention to specific forms.** After students have completed rough drafts of an essay assignment, guide them through a self-editing exercise. With the handbook open for guidance, students can, for example, underline the subject and the verb in each sentence in their draft to check for agreement or underline every noun to determine the type of article needed.

- **Short writing assignments that require students to focus on specific linguistic forms.** You can design writing assignments that require students to practice specific grammatical patterns. For example, the prompt "Describe how you have changed since you enrolled in college" requires students to practice the use of the present perfect tense. Several similar prompts are listed in section E4-b in *Resources for Multilingual Writers and ESL.*

- **Editing logs.** For students who continue to make numerous surface-level errors, you can assign editing logs. Rather than correcting mistakes on students' essays, identify errors by highlighting or underlining them. Later, ask students to submit a log with copies of these original sentences along with corrections and explanations of the rule used to fix the sentence.

  For editing log lesson ideas and a blank log, see Module 13.

- **Dictation and text-reconstruction activities.** Another way to focus on specific forms is through traditional or modified dictation. Try replacing all the prepositions in a short passage with blank lines. Read the passage at a conversational pace, and ask students to fill in the blanks with the prepositions they hear. When the students are finished, reveal the original passage, and follow up with a discussion. Ask students to identify what was new or unexpected and to share what they learned about their own linguistic patterns. Discuss forms that were difficult to discern as well as tips for remembering specific patterns. Noticing patterns of error is the first step in self-editing.

Provide direct feedback; try not to ask what "sounds right."   When working with native English speakers, instructors often ask their students to read their own work aloud so that the students can hear their errors. This strategy typically does not work for multilingual writers. What "sounds right" to many of these students is often the source of the problem since they may not notice subtle sounds (such as *a* and *-ed*). When offering feedback to multilingual writers, provide explicit models, including sample sentence revisions, if appropriate, and encourage them to use their handbook for reference as they edit their papers. To provide focused assistance in a conference or on paper, key editing symbols to sections of the handbook.

For more on keying feedback to the handbook, see Topic 4.

Enlisting the help of other campus services

For handouts on using the writing center, visit **bedfordstmartins.com /rewriting.**

Some multilingual writers will have needs that you simply will not have time to address during class meetings and occasional office visits. If a student needs more assistance or coaching than you can reasonably offer, solicit help from the support offices on your campus.

Become familiar with the resources at your school's writing lab. Some students will need one-on-one coaching to see a measurable improvement in their writing skills during one semester. Encourage or require these students to use the writing lab on your campus during each step of the writing process. Familiarize yourself with the lab's location, resources, and procedures so that you can provide the students with specific instructions for making the most of their visits.

Maintain an open line of communication with your school's international or multicultural student services office. Many schools have special support offices with advising, counseling, and tutoring for international and multicultural students. Take advantage of the services at your school. With just a phone call, you might be able to arrange language tutoring or special advising for your students.

Be aware of signs of learning disabilities. Not all linguistic concerns stem from second-language learning. Be alert for statements such as "I cannot focus," "I can't spell in my native language either," or "I have trouble organizing an essay in my native language, too." If you suspect that a student has a learning disability, seek assistance from your school's disabilities service office.

Topic 6
Addressing writing in the disciplines

by Terry Myers Zawacki

Most students in first-year composition have had little experience meeting expectations that reflect the disciplines in which their teachers have been trained. The advice in this topic, beginning with a discussion of some of the key terms associated with writing in the disciplines, is aimed at helping you prepare students for the complex writing and rhetorical tasks they will encounter in courses across the curriculum.

Understanding key terms and concepts related to writing in the disciplines

When preparing students for the writing assignments they will encounter in courses across the curriculum, it is useful to understand some of the key terms and concepts associated with writing in the disciplines, or WID, as this field of study is often abbreviated. A more nuanced understanding of WID will, in turn, help you explain to students the complexity and value of the wide range of writing and rhetorical tasks they will undertake in your course and throughout their college careers.

The term *discipline* itself is interesting to consider. While members of a discipline generally agree about core methods, genres, and preferred textual conventions, disciplines are not bound by set rules for building and writing about knowledge. Rather they can expand and change in response to new questions, methods, and social concerns.

Instructors preparing their students for assignments in various disciplines will need to address genres. Genres are much more than rigid formats into which writers pour content. Genre conventions, including rhetorical purposes, formats, and textual features such as structure and tone, differ greatly depending on the aims and motives of the discourse community — the users of particular genres of writing — and the writer's own purpose and audience. For example, a book review in an environmental science or environmental policy course might emphasize the argument the book is making related to science, whereas a book review for a literature course might focus on the author's theme, plot structure, character development, and other literary devices.

For students, learning to write in their chosen discipline occurs gradually over their undergraduate career. With practice, they learn the genres typical of the discipline and the discursive conventions — the approach, tone, structure, and style of writing appropriate for the occasion and the audience. But if students learn all of this through practice in discipline-specific courses, what can the assignments you build for one course teach them about writing in the disciplines?

Instead of teaching students rules and formats for their writing, you can help them become rhetorically aware and attentive to textual features that characterize different ways of knowing and writing in the humanities, social and natural sciences, and applied and technological disciplines such as business and engineering. These textual features include conventions for the structure of the writing (for example, organization and flow); conventions for content, such as typical thesis statements, evidence, methods, and documentation styles of the discipline; and conventions related to tone and language, including how to introduce and refer to sources, when to quote and when to paraphrase, whether to use headings and subheadings, and preferences for paragraph and sentence styles and descriptive language. (For a detailed discussion of these textual differences, see the article by Linton, Madigan, and Johnson in the list of suggested readings at the end of this topic.)

Addressing challenges related to teaching students to write in the disciplines

Because students are usually unfamiliar with the audiences and purposes assumed by their assignments in various disciplines, they may have trouble understanding the genres, conventions, and prose styles their teachers expect. Some students may lose confidence in themselves as writers. They may also become frustrated when they find that assignments of the same genre (a memo or review, for example) may be evaluated by different standards, depending on the discipline and the particular course. If students feel that the wide range of expectations they encounter when writing in various disciplines is arbitrary, they may resist your writing advice or fail to see how your assignments help prepare them for writing in other courses.

Further complicating your task are the "rules" students may have learned for generic academic writing and the attitudes of teachers who believe, sometimes along with the students, that writing should be learned "once and for all" in a composition course. Specifically, students may have trouble breaking away from some of the following:

- organizational templates, like the five-paragraph essay
- formulaic introductions, in which the thesis is only one sentence and must always appear at the end of the first paragraph
- formulaic conclusions that provide no more than a summary
- restrictions on the use of *I* in academic writing
- MLA as the preferred documentation style for the generic "research paper"

When these rules prove to be insufficient or inappropriate for the disciplinary context, students may resign themselves to the idea that teachers are all so different in their expectations that it's hard to predict what they want. (See, for example, the student attitudes reported in Thaiss and Zawacki's *Engaged Writers and Dynamic Disciplines: Reports on the Academic Writing Life*. Full publication information and a list of other readings appear on p. 58.)

One way to help students overcome these challenges is to engage them as active participants in an exploration of academic writing across the curriculum. Help them think about what teachers are expecting them to be able to do as writers and why. Provide students with opportunities to reflect on the rhetorical knowledge they already possess: What do they already know about teachers' expectations and the contexts for those expectations? How will the writing skills they've learned in one context serve them in another?

Helping students become rhetorically aware writers

Invite students to reflect on already acquired rhetorical knowledge.

Active learning and reflection on learning are critical components in the transfer of knowledge from one context to another. Begin by inviting students to reflect on the rhetorical knowledge, skills, and abilities they have already acquired from previous writing experiences. Even students fresh out of high school should be able to draw on writing assignments they've completed for a variety of courses across the curriculum.

Here are some questions you might ask students to guide their self-reflection:

- What kinds of writing assignments have you been asked to do in courses across the curriculum? Which ones were most enjoyable? Why? Which were least enjoyable? Why?

- What assignments have you written with the most confidence? Why did you feel confident about them? Which ones have made you feel less than confident about your writing? Why did you feel unsure?

- How would you describe the characteristics of academic writing, as teachers have taught it or described it to you?

- What are some of the biggest differences you've noticed in the assignments teachers give and the expectations they seem to have? How would you explain these differences?

- What strategies do you use to analyze new or unfamiliar academic writing tasks and audiences?

- What writing skills do you rely on to accomplish your goals, no matter what the task?

- Have you noticed differences in the advice teachers give you regarding format, tone, and style? For example, what have various teachers told you about using *I* and contractions in your writing? Have you learned a variety of approaches toward introductions, thesis statements, and conclusions? Have teachers differed on recommended paragraph and sentence lengths?

- Do any of the differences in writing advice you've been given seem clearly related to the subject being taught? Explain.

Students will likely benefit from sharing their insights and discoveries with their peers. Explaining their experiences gives them the opportunity to analyze their own responses and expand their understanding by finding connections between their self-reflection and what they hear from their peers.

You may want to model this reflective process for your students before they begin. Think about your own academic writing experiences and how you learned to write with confidence in a variety of genres and for readers who may have had very different expectations of your writing. Students will also benefit from hearing about how you learned to become a confident writer and writing teacher.

Here are some questions to guide your own self-reflection:

- What kinds of texts do I routinely write as a scholar and a teacher? Which ones do I enjoy the most? Why?

- What writing skills do I rely on to accomplish my goals, no matter what the task?

- What strategies do I use to analyze unfamiliar writing tasks and audiences?

- How do I define academic writing based on the writing I typically do? How does my definition change when I write for different audiences and purposes?

- When it comes to stylistic conventions, is my academic writing usually formal (for example, not using *I* or contractions) or informal? How do I typically write introductions and conclusions? How do I phrase a thesis? Do my paragraphs tend to be relatively short (no more than five sentences) or longer than five sentences? Do I tend to write longer, more complex sentences, or do I prefer shorter, more concise sentences?

- To what extent and in what ways might my preferences be typical of the preferences of teachers across disciplines? How might they reflect my own disciplinary training?

Reflection helps us better understand ourselves as learners and writers: We can identify and define problems, discern patterns in learning situations and find new ways to think about them, and become agents of our own learning. Reflection is central to our ability to transfer knowledge from one context to another.

It may be helpful to create an inventory of the rhetorical knowledge, skills, and abilities your students identify in this discussion. Record their definitions of academic writing, indicating which features cut across disciplines and which ones reflect disciplinary preferences. (Be sure to acknowledge that teachers may vary, even within the same discipline, based on their own individual preferences and local contexts.) In addition, you may want to record the writing skills, abilities, and strategies your students rely on to write papers for teachers across the curriculum. To expand their rhetorical awareness, ask students to revisit the self-reflection questions and to add to these lists throughout the semester as they become more experienced writers in other disciplines.

Ask students to analyze teachers' assignments and expectations across disciplines.   Early in the semester, ask students to engage in a collaborative exploration of teachers' assignments across disciplines, including yours. As with the self-reflection exercise, the goal of this exploration is to help them identify and draw on already acquired rhetorical and genre knowledge to analyze the writing task and respond appropriately. Remind them of the features that are common to academic writing across disciplines (reasoned analysis and claims supported by evidence) and those that are discipline-specific (genres, use of evidence, and textual conventions for structure and style). Here are some strategies you might consider using:

- With your students, analyze one or more of your assignments. Ask students to underline key words in the assignment that help them understand the genre (for example, literacy narrative) and the purpose of the writing, the rhetorical modes (such as narration, description), and the textual features they associate with this kind of writing. Discuss with students the contexts and mix of variables that influence your assignment and expectations, including your sense of the standards for generic academic writing, the discipline and subdiscipline in which you've been trained (for example, English and composition studies), departmental guidelines, and even personal goals you may have for them as writers. Ask them to consider how the rhetorical strategies, genre conventions, and other writing skills they are practicing in your course will transfer to the assignments they are encountering in other courses.

- Ask students to analyze the descriptions of disciplinary genres and sample student papers that appear in *Writing in the Disciplines: Advice and Models*, a Hacker Handbooks Supplement. How are the genres structured? What topics and questions do they address? Which genre features seem familiar, and which are unfamiliar? Students can work in groups assigned to different disciplines to analyze how the sample student papers reflect disciplinary genres and conventions (such as formal or informal tone; style of introduction, thesis, and conclusion; use of evidence; and documentation style).

- Ask students to perform a similar analysis on a professional piece of writing for a specific discipline. Have students describe the writer's purpose and how it relates to the rhetorical strategies the writer uses (for example, narration, comparison, or classification). Ask students if they can identify conventions for structure, content, tone, and language (see "Understanding key terms and concepts related to writing in the disciplines" on p. 51 for more on these conventions). If the writer uses the first-person point of view, have students describe the purpose and effect.

- Ask students to analyze the different expectations of teachers in courses across the curriculum by collaboratively examining assignments they have been given. This analysis should address questions such as the following:

    Why am I being given this assignment?

    What kind of writing am I being asked to do?

    What key words in the assignment help me understand what my teacher expects me to do as a writer?

    How does this writing reflect the disciplinary focus of the course and the genres typical of the discipline?

    How does this assignment fit in with other activities and writing assignments in the course?

    What do I already know how to do that will help me meet the teacher's expectations?

- Ask students to generate a list of questions they can ask teachers across disciplines about the contexts for their assignments and expectations for good writing, including those that are generic to academic writing, discipline-specific, or derived from other values and goals for writers. (For a list of questions students can ask teachers about writing in their disciplines, see "Learning from your students about writing in the disciplines" on p. 57.)

Reflecting on your own assignments and expectations

When you construct an assignment, you may have an implicit understanding of what you want students to learn, though you might not always state your learning goals and expectations explicitly. Even when you do make your learning goals explicit, you might not be fully aware of the complex mix of variables that influence your expectations, including your sense of the standards for generic academic writing, the discipline and subdiscipline in which you've been trained, departmental guidelines, and even personal preferences based on your sense of what should happen in a general composition course.

The following prompts ask you to reflect on your goals for student writers, the assumptions about academic writing that these goals represent, and the influences that shape the lessons you teach and the assignments you give. These prompts can help you identify and articulate, if you haven't already done so, how the rhetorical knowledge and writing skills students are learning in your course will transfer to the writing tasks they are given in courses across the curriculum. Finally, it's always a good practice to try out an assignment yourself before giving it to students.

Ask yourself the following questions about the assignments you give:

- What do I want students to learn by doing this assignment?

- Do my assignment goals reflect my sense of generic academic skills and rhetorical practices students must learn to be successful writers, no matter what the writing task?

- Do my assignment goals reflect learning outcomes set by the institution, the department, or the composition committee?

- Do my assignment goals reflect my sense of the different genres, formats, and documentation practices students must learn to be successful writers in courses across the curriculum?

- Do my assignment goals reflect other more personal preferences and values (for example, a sense that students need practice in writing for nonacademic audiences in nonacademic genres)?

- Will the rhetorical modes (narration, description, argument) and analytical strategies (definition, comparison and contrast, cause and effect) that I'm teaching students to write be useful to them when they write in other courses? In what way? For example, will these rhetorical modes and analytical strategies be useful when students write case studies or empirical reports based on observation and description?

- How will the genres I'm teaching students to write help them when they write in other courses? How might expectations for genres such as essays, abstracts, annotated bibliographies, book reviews, and researched reports differ from one course to the next?

- What kinds of introductions, thesis statements, and conclusions do I want my students to write? What kind of supporting evidence do I expect my students to use? How are these expectations similar to and different from those of teachers in other disciplines?

- What tone, style, format, and other academic conventions are appropriate for this assignment and this genre of writing? To what extent are they generic to academic writing across the curriculum, and to what extent are they determined by other contexts?

- What do my students need to know about the ways in which my expectations may be similar to or different from those of teachers in other courses across the curriculum?

Learning from your students about writing in the disciplines

Addressing WID in your writing course may seem daunting. How can you begin to grasp the purposes, methods, genres, textual conventions, and other expectations for so many disciplines, courses, and teachers across your institution? It's important to remember how much your students can teach you. You can learn about the kinds of writing your students will be asked to do in their majors if you engage them as active participants in an investigation of academic writing across the curriculum. Their investigation may include interviews with professors, an analysis of their assignments, an exploration of the kinds of professional writing people do in the discipline, and the books and journals their professors write for and read. You might even want to expand this exploration to workplace documents or documents produced in social settings such as organizations and clubs.

Here are some suggestions for questions students might ask a professor in their major:

- How would you describe your discipline and your particular area of interest in the discipline?

- What kinds of questions and methods are typical of your discipline? What type of evidence is most typically used?

- How important is writing in your discipline?

- In what genres do you and your colleagues typically write and for what audiences?

- Do you or your colleagues sometimes write for audiences and in genres that are not typical of your discipline?

- Do you ever use the first-person point of view when you write? If so, when is first person acceptable?

- Does everyone in your discipline follow standard conventions and documentation styles? If so, what are they? If not, what are some of the variations?

- What do you consider to be good writing in your discipline?

For further discussion of the advice and strategies discussed in this topic, see the following readings:

Beaufort, Anne. *College Writing and Beyond: A New Framework for University Writing Instruction.* Logan: Utah State UP, 2007. Print.

Carter, Michael. "Ways of Knowing, Doing, and Writing in the Disciplines." *College Composition and Communication* 58.3 (2007): 385 – 418. Print.

Linton, Patricia, Robert Madigan, and Susan Johnson. "Introducing Students to Disciplinary Genres: The Role of the General Composition Course." *Language and Learning across the Disciplines* 1.2 (1994): 63 – 78. Print.

Russell, David. "Rethinking Genre in School and Society: An Activity Theory Analysis." *Written Communication* 14.4 (1997): 504 – 54. Print.

Thaiss, Chris, and Terry Myers Zawacki. *Engaged Writers and Dynamic Disciplines: Research on the Academic Writing Life.* Portsmouth: Boynton, 2006. Print.

Yancey, Kathleen Blake. *Reflection in the Writing Classroom.* Logan: Utah State UP, 1998. Print.

Modules

The modules in Part II offer strategies and lesson plans for everyday classroom use.

Notes

Module 1
Teaching assignment analysis

Challenges

To approach an assignment effectively and complete it successfully, students must understand both the purpose and the learning objective of the assignment. College writers, often pressed for time with full work and class loads, may have a tendency to dive into an assignment without first having read and reflected on it carefully. They might not pause to think about how the assignment relates to their work in the course or to other writing they have done. They might begin drafting before understanding what their instructor means by language such as "discuss" or "synthesize" or "compare." As a result, you may encounter some of the following challenges as your students approach new assignments:

In this module:

Challenges 61

Strategies 61

■ Sample lesson
for Strategy 1 62

Resources 65

- Students interpret an assignment inaccurately. For example, a student might set out to write a report when the assignment actually calls for a position paper.

To find coverage on working with assignments, see Resources at the end of this module.

- Students are unsure of whether an assignment is calling on them to express a personal opinion or to project conclusions based on evidence from secondary sources. A question students frequently ask is "Should I put my own opinion into my essay?"

- Students may fail to transfer skills and feedback from one assignment to the next. They often don't see how one assignment is related to another, particularly if the genres differ. For example, students should apply what they learn about integrating quotations in a textual analysis to their next research assignment.

- Students define their topics too narrowly or too broadly for a particular assignment prompt.

Strategies

Writing courses should teach students to critically read an assignment and develop an effective response to it. The following strategies can help you teach students how to analyze an assignment:

1. Have students read an assignment prompt and define the directives. Students should become familiar with the meanings of commonly used verbs in assignment prompts: *describe, explain, summarize, discuss, define, compare, contrast, trace, predict, analyze, synthesize, argue, propose, recommend, evaluate.* The student writers must consider whether the prompt is narrow or open-ended—how much freedom do they have with their response? They should also look for any implied questions.

2. Provide students with a model paper they can evaluate in light of the assignment's purpose, directions, requirements, outcomes, expectations, and format. What do they notice about the writer's approach to the assignment? Did the writer fail to meet any requirements of the assignment or address them in an unexpected way?

3. Encourage students to develop action plans before they begin an assignment and to generate assignment checklists for reference during the drafting process. (See the Resources chart at the end of this module and the checklist "Understanding an assignment," if your handbook includes it.)

4. Have students summarize what the assignment asks them to do and reflect on how the assignment builds on previous writing experiences and prepares them for new ones.

Sample lesson for Strategy 1: Understanding an assignment prompt

Lesson planning:	
Sequencing:	Use this lesson when you introduce a new assignment and before students begin drafting.
Student level:	This lesson targets students who are unfamiliar with analyzing an assignment. Students do not need prior experience for this lesson. For students who do have experience with college-level writing assignments, this lesson will help them refine strategies for approaching new assignments.
Learning objectives:	Students will be able to • Prepare for a specific writing assignment • Identify and explain the purpose of an assignment • Identify and define verbs in an assignment • Determine whether an assignment is specific (something like *Compare Samsung's Galaxy S3 ad with Apple's iPhone 5 ad*) or open-ended (such as *Compare two recent advertisements*) • Consider implied questions in an assignment prompt
Time required:	One session of at least fifty minutes with follow-up

Materials/ resources:	• The handbook (See the Resources chart at the end of this module.)
	• Refer to the following guidelines and checklists, if your handbook includes them:
	• Understanding an assignment
	• Approaching assignments in the disciplines

Lesson steps:

Preparation for session:	Ask students to think about a writing assignment they have responded to recently. The assignment could be any kind of writing from any course. Examples might include lab reports, case studies, position papers, critical responses, or research projects from general studies courses, elective courses, or courses in the students' majors. To prepare for Session 1, students should write responses to these questions about the assignment:
	• What topic did you write about?
	• What do you remember saying about that topic?
	• What were the challenges in completing the assignment?
	• Could the assignment have included additional information that would have helped you overcome those challenges? If so, what kind of information?
	Students should bring a copy of their responses to class. (To gauge student preparedness, you might want to ask them to submit their responses to you by e-mail as well before class begins.)
Session:	1. Have a few volunteers share their written responses with the whole class. Spend about fifteen or twenty minutes on this warm-up.
	• Volunteers should describe the assignment they decided to write about. What do they recall saying about that topic?
	• Ask volunteers to explain what the challenges were. Was it difficult to get started, think of a topic, form an opinion, find sources, etc.? What information could have helped them respond to those challenges?
	• As the challenges are mentioned, record them on the board or on the screen.
	• Once students have compiled a list of challenges, ask them to notice any patterns.
	• Introduce students to the idea that an assignment is a text that can be understood and analyzed. Assignment analysis can help them resolve or avoid some of the challenges they've listed.
	• Emphasize that when students think about what the assignment is asking them to do before they begin drafting, they save themselves time and have a better chance of successfully completing the assignment.
	• Encourage students to ask any questions they still have after thinking through the assignment. Some writing challenges can be traced back to a lack of clarity or information in the assignment. Instructors benefit from the opportunity to improve their assignments when students identify problems.
	2. Explain that most assignments include key terms that identify the purpose. Give students a list of these words: *describe, explain, summarize, discuss, define, compare, contrast, trace, predict, analyze, synthesize, argue, propose, recommend, evaluate.* Ask students what these verbs mean to them. Have they encountered them in assignments or essay exams? What do these words ask them to do as writers?

3. If your handbook includes it, direct students to coverage of understanding writing assignments in the disciplines (see the Resources chart at the end of this module) for sample assignments and key terms.

4. Give students the opportunity to practice identifying purpose and key terms in a sample assignment. (Allow at least twenty minutes for this step. You may need to carry it over to the next class period.)

   - Distribute a writing assignment for your course. Divide the class into small groups of two or three.

   - If your handbook includes it, ask students to refer to the checklist "Understanding an assignment" during this step.

   - Each group should appoint one member to record the group's responses. Have each group identify the following elements in the assignment:

     - The key terms in the prompt

     - The purpose of the assignment and any verbs that communicate that purpose

     - The *how* or *why* question that asks the writer to take a position

   - Ask students to identify any implied questions. For example, when assignments ask students to discuss, analyze, or consider a topic, they often require students to answer a *how* or *why* question that is not explicitly stated. A prompt such as "Discuss the effects of larger class sizes on education in kindergarten through eighth grade" is another way of saying "*How* have larger class sizes affected students and teachers in kindergarten through eighth grade?" A general term such as "discuss" might imply that the writer should perform a more specific task such as identifying a cause, making a prediction, or stating a position.

   - Have the groups share their findings with the whole class.

   - Use the concluding time to ask students if there are any aspects of the assignment that require clarification. At this time, remind students that the best way to confirm their understanding of an assignment is to check with their instructor and ask questions about anything in the assignment they do not understand.

Follow-up:	For homework, students can write a brief paragraph in response to the questions "What is this assignment asking me to do?" and "How should I approach it?" Their notes can serve as a rough action plan that will help them begin drafting.

Encourage students to apply what they've learned in this lesson to analyzing writing assignments in other courses. |

Resources

Handbook coverage

The Bedford Handbook, 9th ed.	*A Writer's Reference*, 7th ed.	*Rules for Writers*, 7th ed.	*A Pocket Style Manual*, 6th ed.	*Writer's Help* (writershelp.com)
Assessing the writing situation (1a) Exploring your subject (1b) Drafting a plan (1d) Approaching writing assignments in the disciplines (65)	Assessing the writing situation (C1-a) Exploring the subject (C1-b) Sketching a plan (C1-d) Understanding writing assignments in the disciplines (A4-f)	Assessing the writing situation (1a) Exploring the subject (1b) Sketching a plan (1d)		T Composing and revising **Planning** Assessing the writing situation S *writing situation; assignments*

T = *Writer's Help* table of contents
S = Search terms in *Writer's Help*

Practice, models, and more

hackerhandbooks .com/bedhandbook	hackerhandbooks .com/writersref	hackerhandbooks .com/rules	hackerhandbooks .com/pocket	*Writer's Help* (writershelp.com)
e The writing process **As you write** Exploring a subject **Exercises** 1–3 Purpose and audience e Writing in the disciplines **As you write** Examining a writing assignment from one of your courses	Practice exercises **Composing and revising** C1–3 Purpose and audience	Practice exercises **The writing process** 1–3 Purpose and audience		Exercises **Composing and revising** Purpose and audience

e Students can access integrated media with the purchase of a new handbook (or with standalone purchase online).
NOTE: Instructor registration grants you access to all media for your handbook.

Module 2
Teaching prewriting strategies

Challenges

To find coverage in your handbook, see Resources at the end of this module.

After receiving an essay assignment, many student writers move directly into the drafting stages because they don't see the point of taking "extra time" to explore and expand upon their ideas prior to drafting. Avoiding prewriting can contribute to students' likelihood of experiencing writer's block or of producing a one-dimensional, uninspired first draft. In any writing-intensive class, you are likely to encounter some of the following challenges:

- Students incorporate prewriting into their wWriting processes sporadically, if at all.

- Students assume that prewriting adds too much additional time to the writing process.

- Students don't see the value of discovery, the opportunity that prewriting provides.

- Students distrust the openness of some prewriting techniques or find prewriting in general irrelevant to the goal of finishing the final "product."

- Some students have limited experience with the variety of prewriting techniques and rely heavily on one.

- Some experienced or capable student writers feel that prewriting techniques are more applicable to their peers and thus miss an opportunity to discover challenging or innovative subject matter.

Strategies

Students often view academic writing as a chore rather than a creative endeavor or learning opportunity, so they require repeated assurances that the first part of the writing process, though often messy, will be productive. Many students also must be convinced that exploring topics through prewriting strategies can actually shave time off the writing process by reducing the chance of writer's block and result in a better final paper. You can use the following activities to demonstrate the benefits of prewriting techniques to your students:

1. If your handbook covers prewriting, review that coverage with your students. Note that the variety of prewriting techniques makes it easy for students to identify one or two approaches that they will find fruitful and suited to their individual writing processes.

2. Assign one or two specific prewriting techniques per paper and grade these on a complete/incomplete basis. For example, a rhetorical analysis assignment could be prefaced with an assignment that requires students to read and annotate a hard copy of the text they are going to analyze. A descriptive or narrative paper might begin with a prewriting assignment asking students to answer the journalist's questions (Who? What? When? Where? Why? How?) on their topics.

3. If a writing assignment lets students choose from several prompts, ask them to pick their two top choices and list ideas for each one.

4. Assign a brief essay about the usefulness of prewriting techniques, such as Peter Elbow's "Freewriting," to encourage discussion of how prewriting can eliminate premature and counterproductive self-editing.

5. To generate specific topics for essays within a given subject, complete a clustering activity with the class. Be sure to point out any surprising topics that may be generated as proof that prewriting can reveal the unexpected.

6. Assign students to blog in response to class readings and discussions. Require students to comment on each other's blogs.

Sample lesson for Strategy 5: Prewriting techniques

Lesson planning:	
Sequencing:	Use this lesson one or two class periods after students have received the writing prompts for an essay assignment early in the term.
Student level:	This lesson will benefit novice writers who may be unfamiliar with prewriting techniques as well as experienced writers who use prewriting techniques but may be looking to expand their repertoire.
Learning objectives:	Students will be able to • Describe prewriting techniques as identified in the handbook or in lecture • Use several prewriting techniques to generate ideas for an essay
Time required:	One session of at least fifty minutes
Materials/ resources:	The handbook A chalkboard, erasable whiteboard, or projection technology Copies of an essay assignment that includes a choice of several writing prompts. (See "Sample assignments" on pp. 231–43 for ideas.)

Lesson steps:	
Session 1:	1. Observe that many prewriting exercises can be completed in less than fifteen minutes, and spending this time leads to better first drafts and a decreased chance of writer's block while drafting.

2. On one side of the board, write a list of prewriting techniques such as talking and listening, reading, listing, clustering, freewriting, journaling, and blogging. (To find discussions of these techniques, see the Resources chart at the end of this module.) Briefly describe each one, pausing to ask if students have used the technique before and to encourage them to share any observations about their experiences.

3. Explain that the class will focus on experimenting with some of these prewriting techniques. First, ask students to complete a five- to ten-minute open freewrite. Before they begin, explain that an open freewrite should not have a predetermined topic and should be as faithful to their stream-of-consciousness thought processes as possible. Students will put pen to paper and simply write for the designated amount of time. If nothing comes to mind, they can write the same word or phrase repeatedly until something else surfaces. Emphasize that this technique is useful when trying to generate spontaneous, unique ideas for an open-topic writing assignment or as a general warm-up to reduce the writing jitters prior to prewriting on a specific subject. After the freewrite, ask students to share any promising or surprising ideas or topics they generated.

4. Before moving to more focused prewriting, review the writing assignment with students, pausing to answer any questions.

5. Pick one of the prompts from the writing assignment and demonstrate the clustering technique on the board. Note that students may have used this technique before, but they may have called it a "web" or "webbing." Write a shortened version of the prompt or its main concern in a central bubble and then ask students to begin offering related ideas. Write these ideas (in abbreviated form if necessary) in bubbles that radiate from the central idea. Try to follow each cluster out into subpoints if possible. If students' responses are too rapid, ask for an assistant scribe to help you at the board. After this exercise, remark on any unexpected directions the clustering took and note how collaborating can often generate more ideas than individual brainstorming. Point out that clustering can be an effective technique to alleviate writer's block during the drafting process, too, because it is nonlinear and can help writers tackle challenging sections of a draft by reducing the anxiety of facing a blank page or screen.

6. Transition from general prewriting exercises completed as a class to exercises that help students choose and explore their own topics. Ask students individually to pick two prompts from the writing assignment and to quickly (in about five to ten minutes) generate a list of ideas related to each prompt. After they have generated their lists, tell them to pick a partner and share their results, asking questions and adding additional ideas to their partner's list.

7. Based on the results of the listing/talking and listening exercise, have students pick *one* of their two prompts to explore further. Then ask them to identify *one* general or abstract idea in need of elaboration from the list they made for their chosen topic. For example, for a writing prompt that asks students to "Write an essay exploring how language can be used as a means of attaining (or maintaining) power," students may respond with lists including such general or abstract ideas as "racial slurs," "suggestive language," "sucking up," "correct English," and so on. After students |

Session 1, *continued*:	have picked a general or abstract idea from their lists, ask them to cluster or ask journalist's questions about this idea for five minutes. This technique will give students practice exploring and refining the general ideas that often crop up in initial listing exercises. When they finish, discuss how this technique was able to help them generate further details and specific examples. 8. Finally, ask students to do a ten-minute focused freewrite on their chosen prompt, assuring them that they are not necessarily wedded to the topic if they want to change it after today's work. Students will end the class with a list of ideas on their chosen prompt, a method of elaborating on each of these by clustering or asking journalist's questions, and a ten-minute freewrite that has already germinated some writing on their potential topic.
Follow-up:	After distributing each essay assignment, incorporate at least fifteen minutes of prewriting time into the class session to emphasize the importance of prewriting and to ensure that students are continuing to practice this part of the writing process. Some prewriting techniques may be more fruitful than others for particular assignments. Encourage students to experiment with a variety of techniques from one assignment to the next.
Variations:	• For an alternative Step 5, introduce the students to clustering by either projecting the cluster diagram or referring the students to the diagram in their handbook (if your handbook includes it) as you briefly explain the technique. Then divide students into groups of three or four and assign each group one writing prompt to cluster on for five minutes (with one group member acting as the scribe). Have groups that worked on the same prompt compare their clusters. The small-group approach may encourage more students to participate than the full-class exercise and thus generate more ideas. • At the beginning of Step 1 ask students to write down any situations outside of the classroom in which they have had to brainstorm ideas to help them compose their words ahead of time — for example, before writing a cover letter or asking for a raise, before asking someone on a date, or before asking parents for help with a large purchase. Ask students to explain how they went about generating ideas: Did they write lists, rehearse major talking points in their heads, or discuss their ideas with friends? Then ask for volunteers to share their responses and point out that this kind of brainstorming is similar to prewriting for academic papers; both help an individual generate (or, if necessary, discard) words and ideas prior to their delivery in a "final draft" setting. • If you are using an online platform, reserve a discussion board for students to post their initial essay ideas and respond to others'. You can also assign blog entries that require students to practice specific prewriting techniques.

Resources

Handbook coverage

The Bedford Handbook, 9th ed.	A Writer's Reference, 7th ed.	Rules for Writers, 7th ed.	A Pocket Style Manual, 6th ed.	Writer's Help (writershelp.com)
Exploring your subject (1b)	Exploring the subject (C1-b)	Exploring the subject (1b)		🅣 **Composing and revising**
Reading a text actively (4a)	Reading actively; annotating the text (A1-a)	Reading actively; annotating the text (5a)		**Planning**
Reading a multimodal text actively (5a)	Sketching an outline (A1-b)	Sketching an outline (5b)		Exploring the subject
Outlining a text (4b)	Summarizing to demonstrate understanding (A1-c)	Summarizing to demonstrate understanding (5c)		Outlining
Outlining an image (5b)				🅣 **Academic writing**
Summarizing a text (4c)	Analyzing to demonstrate critical thinking (A1-d)	Analyzing to demonstrate critical thinking (5d)		**Writing about texts**
Summarizing a multimodal text (5c)	Sample annotated article (A1-a)	Sample annotated article (p. 72)		Active reading
Analyzing a text (4d)	Sample annotated advertisement (A1-a)	Sample annotated advertisement (p. 73)		Outlining a written or a visual text
Analyzing a multimodal text (5d)				Summarizing a written or a visual text
Reading actively about literature (7a)				Analyzing a written or a visual text
Sample annotated article (pp. 111–12)				🅣 **Writing about literature**
Sample annotated advertisement (p. 131)				🅣 **Understanding and composing multimodal projects**
				🅢 *exploring; outlining; annotating; writing about texts; summarizing texts; analyzing texts; interpretation of literature; multimedia*

🅣 = *Writer's Help* table of contents
🅢 = Search terms in *Writer's Help*

Practice, models, and more

hackerhandbooks.com/bedhandbook	hackerhandbooks.com/writersref	hackerhandbooks.com/rules	hackerhandbooks.com/pocket	*Writer's Help* (writershelp.com)
e **The writing process**				
As you write				
Exploring a subject				
e **Academic reading and writing**				
As you write				
Reading actively				
Analyzing a text				
Reading visual texts actively				
Analyzing an image or a multimodal text				

e Students can access integrated media with the purchase of a new handbook (or with standalone purchase online).
NOTE: Instructor registration grants you access to all media for your handbook.

Print ancillaries

The Bedford Handbook, 9th ed.	*A Writer's Reference,* 7th ed.	*Rules for Writers,* 7th ed.	*A Pocket Style Manual,* 6th ed.	*Writer's Help* (writershelp.com)
Understanding and Composing Multimodal Projects, a Hacker Handbooks Supplement	*Writing about Literature,* a Hacker Handbooks Supplement *Understanding and Composing Multimodal Projects,* a Hacker Handbooks Supplement	*Writing about Literature,* a Hacker Handbooks Supplement *Understanding and Composing Multimodal Projects,* a Hacker Handbooks Supplement	*Writing about Literature,* a Hacker Handbooks Supplement	

Module 3
Teaching critical reading

Challenges

To find coverage on critical reading in your handbook, see Resources at the end of this module.

Every college course asks students to learn, to some extent, by reading the findings, ideas, and experiences of others. Reading may not be a new experience for your students; *critical* reading, however, may be. You may need to introduce students to the idea that critical reading asks them to engage with a text, questioning the author as they read, interrogating the claims and evidence presented, noting surprising conclusions, and perhaps making connections with other texts, ideas, or related real-world or personal scenarios. Help students recognize that critical reading enhances understanding, encourages analytical thinking and better writing, and is a useful college habit.

When you initiate a discussion about a reading assignment in class, one or more of these issues might surface:

- Students are accustomed to skimming, scanning, or reading very short pieces and works of fiction. It can be a challenge to remain focused and engaged with a long text or a text that develops ideas rather than a narrative thread.

- Students are resistant to certain topics, new information, or opposing opinions.

- Students do not understand the vocabulary or they struggle in general with the level of difficulty of a text.

- Students are inexperienced with identifying or analyzing a written text's purpose, argument, and assumptions.

- Students are familiar with reading for information, but they are unfamiliar with analyzing and evaluating texts and expressing opinions about them.

- Students are intimidated by the idea of questioning a published author, perhaps an expert in his or her field.

Strategies

You can assist your students in overcoming these challenges. By inviting them occasionally to participate in the process of selecting texts, you can engage them in readings that interest them. By preparing them to read particular texts, you can build their confidence with reading. By giving your students opportunities to respond not only analytically but also personally to their reading assignments, you can invite them to become more invested in the reading they do.

Help students understand that reading, like writing, is a process. Before they begin reading, they should take time to jot down what they know about the author and what the author is writing about and reflect on any notions they have already formed about the topic. Reading is the next step, and they should be active rather than passive readers, making notes as they go along. Explain to students that reading doesn't end with the last word on the page. After they've read the work once or twice, they should spend time reflecting on the text, asking themselves questions about what they've learned, where the piece is strong or weak, and so on.

The following strategies can help you engage students in their readings and in the process of reading:

1. Before students read a text, take time in class to prepare them for the reading they will do. Present them with the topic of the text and open it for some preliminary discussion. Have students read and discuss a few short, representative passages in class. You can choose a passage from the beginning to get them started, or choose a passage from a place deeper in the text to create a different effect on their reading. Define any major terms they might find challenging.

2. To promote active reading, have students annotate while they read, outline and/ or summarize as they conclude the reading assignment, and write reflectively as a follow-up. Assigning such activities for homework can help ensure that students come to class prepared to discuss readings.

3. As students read, ask them to identify the author's purpose, main claims, evidence, and strategies. Ask them to evaluate how effectively the author supports the thesis and employs those strategies.

4. Give students opportunities to express their personal reactions to a text as well as more analytical responses. Create time in class for discussion and debate.

5. Help students connect to a text and its author by viewing a video clip of the author or by reading a short biographical piece together in class.

6. Have students read and evaluate a sample student paper that analyzes a text. You can, for example, refer students to Emilia Sanchez's essay "Rethinking Big-Box Stores" in the handbook. If your handbook does not include the essay, project the PDF on your book's companion Web site or distribute copies (see the Resources chart at the end of this module).

Sample lesson for Strategy 1: Preparing to read a text critically

Lesson planning:	
Sequencing:	Use this lesson to introduce a reading assignment.
Student level:	This lesson targets students who are inexperienced readers, but it is also useful for more advanced students. Students do not need prior experience for this lesson. For students who are more experienced with college-level reading assignments, this lesson will provide review and guide them into new readings.
Learning objectives:	Students will be able to • Read actively • Identify the basic features and structure of a text • Read to discover meaning • Apply critical thinking strategies to a text
Time required:	Two fifty-minute sessions with follow-up
Materials/ resources:	• The handbook (See the Resources chart at the end of this module.) • The chart "Guidelines for Active Reading," if your handbook includes it • Opinion articles or essays (handouts, online, or in a textbook)

Lesson steps:	

Session 1:	Invite students to participate in the selection of texts they will read for the following class period. Giving students the option to select among several choices encourages them to feel more invested in the reading assignment. It allows them to look for texts that interest them.
	
	Tell the students you will also read the article they select for their assignment. The students are deciding on a reading assignment both for you and for themselves. Students enjoy the experience of producing an assignment as a departure from their usual practice of being given assignments.
	
	1. Selection of reading assignment
	
	   The task for the entire class is to decide on a text they all will read and discuss. Give your students the option of selecting one text from a choice of two or three by following these steps:
	
	   • Divide the class into small groups. Distribute the readings to each group or ask them to access the texts online.
	
	   • Each group should quickly evaluate the readings and come up with a recommendation for the class. Ask each group to share their recommendation and to explain their choice. (Considerations will likely include interest in the topic, length, and the perceived level of difficulty.) Groups may want to respond to recommendations and try to persuade each other; allow a little time for discussion.

Session 1, *continued*:	• After every group has presented a case, ask students to vote individually with a show of hands. The article that wins the vote is the reading assignment for the next class period.
	Familiarize students with the following questions that they should consider for active reading:
	• What kind of text are you reading? An essay? An editorial? A scholarly article? An advertisement? An image?
	• What is the author's purpose? To inform? To persuade? To call to action?
	• Who is the audience? How does the author attempt to appeal to the audience?
	• What is the author's thesis? What question does the text attempt to answer?
	• What evidence does the author provide to support the thesis?
	2. Begin with the first paragraph of the essay.
	• To get students started in the reading, begin reading the first sentence(s) aloud.
	• Pause and ask:
	• Can you determine what the author's purpose is from these sentences?
	• Can you determine who the intended audience might be?
	• Do you know what the author's thesis is yet?
	• Is it possible to determine what question the author may be attempting to answer with this essay?
	• Task a student to resume reading the next sentence(s).
	• Pause and ask:
	• What does the author's purpose seem to be now? Has your perception of the purpose changed?
	• How does the author seem to be attempting to appeal to the audience?
	• Can you identify the thesis yet or the question the text is responding to?
	3. Tell students that they will continue reading on their own. An important part of active reading is annotating. Ask students to open their handbooks to Emilia Sanchez's notes on "Big Box Stores Are Bad for Main Street." If your handbook does not include the annotated article, project the PDF on your book's companion Web site or distribute copies (see the Resources chart at the end of this module). Point out the different kinds of marks the reader uses to annotate the text. Ask students to describe the different kinds of annotations. Some of them state what the text or author is doing. Some of them express opinions. Some of them ask questions.
	4. Next, ask students to complete the following steps on their own as preparation for the next class period:
	• Finish reading the article the class selected.
	• Annotate the article while they are reading. Have students refer to questions in steps 1 and 2 for ideas about what to comment on. (If your handbook includes it, students can refer to "Guidelines for Active Reading.")
	• Make a photocopy of the article with the annotations to hand in for credit.

Session 2:	1. Ask students to have their annotated articles available for discussion. Follow these steps: • Freewriting: For five minutes, have students freewrite a response to some or all of the following questions: Has the author revealed a fact or made a point that counters your assumptions? Is anything surprising? Does the reading make you think about something that you'd never thought about before? Does the author present any contradictions that need to be resolved? What are they? • Divide the class into small groups. Ask students to share their responses to the freewriting with two other students near them. Have each group choose at least one response to share with the class. • Ask each group to report on their responses. Encourage them to examine their reactions to the reading. Why had they assumed a point was true? Did the author persuade them to think differently? What did the author do to challenge their assumptions? Encourage a variety of responses. 2. Extend the freewriting discussion activity with these three questions from "Guidelines for Active Reading" (see the Resources chart at the end of this module): • Has the author made a generalization you disagree with? Can you think of evidence that would challenge the generalization? • Are there any contradictions or inconsistencies in the text? For example, has the author made any statements that seem to disagree with each other or any statements that seem out of place? • Are there any words, statements, or phrases in the text that you don't understand? If so, what reference materials do you need to consult? (Note: For difficult readings, the freewriting and discussion exercises could begin rather than conclude with this question about parts of the text that are difficult to understand. Identifying points of confusion or difficulty can be another entry point into reading a text critically.) 3. Ask students to share their annotated copies of the article. (If you have a document camera in the classroom, you can display them on the screen. Or before class, you can select and scan a few to display to the class.) In a brief workshop on their annotations, ask students to note how different readers in the class have annotated differently. Ask the students to explain why they chose to annotate certain points in the text the way they did. 4. To conclude, ask students what they've learned about the nature and value of critical reading. Remind students that critical reading involves questioning an author's positions, assumptions, evidence, and conclusions and that doing so will help them understand and interact with the ideas in a reading well enough to be able to write about them.
Follow-up:	Ask students to come up with two or three critical comments or questions about each reading for homework before class discussions. This practice will help students come prepared to discuss the reading. You can choose to assign a participation or homework point value to each set of comments or questions. Having students write a brief response to the reading after class discussion may help them further digest the reading, their ideas about the reading, and the responses and questions of their peers.
Variations:	This lesson can be continued with visual texts, advertisements, and Web sites. See your handbook and your handbook's companion Web site for examples of annotated visuals and Web sites.

Resources

Handbook coverage

The Bedford Handbook, 9th ed.	A Writer's Reference, 7th ed.	Rules for Writers, 7th ed.	A Pocket Style Manual, 6th ed.	Writer's Help (writershelp.com)
Reading a text actively (4a) Reading a multimodal text actively (5a) Outlining a text (4b) Outlining an image (5b) Summarizing a text (4c) Summarizing a multimodal text (5c) Sample annotated article (pp. 111–12) Sample annotated advertisement (p. 131) Reading and writing arguments (6a–6c) Reading actively about literature (7a)	Reading actively; annotating the text (A1-a) Sketching an outline (A1-b) Summarizing to demonstrate understanding (A1-c) Analyzing to demonstrate critical thinking (A1-d) Sample annotated article (A1-a) Sample annotated advertisement (A1-a) Evaluating arguments (A3)	Reading actively; annotating the text (5a) Sketching an outline (5b) Summarizing to demonstrate understanding (5c) Analyzing to demonstrate critical thinking (5d) Sample annotated article (p. 72) Sample annotated advertisement (p. 73) Evaluating arguments (7)		▧ **Academic writing** **Writing about texts** Active reading Outlining a written or a visual text Summarizing a written or a visual text Analyzing a written or a visual text More help with Writing about texts (charts, visuals, models) **Evaluating arguments** ▧ **Writing about literature** ▧ **Understanding and composing multimodal projects** ▨ *exploring; outlining; writing about texts; summarizing texts; analyzing texts; evaluating arguments*

▧ = *Writer's Help* table of contents
▨ = Search terms in *Writer's Help*

Practice, models, and more

hackerhandbooks.com/bedhandbook	hackerhandbooks.com/writersref	hackerhandbooks.com/rules	hackerhandbooks.com/pocket	*Writer's Help* (writershelp.com)
e Academic reading and writing **As you write** Reading actively Analyzing a text Reading visual texts actively Analyzing an image or a multimodal text Evaluating ads for logic and fairness Identifying appeals Evaluating an argument Asking questions about literature **Exercises** 6–1 Evaluating arguments **Sample student writing** Sanchez, "Re-thinking Big-Box Stores" (analysis of an article) Yoshida, "Some-times a Cup of Coffee Is Just a Cup of Coffee" (analysis of an advertisement) Jacobs, "From Lecture to Conversation: Redefining What's 'Fit to Print'" (argument) Larson, "The Transformation of Mrs. Peters: An Analysis of 'A Jury of Her Peers'" (literary analysis)	**Model papers and other sample documents** Sanchez, "Re-thinking Big-Box Stores" (analysis of an article) Jacobs, "From Lecture to Conversation: Redefining What's 'Fit to Print'" (argument) Larson, "The Transformation of Mrs. Peters: An Analysis of 'A Jury of Her Peers'" (literary analysis) Peel, "Opposing Voices in 'Ballad of the Landlord'" (literary analysis)	**Model papers and other sample documents** Sanchez, "Re-thinking Big-Box Stores" (analysis of an article) Jacobs, "From Lecture to Conversation: Redefining What's 'Fit to Print'" (argument) Larson, "The Transformation of Mrs. Peters: An Analysis of 'A Jury of Her Peers'" (literary analysis) Peel, "Opposing Voices in 'Ballad of the Landlord'" (literary analysis)	**Model papers and other sample documents** Sanchez, "Re-thinking Big-Box Stores" (analysis of an article) Jacobs, "From Lecture to Conversation: Redefining What's 'Fit to Print'" (argument) Larson, "The Transformation of Mrs. Peters: An Analysis of 'A Jury of Her Peers'" (literary analysis) Peel, "Opposing Voices in 'Ballad of the Landlord'" (literary analysis)	**T MLA papers** **Directory to MLA model papers** Sanchez, "Re-thinking Big-Box Stores" (analysis of an article) Jacobs, "From Lecture to Conversation: Redefining What's 'Fit to Print'" (argument) Larson, "The Transformation of Mrs. Peters: An Analysis of 'A Jury of Her Peers'" (literary analysis) Peel, "Opposing Voices in 'Ballad of the Landlord'" (literary analysis) **S** *model papers*

T = *Writer's Help* table of contents
S = Search terms in *Writer's Help*
e Students can access integrated media with the purchase of a new handbook (or with standalone purchase online).
NOTE: Instructor registration grants you access to all media for your handbook.

Print ancillaries

The Bedford Handbook, 9th ed.	A Writer's Reference, 7th ed.	Rules for Writers, 7th ed.	A Pocket Style Manual, 6th ed.	Writer's Help (writershelp.com)
Understanding and Composing Multimodal Projects, a Hacker Handbooks Supplement	*Writing about Literature,* a Hacker Handbooks Supplement *Understanding and Composing Multimodal Projects,* a Hacker Handbooks Supplement	*Writing about Literature,* a Hacker Handbooks Supplement *Understanding and Composing Multimodal Projects,* a Hacker Handbooks Supplement	*Writing about Literature,* a Hacker Handbooks Supplement *Understanding and Composing Multimodal Projects,* a Hacker Handbooks Supplement	

Module 4
Teaching thesis statements

Challenges

Inexperienced with academic genres, novice college writers sometimes lack the rhetorical and audience awareness needed to write strong thesis statements. They may be new to defining a thesis as an answer to a question they've posed, the solution to a problem they've identified, or their position in a debate. If they do not understand the persuasive nature of some academic writing, they might write thesis statements as observations rather than assertions, or claims. Students who have had some high school instruction in writing thesis statements may knowingly or unknowingly resist your attempts to further develop their skills; they may assume that the instruction they received in high school is sufficient. You may see some of the following patterns emerge as students grapple with writing thesis statements:

- The thesis is too vague or broad, leading to an unwieldy paper.

- The thesis is too narrow or factual and cannot be developed into a full paper.

- Students write purpose statements (*In this paper, I will . . .*) instead of claims.

- Students neglect to take a stance on an issue; they write observations, which are not debatable, instead of claims, which are debatable.

Strategies

A clear and compelling thesis is the foundation of most college writing assignments. You can help students master thesis statements with extensive modeling and guided practice, using the following strategies:

1. Provide multiple models of thesis statements in the rhetorical style required by the assignment. When possible, present thesis statements in the context of complete texts.

2. For argument papers, use role playing so that students can practice taking a stance on an issue and arguing their points.

3. Help students frame questions that lead to an appropriate thesis statement. See the sample lesson for this strategy.

To find sample thesis statements in your handbook, see Resources at the end of this module.

Sample lesson for Strategy 3: Drafting a working thesis for an argument essay

Lesson planning:	
Sequencing:	Use this lesson near the beginning of the term, before the first essay assignment is due. You can adapt the content to fit your first essay assignment.
Student level:	This lesson targets students who are not familiar with thesis statements or who are accustomed to writing purpose statements (for example, *In this essay, I will . . .*) instead of claims.
Learning objectives:	Students will be able to • Draft a working thesis for their paper • Evaluate whether sample thesis statements and other students' thesis statements contain claims that are debatable
Time required:	One session of at least fifty minutes
Materials/ resources:	Instructions for the assignment or possible topics (For this lesson, you don't need the printed instructions, but students should understand the purpose of the essay assignment before you begin.)

Lesson steps:	

	1. Begin the session by discussing the purpose of a thesis for both readers and writers. Cover the following ideas, and encourage participation as you present each point:
	
	  • The thesis (made up of one or more sentences) is the most important part of the paper because it asserts the controlling idea that is proved or supported in the body of the work. The remaining ideas in the paper — especially subpoints contained in topic sentences — relate directly to this main idea.
	
	  • Because it contains the controlling idea, the thesis provides necessary direction for the reader.
	
	  • In the early stages of the writing process, a working thesis serves as an anchor for the writer, who can revisit the thesis throughout the drafting process to keep the content focused.
	
	2. Emphasize the debatable nature of the thesis in most academic papers. Explain that a claim is a stand on a particular topic, a statement that reveals a point of view that others might disagree with. It is not an observation; it is an arguable position.
	
	If some students have been exposed to purpose statements (for example, *In this paper, I will . . .*), you can also use this time to contrast such introductory sentences with claims. For example, you can point out that others would not disagree with a statement that begins with *In this paper, I will . . .* or *This paper will show that. . . .*
	
	3. Briefly review your assignment with students and explain that they will use this session to draft a working thesis for their paper.

NOTE: Your assignment may call for a basic **proposal** ("The state legislature should do x . . .") or an **evaluation** ("The new guidelines for y are not an effective solution to the problem of z . . .") as a thesis statement. See the chart on page 84 for examples of other types of thesis statements.

4. Elicit subjects appropriate for your assignment, writing a few contributions on the board. Using one subject from the board as an example, ask students to suggest questions about the subject that might lead to a position. (If students have difficulty generating questions, encourage them to ask "should" questions about the subject to get started. Once they understand the objective, you can branch out into other suitable question types.) Here are a few examples:

   - Subject: Global climate change

     Question: What action, if any, should the US government take to reduce global climate change?

   - Subject: Childhood obesity

     Question: What should schools do to curb the childhood obesity epidemic?

5. Ask students to make an assertion by answering each question in a single complete and specific sentence. (A thesis may be longer than one sentence, of course, but this exercise is usually more successful when students focus on one sentence at this point.) Even if the students don't have strong views on the subject, ask them to take a stance for the exercise. Students may need to see several models before they can write a sentence of their own. Work as a group to create one or more sample sentences, such as these, and write them on the board:

   - The US government should impose restrictions on industrial emissions to mitigate the warming effects of carbon in the atmosphere.

   - To combat the growing rate of childhood obesity, schools should organize daily physical activities, offer healthy meals in the cafeteria, and counsel parents on healthy eating habits.

6. As a class, test the sample assertions by asking if the positions can be opposed. You can ask students to offer their own opposing ideas, or you can ask them to role-play what the opposition might say. Allow students to refine the samples as necessary, making changes on the board that reflect their suggestions.

7. Give students a few minutes to write their own working thesis. After about five minutes, elicit a few examples from willing students. Again, as a class, test whether the sentences contain debatable assertions (see Step 6).

8. Remind students that they can revise or change their thesis statements at any point during the writing process, especially as they find more information and further develop their own ideas.

Follow-up:	• For homework, ask students to revise their working thesis statements and submit them for preliminary approval.
	• As students develop the supporting points and body of the paper, ask them to refine their thesis by building in some direction for the major parts of the paper.
Variations:	• Once students have drafted their working thesis, conduct a peer review. Ask the peers to provide an opposing position to the thesis; if they can't, then it may need revision.
	🖥 If you are teaching online, you can create brief quizzes that ask students to test whether sample thesis statements contain debatable assertions. You can also ask students to post their tentative thesis statements on the discussion board for peer review.

Sample thesis statements:

	Subject	Question	Sample thesis statement
Definitional	Voter ID laws	Are new voter identification laws a form of voter suppression?	Voter identification laws are/are not a form of voter suppression.
Analytical	News media	As new methods of gathering and reporting news are developed, do newspapers continue to remain relevant?	Although methods of gathering and reporting have changed, newspapers continue to remain relevant.
Causal	Global climate change	What are the possible causes of global climate change?	Industrial carbon emissions are/are not the primary cause of global climate change.
Predictive	The Affordable Care Act	What are the potentially positive/negative consequences of the Affordable Care Act on the health and economy of the United States?	The Affordable Care Act will have positive/negative effects on the health and economy of the United States.
Evaluative	The electoral college	Is the electoral college a fair and effective way to conduct presidential elections?	The electoral college is/is not a fair and effective way to conduct presidential elections.
Proposal	Childhood obesity	What should schools do to curb the childhood obesity epidemic?	To combat the growing rate of childhood obesity, schools should organize daily physical activities, offer healthy meals in the cafeteria, and counsel parents on healthy eating habits.

Resources

Handbook coverage

The Bedford Handbook, 9th ed.	*A Writer's Reference*, 7th ed.	*Rules for Writers*, 7th ed.	*A Pocket Style Manual*, 6th ed.	*Writer's Help* (writershelp.com)
Drafting and revising a working thesis (1c)	Drafting a working thesis (C1-c)	Drafting a working thesis (1c)	Supporting a thesis [MLA] (29)	▯ **Composing and revising**
Backing up your thesis (6g)	Drafting an introduction and a thesis (C2-a)	Drafting an introduction and a thesis (2a)	Supporting a thesis [APA] (35)	**Planning**
Drafting a working thesis for a literary analysis (7c)	Backing up your thesis (A2-d)	Backing up your thesis (6d)	Supporting a thesis [*Chicago*] (40)	Drafting a working thesis
Supporting a thesis [MLA] (53)	Supporting a thesis (MLA-1)	Supporting a thesis [MLA] (56)		**Drafting**
Supporting a thesis [APA] (58)	Supporting a thesis (APA-1)	Supporting a thesis [APA] (61)		Drafting an introduction with thesis
Supporting a thesis [*Chicago*] (63a)	Supporting a thesis (CMS-1)			▯ **Academic writing**
				Constructing reasonable arguments
				Stating your position in your introduction
				Backing up the thesis with lines of argument
				Supporting claims with evidence
				▯ **Writing about literature**
				Planning an interpretation of literature
				Drafting an interpretive thesis
				▯ *main point; thesis; interpretation of literary work*

▯ = *Writer's Help* table of contents
▯ = Search terms in *Writer's Help*

Practice, models, and more

hackerhandbooks.com/bedhandbook	hackerhandbooks.com/writersref	hackerhandbooks.com/rules	hackerhandbooks.com/pocket	*Writer's Help* (writershelp.com)
ⓔ The writing process **As you write** Revising a thesis **Exercises** 1–5 and 1–6 Thesis statements **ⓔ Academic reading and writing** **As you write** Drafting and revising an analytical thesis Drafting and revising an analytical thesis (for multimodal texts) **Exercises** 7–1 Thesis statements in literature papers	**Practice exercises** **Composing and revising** C2–2 and C2–3 Thesis statements **MLA** MLA 1–1 and MLA 1–2 Thesis statements in MLA papers **APA** APA 1–1 and APA 1–2 Thesis statements in APA papers **CMS (*Chicago*)** CMS 1–1 and CMS 1–2 Thesis statements in CMS (*Chicago*) papers	**Practice exercises** **The writing process** 2–2 and 2–3 Thesis statements **MLA** 56–1 and 56–2 Thesis statements in MLA papers **APA** 61–1 and 61–2 Thesis statements in APA papers	**Practice exercises** **MLA** 29–1 and 29–2 Thesis statements in MLA papers **APA** 35–1 and 35–2 Thesis statements in APA papers ***Chicago*** 40–1 and 40–2 Thesis statements in *Chicago* papers	**Exercises** **Composing and revising** Thesis statements 1 and 2 **Academic writing** Thesis statements in literature papers **MLA papers** Thesis statements in MLA papers 1 and 2 **APA papers** Thesis statements in APA papers 1 and 2 ***Chicago* (CMS) papers** Thesis statements in *Chicago* (CMS) papers 1 and 2

ⓔ Students can access integrated media with the purchase of a new handbook (or with standalone purchase online).
NOTE: Instructor registration grants you access to all media for your handbook.

Print ancillaries

The Bedford Handbook, 9th ed.	*A Writer's Reference*, 7th ed.	*Rules for Writers*, 7th ed.	*A Pocket Style Manual*, 6th ed.	*Writer's Help* (writershelp.com)
	Writing about Literature, a Hacker Handbooks Supplement	*Writing about Literature*, a Hacker Handbooks Supplement	*Writing about Literature*, a Hacker Handbooks Supplement	

Module 5
Teaching essay structure

Challenges

Some students approach their writing assignments haphazardly, often because they don't see the value of taking the time to plan their thoughts or haven't been taught how to do so. Some student writers confess to sitting at their laptops and rambling on with their fingers until a main idea emerges — for lack of a better strategy. While this brainstorming activity can help students identify and clarify their own thoughts on a topic, the writing that results from the brainstorming shouldn't become the student's draft. If it does, there's a danger that it will lack structure — that it will meander ineffectively. Students need to structure their thoughts to achieve a specific purpose and meet the needs of their audience.

Strategies

To help students structure their ideas effectively, plan activities such as the following that make them aware of the rhetorical features and forms their audiences will most likely expect. Use these activities early in the writing process of any project.

1. Introduce novice writers to key terms (such as *thesis*, *topic sentence*, and *paragraph*) using explicit models, such as those in your handbook.

2. Review two or more sample essays that use different organizational approaches to achieve similar goals, and discuss the features that make them effective or ineffective.

3. Assign outlines to be submitted to you or reviewed by peers before a preliminary draft is due.

4. Use graphic organizers (charts that visually represent the structure of an essay) to plan essays in class. See the sample lesson for this strategy.

5. Use storyboards to plan essays. A storyboard, often associated with cartoons, is a series of boxes ("panels") that students can use to experiment with sequencing the key ideas for their essay. Students can use a combination of text and images to fill in these boxes. Although storyboards can help organize any essay, they may be particularly useful in helping students identify key scenes for a narrative essay or for a digital storytelling assignment.

To find coverage in your handbook, see Resources at the end of this module.

6. Use idea maps to plan essays. An idea map might be considered a more elegant, formal, and involved version of the clustering technique, in which images, text, and colors are combined into a complex and artful representation of the author's flow of ideas. Generally, an idea map would be used after the prewriting stage to help students visually organize ideas they have already generated. This technique is particularly useful for students who are predominantly visual learners.

Sample lesson for Strategy 4: Planning an essay with a graphic organizer

Lesson planning:	
Sequencing:	Use this lesson during the planning stages of any essay assignment.
Student level:	Novice writers working on any essay or experienced writers encountering new rhetorical forms
Learning objectives:	Students will be able to • Identify features of sample essays using the key terms (such as *thesis* and *topic sentence*) that have been introduced • Understand the rhetorical connections between parts of an essay (such as the thesis and topic sentences) • Identify the strengths and weaknesses of the organizational patterns in sample essays • Plan a well-structured essay draft
Time required:	Two consecutive sessions of at least fifty minutes
Materials/ resources:	• One or more sample essays in the same rhetorical form as the assignment (Use samples from your handbook or from previous semesters.*) • A blank graphic organizer for each student (See Resources at the end of this module for samples.) • A slide** of the graphic organizer your students will use and a projector • Your handbook * If you have not taught the course before, you might be able to obtain samples from other instructors. ** If you don't have projection technology, you can sketch a large graphic organizer on the board.
Lesson steps:	
Session 1:	1. Introduce students to the target rhetorical form (such as an analysis essay, a compare-and-contrast essay, or an argument essay) by explaining its purpose and defining key terms (such as *thesis*, *topic sentence*, *argument*, and *counterargument*) that students will need to use. Refer to the handbook for definitions and models. 2. Review one or more sample essays in the target rhetorical form, discussing the strengths of the models. Ask students to point out patterns (such as paragraph order

Session 1, *continued*:	or the order of ideas within paragraphs) and cohesive structures (such as transitional elements or strategic repetition of main ideas) that advance the purpose and help readers understand the writer's ideas. 3. Using the projector (or the board), introduce the graphic organizer that your class will use. Ask students to suggest ways to fill in the graphic organizer with information from the sample essay. Point out the consistency between the thesis and the topic sentences, for example, so that students can visualize the rhetorical connections. **Sample essay** **Graphic organizer** …Adopting a slow food lifestyle benefits not only an individual's health but the health of local communities and the environment. Although people may save time by eating fast food, they will likely add years to their life by eating slow food, which is made from healthy, fresh, local ingredients… **THESIS:** Adopting a slow food lifestyle benefits not only an individual's health but the health of local communities and the environment. **TOPIC 1:** A slow food lifestyle is healthy. **TOPIC 2:** A slow food lifestyle benefits local communities. **TOPIC 3:** A slow food lifestyle is environmentally responsible. 4. Provide students with blank graphic organizers, which they can fill with their own ideas about their writing assignment. (A few samples are provided on pp. 93–97.) If your class period is short, ask students to complete the graphic organizer for homework; if your class period is long enough, have students begin the process in class.
Session 2:	1. After students have filled their graphic organizers with working thesis statements and supporting points, conduct a peer review. Ask students to identify the strengths of a peer's work and to provide at least one concrete suggestion for improvement. You may guide students to answer questions such as the following or any others that fit your assignment. *For additional tips on guiding peer review sessions, see Module 14.* a. Is the thesis clear? Is it debatable? b. Do the main points advance the thesis? c. Are ideas presented in a logical order? 2. After the peer exchange, ask a few willing students to share their samples with the class. Again, identify the strengths of each sample, and diplomatically offer concrete suggestions for improvement. 3. Ask students to revise their graphic organizer plans during any remaining class time or for homework. Encourage them to aggressively shape their work at this point; let them know that they can omit ideas they have determined are unnecessary and can expand discussions that advance the main idea of their essays. Some students may even need to start over if they discover that their original plan does not adequately reflect their ideas or address the assignment requirements. They should make their plan as solid as possible at this stage, bearing in mind that they will need to stay flexible as they revise.

Follow-up:	Encourage students to use the graphic organizers as they begin drafting. Remind them not to feel bound to this plan as they make later revisions, but encourage them to structure at least their first draft according to this plan, which has been peer-reviewed for logic and sense. Ask students to bring the graphic organizers to future revision workshops to refer to if necessary. Students should submit their graphic organizers along with their final drafts.
Variations:	• After introducing graphic organizers, ask students to create their own for each assignment instead of an outline. 🖥 If you are teaching online and your students use compatible word processing programs, you can provide sample essays and corresponding graphic organizers with tables or text boxes to fill in. Students can peer-review each other's work using comment fields.

Resources

Handbook coverage

The Bedford Handbook, 9th ed.	*A Writer's Reference*, 7th ed.	*Rules for Writers*, 7th ed.	*A Pocket Style Manual*, 6th ed.	*Writer's Help* (writershelp.com)
Writing a first draft (1c, 1e–1g) Building effective paragraphs (3) Reading and writing arguments (6) Reading and writing about literature (7) Supporting a thesis [MLA] (53) Supporting a thesis [APA] (58) Supporting a thesis [*Chicago*] (63a)	Drafting (C2) Writing paragraphs (C4) Constructing reasonable arguments (A2) Supporting a thesis (MLA-1) Supporting a thesis (APA-1) Supporting a thesis (CMS-1)	Drafting the paper (2) Build effective paragraphs (4) Constructing reasonable arguments (6) Supporting a thesis [MLA] (56) Supporting a thesis [APA] (61)	Supporting a thesis [MLA] (29) Supporting a thesis [APA] (35) Supporting a thesis [*Chicago*] (40)	🅣 **Composing and revising** **Planning** Drafting a working thesis Writing paragraphs 🅣 **Composing and revising** **Drafting** 🅣 **Academic writing** **Constructing reasonable arguments** 🅣 **Writing about literature** 🅢 *drafting*; *main point*; *thesis*; *paragraphs*; *storyboard*; *argument*; *writing about literature*

🅣 = *Writer's Help* table of contents
🅢 = Search terms in *Writer's Help*

Practice, models, and more

hackerhandbooks.com/bedhandbook	hackerhandbooks.com/writersref	hackerhandbooks.com/rules	hackerhandbooks.com/pocket	*Writer's Help* (writershelp.com)
e The writing process	**Practice exercises**	**Practice exercises**	**Practice exercises**	**Exercises**
As you write	**Composing and revising**	**The writing process**	**MLA**	**Composing and revising**
Revising a thesis	C2–2 and C2–3 Thesis statements	2–2 and 2–3 Thesis statements	29–1 and 29–2 Thesis statements in MLA papers	Thesis statements 1 and 2
Revising an introduction	C2–4 Introductions	2–4 Introductions	**APA**	**Academic writing**
Revising a conclusion	C4–2 Topic sentences	4–2 Topic sentences	35–1 and 35–2 Thesis statements in APA papers	Thesis statements in literature papers
Creating unity	C4–3 Transitions	4–3 Transitions	*Chicago*	**MLA papers**
Using transitions	**MLA**	**MLA**	40–1 and 40–2 Thesis statements in *Chicago* papers	Thesis statements in MLA papers 1 and 2
Exercises	MLA 1–1 and MLA 1–2 Thesis statements in MLA papers	56–1 and 56–2 Thesis statements in MLA papers		**APA papers**
1–5 and 1–6 Thesis statements	**APA**	**APA**		Thesis statements in APA papers 1 and 2
1–7 Introductions	APA 1–1 and APA 1–2 Thesis statements in APA papers	61–1 and 61–2 Thesis statements in APA papers		*Chicago* (CMS) **papers**
3–2 Topic sentences	**CMS (*Chicago*)**			Thesis statements in *Chicago* (CMS) papers 1 and 2
3–3 Transitions	CMS 1–1 and CMS 1–2 Thesis statements in *Chicago* papers			
e Academic reading and writing				
As you write				
Drafting and revising an analytical thesis				
Drafting and revising an analytical thesis (for multimodal texts)				
Drafting your central claim and supporting claims				
Asking questions about literature				
Evaluating a working thesis				
Exercises				
7–1 Thesis statements in literature papers				
e Researched writing				
Exercises: MLA papers				
53–1 and 53–2 Thesis statements in MLA papers				

e Students can access integrated media with the purchase of a new handbook (or with standalone purchase online).
NOTE: Instructor registration grants you access to all media for your handbook.

Practice, models, and more (*continued*)

hackerhandbooks .com/bedhandbook	hackerhandbooks .com/writersref	hackerhandbooks .com/rules	hackerhandbooks .com/pocket	*Writer's Help* (writershelp.com)
Exercises: APA papers 58–1 and 58–2 Thesis statements in APA papers **Exercises: *Chicago* papers** 63–1 and 63–2 Thesis statements in *Chicago* papers				

Print ancillaries

The Bedford Handbook, 9th ed.	*A Writer's Reference*, 7th ed.	*Rules for Writers*, 7th ed.	*A Pocket Style Manual*, 6th ed.	*Writer's Help* (writershelp.com)
	Writing about Literature, a Hacker Handbooks Supplement	*Writing about Literature,* a Hacker Handbooks Supplement	*Writing about Literature,* a Hacker Handbooks Supplement	

Sample graphic organizer for a basic essay

These boxes are meant to help you organize your thoughts. They do not necessarily represent individual paragraphs.

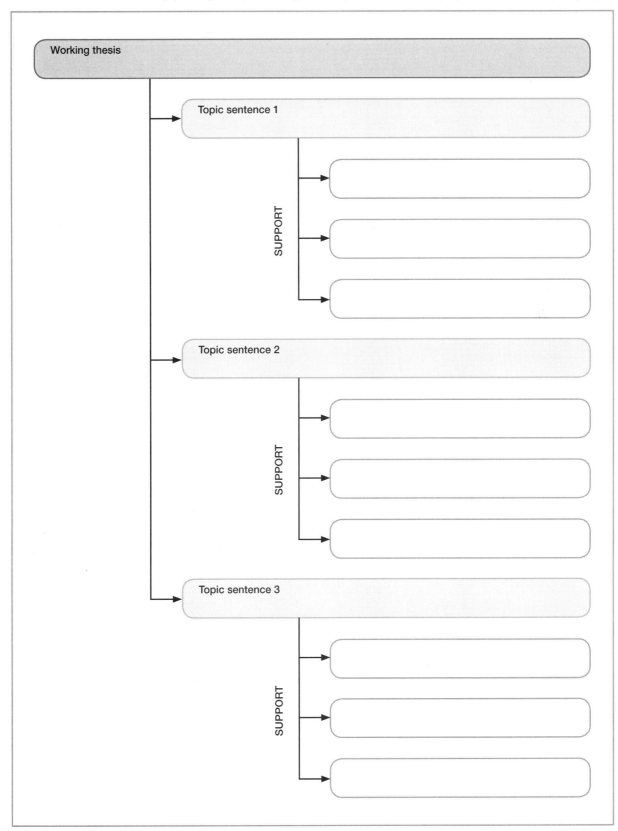

Sample graphic organizer for an analytical essay

These boxes are meant to help you organize your thoughts. They do not necessarily represent individual paragraphs.

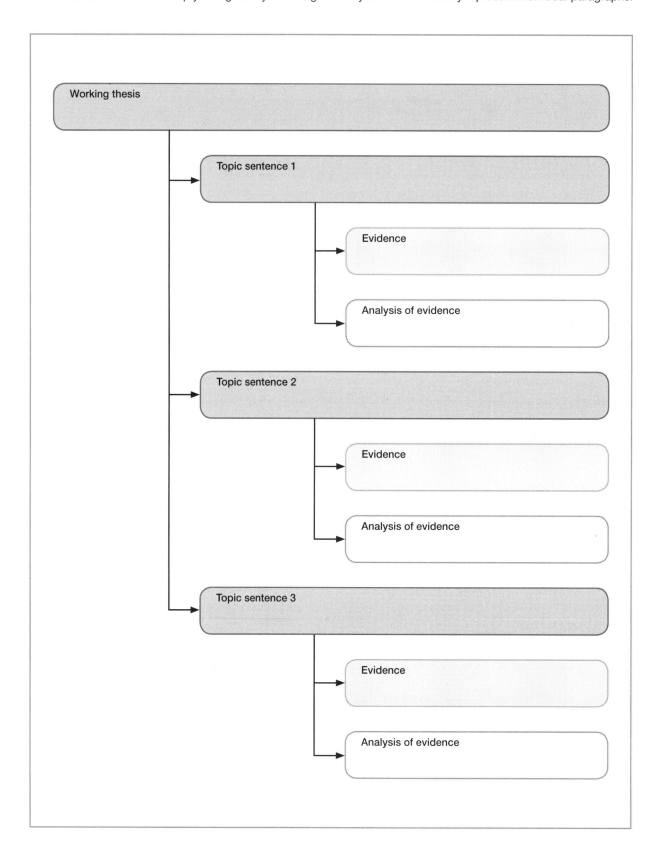

Sample graphic organizer for a compare-and-contrast essay

These boxes are meant to help you organize your thoughts. They do not necessarily represent individual paragraphs.

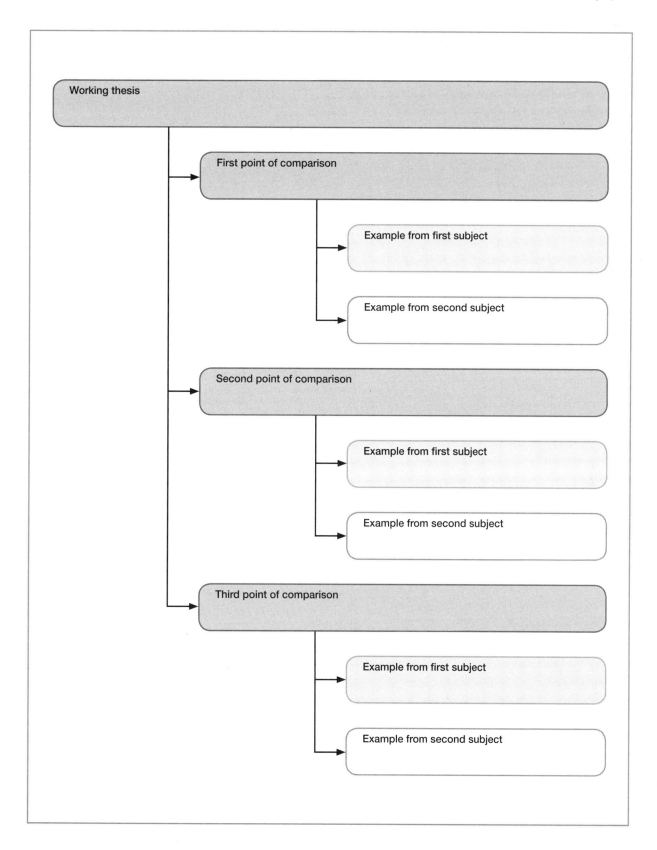

Sample graphic organizer for an argument essay (Option 1)

These boxes are meant to help you organize your thoughts. They do not necessarily represent individual paragraphs.

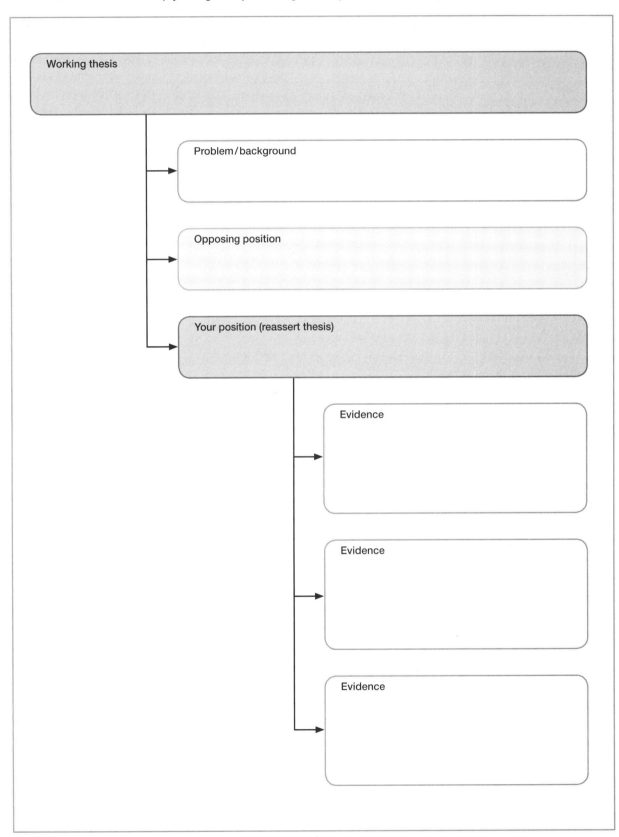

Sample graphic organizer for an argument essay (Option 2)

These boxes are meant to help you organize your thoughts. They do not necessarily represent individual paragraphs. Be aware that you may address counterarguments at the beginning of the essay (see Option 1 on p. 96), as you work through individual reasons in support of your own position, or at the end of the essay. (This organizer provides opportunities to address counterarguments with each supporting reason.) Where and how you address counterarguments will depend on your topic and argumentative strategy.

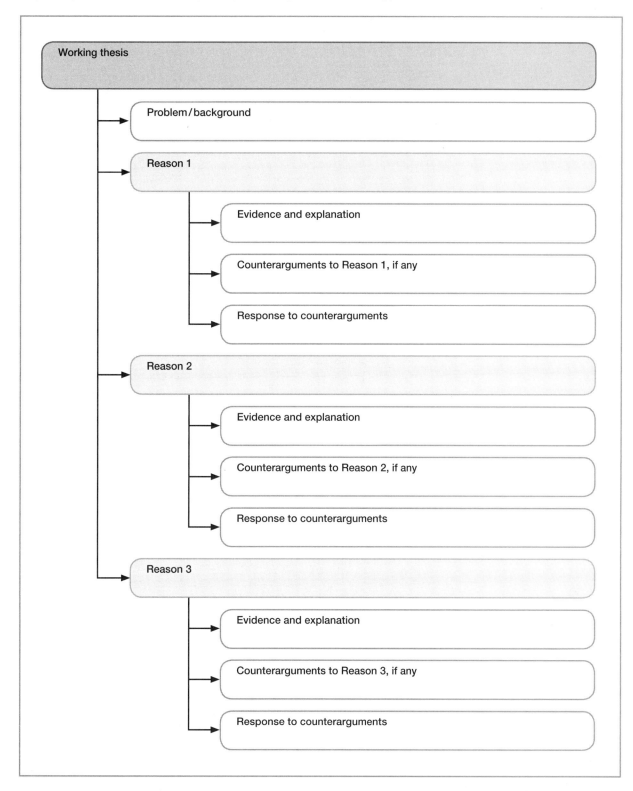

Working thesis

Problem / background

Reason 1

Evidence and explanation

Counterarguments to Reason 1, if any

Response to counterarguments

Reason 2

Evidence and explanation

Counterarguments to Reason 2, if any

Response to counterarguments

Reason 3

Evidence and explanation

Counterarguments to Reason 3, if any

Response to counterarguments

Module 6
Teaching paragraphs

by Elizabeth Canfield

Challenges

Teaching paragraphs can be challenging; as experienced writers, we may have internalized essay and paragraph structure. Because we understand the relationship between organization and meaning and can anticipate readers' needs, we may struggle to explain effective paragraphing techniques to students who are not as aware of their audience and how to reach them. Especially in a first-year writing class, students will have varying levels of experience with thinking about or writing cohesive and organized paragraphs.

When paragraphing, students might face some of the following challenges:

- Readers expect paragraphs to guide them from one clearly stated and developed idea to the next. If students write without a sense of organization and simply lump their prose into paragraphs, readers will find those paragraphs disorganized and confusing. What seems natural to the writer may not be logical for the reader.

- Many students have internalized a five-paragraph essay form that inhibits their ability to write expansive or detailed pieces; they may not understand how to break long discussions into more than three body paragraphs.

- Students might not have a sense of when a paragraph break is needed. Thus, some paragraphs may be too long and in need of a break; other paragraphs may be too short and in need of combining.

- Students might not use transitions between paragraphs that guide readers smoothly to new information from information given in the previous paragraph. Novice writers might use a transitional word at the beginning of a paragraph (*however* or *next*, for example), but the word might be out of place if the paragraphs are not logically connected.

- Some students will produce pieces of writing with no paragraphs at all.

Strategies

Although at first it might seem desirable to teach students what paragraphs are (by showing them models of paragraphs with topic sentences and supporting sentences), helping students see the relationships between ideas and how ideas can be grouped together might be more beneficial. The following strategies can help students grasp how paragraphs work:

See the Resources chart at the end of this module for paragraph coverage, including samples.

1. Help students understand that they should not think of paragraphs as a template into which they must force their ideas.

2. Discuss paragraphing in the context of a larger conversation about how structure reveals and reinforces relationships between ideas (from the sentence level to the essay level). Show students samples of paragraphs that reflect different relationships among ideas.

3. Take a student draft and remove the paragraph structure. Ask students to read through the draft without paragraphs and think about where breaks and transitions would help readers and the writer.

4. Have students revise paragraphs and rearrange the order of paragraphs so that each idea in an essay transitions smoothly into the next idea.

5. Have students workshop topic sentences and build paragraphs to support them. See the sample lesson for this strategy.

Sample lesson for Strategy 5: Topic sentence and paragraphing workshop

Lesson planning:	
Sequencing:	Students should have already completed at least one draft of their first writing assignment.
Student level:	Novice writers, though more experienced writers could also benefit from this lesson
Learning objectives:	Students will be able to • Discuss the purposes of paragraphs • Practice writing topic sentences and subordinate and coordinate ideas in the context of a draft-in-progress
Time required:	Two sessions of at least fifty minutes
Materials/ resources:	• Overhead projector (and transparency), laptop projector or document camera • Bring a sample student essay or reader selection to Session 1 (see Session 1, step 1). If possible, have an electronic file or transparency available for projection. Students should come to Session 2 with an essay draft. The suggested activity for Session 2 will work best if students write on similar topics or in response to the same readings.

Lesson steps:	

Session 1:	1. Provide students with a sample essay or a reader selection. Ask them to identify a paragraph they find effective. Give them time to write a short response explaining their choice. (This step can be completed as homework for Session 1.)
	
	2. In small groups, have the students read their favorite paragraphs aloud to their peers and briefly explain their choice. Each group should then choose one paragraph to focus on. Each group should discuss the following questions about the paragraph they've chosen:
	
	   • Why did you choose this paragraph?
	   • How does the writer group ideas together? Describe the order of the sentences within the paragraph. How does the paragraph begin? How does it end?
	   • How do the sentences work together within the paragraph? What is each sentence's "job" for creating meaning?
	   • How does the paragraph follow logically from the paragraph that precedes it and lead into the next paragraph?
	
	3. Ask groups to share their responses with the class. (If projecting the paragraph is not an option, make sure every student has a copy of the essay.)
	
	4. To prepare for Session 2, provide students with a handout that lists some characteristics of topic sentences. Students should add to the list and match up each characteristic with an appropriate topic sentence from the paragraphs discussed in Session 1. To get your students started, you can list a few of the following characteristics: (a) Topic sentences don't have to be the first sentence of a paragraph. (b) Topic sentences can express a question, which the rest of the paragraph answers. (c) Topic sentences can express an opinion, a fact, or an attitude, which other sentences support or discuss. (d) Topic sentences can present a problem, which the paragraph addresses. (e) Topic sentences can summarize what other sentences explore in detail.

Session 2:	1. Take a few minutes to discuss the characteristics and examples students gathered in preparation for this session. Record some characteristics on the board.
	
	2. To begin the topic sentence workshop, ask students to take out their drafts. (The following suggested steps work best if students have written on the same topic or in response to the same readings.)
	
	   • Ask students to write a possible topic sentence for a paragraph for their essay-in-progress on a separate sheet of paper, using their topic sentence handout and the examples on the board to guide them in creating their topic sentence.
	   • Collect the sheets of paper, and using either the board or a projected laptop, display one student-generated sample topic sentence. (The selected topic sentence should be strong enough to provide clues about the purpose and direction of the paragraph. If the class is writing on a variety of topics, however, the writer of the sample topic sentence may want to provide some additional context about the essay.)
	   • Ask the class to brainstorm sentences that would surround or follow the sample topic sentence, and write them on the board.
	   • Once the paragraph is drafted, ask the class if any of the sentences can be moved around to convey meaning more clearly and effectively.

Session 2, *continued*:	• Process questions: Ask students why they made the choices that they did with *what* they said and *how* they said it.
	• Repeat the steps in this list at least one more time.
	3. Once students have had some practice with the previous exercise, ask them to do one of the following:
	• Repeat the previous exercise on their own with one of the sentences that they generated earlier in the session.
	• Revise an existing paragraph in their essay draft to reflect a strong topic sentence and well-arranged and well-crafted subordinate/coordinate sentences.
Follow-up:	It is helpful to repeat this lesson more than once and to explain the relationship of this exercise to other exercises focused on structuring the essay as a whole.
Variations:	• Session 2 can focus on a later draft. Turn the topic sentence workshop into a revision workshop using paragraphs that students have already generated for their essay. Have them consider the following questions: (1) Look at key words in the topic sentence. What does the topic sentence promise readers that the paragraph will be about? (2) Does the paragraph fulfill that promise? If so, how? If not, where does it fall short? (3) How could the paragraph be revised and/or reordered so that the main idea of each paragraph will flow into the main idea of the next paragraph? (4) What are the strengths and limitations of the draft topic sentence, from a writer's and a reader's point of view?
	🖥 If your course is conducted online, discussion boards or blogs can be a good setting for Session 1. Session 2 requires a collaborative writing space (such as Google Docs).

Resources

Handbook coverage

The Bedford Handbook, 9th ed.	A Writer's Reference, 7th ed.	Rules for Writers, 7th ed.	A Pocket Style Manual, 6th ed.	Writer's Help (writershelp.com)
Drafting a plan (1d)	Planning (C1)	Generating ideas and sketching a plan (1)	Checklist for global revision	🆃 **Composing and revising**
Drafting an introduction, body, and conclusion (1e to 1g)	Drafting (C2)	Roughing out an initial draft (2)		**Planning**
Revising and editing (2a to 2c)	Revising (C3)	Making global revisions (3)		**Drafting**
Building effective paragraphs (3)	Writing paragraphs (4)	Building effective paragraphs (4)		**Revising**
Focusing on a main point (3a)	Focusing on a main point (C4-a)	Focusing on a main point (4a)		**Writing paragraphs**
Developing the main point (3b)	Developing the main point (C4-b)	Developing the main point (4b)		🆂 *paragraphs; drafting; revising*
Choosing a suitable pattern of organization (3c)	Choosing a pattern of organization (C4-c)	Choosing a pattern of organization (4c)		
Making paragraphs coherent (3d)	Making paragraphs coherent (C4-d)	Making paragraphs coherent (4d)		
Adjusting paragraph length (3e)	Adjusting paragraph length (C4-e)	Adjusting paragraph length (4e)		

🆃 = *Writer's Help* table of contents
🆂 = Search terms in *Writer's Help*

Practice, models, and more

hackerhandbooks.com/bedhandbook	hackerhandbooks.com/writersref	hackerhandbooks.com/rules	hackerhandbooks.com/pocket	*Writer's Help* (writershelp.com)
ⓔ The writing process	**Practice exercises**	**Practice exercises**		**Exercises**
As you write	**Composing and revising**	**The writing process**		**Composing and revising**
Revising a thesis	C2–2 and C2–3 Thesis statements	2–2 and 2–3 Thesis statements		Thesis statements 1 and 2
Revising an introduction	C2–4 Introductions	2–4 Introductions		Introductions
Revising a conclusion	C4–2 Topic sentences	4–2 Topic sentences		Topic sentences
Creating unity	C4–3 Transitions	4–3 Transitions		Transitions
Using transitions				
Exercises				
1–5 and 1–6 Thesis statements				
1–7 Introductions				
3–2 Topic sentences				
3–3 Transitions				

ⓔ Students can access integrated media with the purchase of a new handbook (or with standalone purchase online).
NOTE: Instructor registration grants you access to all media for your handbook.

Module 7
Teaching introductions and conclusions

Challenges

Experienced writers in many fields understand the necessity of writing an engaging introduction to spark readers' interest and of finishing a piece with a compelling conclusion to ensure that readers will remember the writer's message or findings. Student writers, however, may be hard-pressed to see introductions and conclusions as providing important opportunities to guide and engage readers, instead treating these sections as hastily written afterthoughts to be appended to the body of the paper. The following are some of the challenges you are likely to encounter while teaching introductions and conclusions:

- Students struggle with conflicting advice they have accumulated about how to write a successful introduction or conclusion.

- Students often keep a weak initial attempt at an introduction or conclusion rather than revising it.

- Students begin an introduction too broadly ("Since the dawn of humankind . . ." or "There are many interesting aspects to the issue of . . .") as they try to provide a general overview of their topic before narrowing it down to their thesis.

- In the introduction, students self-consciously comment on the essay prompt or assignment ("When I first received this assignment . . ."), unaware that this is unconventional for most genres.

- In the conclusion, students simply repeat their thesis or their main points from the body paragraphs verbatim.

- Students omit the conclusion completely.

- Students use a quotation to introduce or conclude an essay but neglect to comment on it or explain how it relates to their topic.

- Students write their way to a thesis by the end of their paper and need help seeing that their draft conclusion might serve as an introduction instead.

Strategies

Convince students that introductions and conclusions perform crucial functions for the writer and reader and are useful for many types of writing, not just academic essays. Introductions can draw readers into a debate, provide background information on a topic, set the scene for a narrative, or describe a problem to be solved. Conclusions can communicate findings, reinforce a call for action, share a lesson learned, offer a recommendation, or pose a question for future investigation. You might encourage student writers to view introductions and conclusions as opportunities to explore their own creativity and to find ways to connect with and to persuade their readers. The following strategies will help students understand the functions of the introduction and conclusion and will offer them practice in writing and revising these sections of the academic essay:

See the Resources chart at the end of this module for coverage of introductory and concluding techniques.

1. As a class, discuss introductory and concluding techniques. (See pp. 108 and 109 for lists of techniques.) Remind students that different techniques will be appropriate for different topics and rhetorical purposes and that two or more techniques can often be blended into a successful introduction or conclusion.

2. Pick one or two introductory techniques that require creative choices and specific detail (such as a vivid example or a description or an image), provide an inviting sample topic and thesis, and ask students to draft a sample introduction. Have students share their introductions with each other in small groups, and then ask them to choose one or two to share in full-class discussion.

3. Ask students to bring in examples of introductions and conclusions in short print or online articles to discuss how writers make careful choices when composing introductions and conclusions and to note any patterns they see in the introductions and conclusions they examine. Use these examples to examine how writers use different techniques for different audiences and rhetorical purposes. See the sample lesson for this strategy.

4. Discuss the techniques for and advice about writing introductions and conclusions that students have encountered in other courses. Some will likely have been taught never to use a question or a quotation in an introduction, and some will have been taught to begin an introduction with a general discussion of the topic. In full-group discussion, have students compile a list of "good advice" and a separate list of "unhelpful/confusing advice" for writing introductions and conclusions. See the sample lesson for this strategy.

5. Review examples of introductions and conclusions from previous semesters as a group. Be sure to include both exemplary work and work in need of various levels of revision so that students can practice critical peer review skills.

6. After students have drafted an essay, assign a revision of the introduction and conclusion, requiring students to choose a different technique for each section than what they've used in the first draft.

Sample lesson for Strategies 3 and 4: Techniques for writing introductions and conclusions

Lesson planning:	
Sequencing:	Use this lesson when students are in the early drafting stages of their first or second essay.
Student level:	This lesson can benefit novice writers who may have difficulty generating ideas for introductions and conclusions as well as experienced writers, who may rely heavily on only a few techniques and will gain flexibility in their writing by practicing some new methods.
Learning objectives:	Students will be able to • list and describe introductory and concluding techniques • understand the functions of introductions and conclusions in academic essays • choose an appropriate introductory and concluding technique for their essay topic • critique models of student work and their peers' introductions and conclusions • evaluate drafts of their own introductions and conclusions and revise as necessary
Time required:	Two sessions of at least fifty minutes each
Materials/ resources:	• Overhead projector, laptop projector, or document camera • Chalkboard or erasable whiteboard • Brief sample essays to provide model introductions and conclusions (can be student work from previous classes, examples of student writing in your handbook or on the handbook's companion Web site, or your own writing) • Introductory and concluding paragraphs from brief print or online articles that students bring to class • The handbook (See the Resources chart at the end of this module.)
Lesson steps:	
Session 1: Writing introductions	1. Begin the session by asking students to list any advice they have been given about writing introductions. Encourage students to volunteer examples from their lists, and write their examples on the board. Discuss each piece of advice as you add it to the list; you will find that some suggestions students have received are beneficial but general (for example, "Try to find something interesting about your topic that will hook your reader") or that some advice may be confusing to students and may contradict what they have seen in the work of experienced writers. For example, "Never begin with a question or quotation" is a likely response from students during this exercise. Assure students that these are viable introductory techniques but that a writer also must comment on a question or quotation rather than simply leave it hanging without elaboration. After discussing the student-generated list, break the advice into categories labeled "Good Advice" and "Unhelpful/Confusing Advice."

Session 1, *continued*:	2. Remind students that the two main functions of an introduction are to hook readers—to get them invested in reading further—and to provide the main point of the essay.
	3. Observe that introductions are common in many genres, including academic essays, magazine articles, and documentaries. Also note for students that within a genre (such as academic journal articles), introductions can have an identifiably similar pattern.
	4. If the handbook you are using includes a list of introductory techniques in the section on drafting an essay, review the list and ask students to provide brief examples of each of the following techniques (even if they have to invent details, facts, or statistics):
	• a startling statistic or an unusual fact
	• a vivid example
	• a description or an image
	• a paradoxical statement
	• a quotation or a bit of dialogue
	• a question
	• an analogy
	• an anecdote
	If your handbook does not include a section on drafting an introduction, you might create a slide presentation that lists these techniques and provides model introductions using some of them. Note that these introductory techniques hinge on specific detail rather than sweeping generalization and that each of them offers opportunities for writers to flex their creativity.
	5. Turn to the examples of introductions that students have brought in from short print or online articles. Have pairs of students identify the type or types of introductory technique being used in their examples (students may identify combinations of techniques or techniques not listed in their handbook). Ask them to reflect on why each writer made the specific choice of introductory technique and to evaluate its success. Reiterate the point that introductions occur in all kinds of writing, not just academic essays, and that the techniques used to introduce a piece of writing are time-tested and used regularly in a variety of genres.
	6. Now that students have a toolbox of introductory techniques with which to work, ask them to write a brief introduction for an argumentative essay during the class period. Assure them that their best introductions will be written in the process of producing and revising a complete essay but that the activity will provide some practice in applying a particular technique to craft an introduction.
	A sample thesis that generates quick, creative responses is "Valentine's Day is overrated because . . ." or "Valentine's Day is a special holiday because. . . ." Students can quickly choose their thesis assertion, fill in the supporting reasons, and then craft an introduction around the thesis that uses one of the techniques they have just learned. Although this exercise may seem rudimentary, it often generates detailed responses and gives students confidence in writing catchy, creative introductions. Encourage students to share these introductions in small groups and pick one introduction from their group to share with the whole class. If time is too short to include this exercise during Session 1, assign it as homework and share in class at the beginning of Session 2.

Session 2:
Writing conclusions
	1. Begin the session by reviewing the introductory techniques learned in Session 1. Assure students that many of these same techniques can be used to help craft their conclusions, although this session will focus on additional techniques. Ask students what advice they have received about writing conclusions, and, as in Session 1, write examples of good advice or unhelpful/confusing advice on the board and discuss them. You may find that some students have been taught to repeat their thesis or main topic sentences from the body paragraphs verbatim in the conclusion.
	
	2. Observe that readers need a sense that the essay is ending and that their time has been well spent in reading it. The conclusion can accomplish this in a variety of ways. Some effective conclusions reiterate the writer's main point or points; in some genres, the conclusion suggests areas for further inquiry. In short, the conclusion can sum up or can leave readers pondering new ideas.
	
	3. If the handbook you are using includes the following list of concluding techniques in the section on drafting an essay, review it with students:
	
	   • briefly summarize your key points
	   • propose a course of action
	   • offer a recommendation
	   • discuss the topic's wider significance or implications
	   • redefine a key term or concept
	   • pose a question for further study
	
	   If your handbook does not include a section on drafting a conclusion, you might create a slide presentation that lists these techniques and provides model conclusions using some of them.
	
	4. Distribute model essays (two or three of each) or project them on the overhead. In full-group discussion, ask students to identify what types of techniques are being used in each conclusion, to evaluate their effectiveness, and to make suggestions for revision. Try to find examples from previous student work that are too vague or broad or that are simply not engaging as well as models that are more specific and well written. Consider adding at least one conclusion that is well crafted but that neglects to connect with the thesis.
	
	5. Ask students to revise one of the weaker concluding models, using one of the concluding techniques presented during this session; for this exercise, students can work individually at first and then pair up or work in small groups to discuss their revisions. Have students choose one revision from the group to share with the whole class, and ask them to be ready to explain why this revision is successful.

Follow-up	• After students have drafted an essay, require them to write an alternative introduction and conclusion to explore different approaches and to reinforce the benefits of significant revision. • During peer reviews, require students to identify and evaluate introductory and concluding techniques in each other's essays.
Variations	• If students have drafts of their own essays to work with, step 6 in Session 1 and steps 4 and 5 in Session 2 can be modified to produce revisions of the students' own introductions and conclusions.

Variations, *continued*:	• Begin Session 1 by viewing a brief introductory clip from a recent documentary and ask how the director chose to introduce the film's main point, focusing if applicable on how specific details can be more compelling than a vague overview of the topic. Consider viewing the documentary's conclusion at the beginning of Session 2 to discuss what choices the director made to reinforce the documentary's main message and to create a feeling of closure for the audience. 🖥 If you are using an online platform, have students post their introductions or conclusions in a discussion forum and respond to each other with suggestions for revision.

Resources

Handbook coverage

The Bedford Handbook, 9th ed.	A Writer's Reference, 7th ed.	Rules for Writers, 7th ed.	A Pocket Style Manual, 6th ed.	Writer's Help (writershelp.com)

Drafting an introduction that includes a thesis (1e)
 	
 Drafting a conclusion (1g)
 	
 Revising with comments: Narrow your introduction (p. 52)
 	
 Establishing credibility and stating your position [argument] (6f)
 	
 Drafting an introduction that announces your interpretation [literature] (p. 184)
 	
 Drafting an introduction for your thesis [MLA] (53d)
 	
 Forming a working thesis [APA] (58a)
 	
 Forming a working thesis [*Chicago*] (p. 740)
	Drafting an introduction that includes a thesis (C2-a)
	
	 Drafting a conclusion (C2-c)
	
	 Revising with comments: Narrow your introduction (p. 24)
	
	 Establishing credibility and stating your position [argument] (A2-c)
	
	 Forming a working thesis (MLA-1a)
	
	 Forming a working thesis (APA-1a)
	
	 Forming a working thesis (CMS-1a)
		Drafting an introduction that includes a thesis (2a)
		
		 Drafting a conclusion (2c)
		
		 Revising with comments: Narrow your introduction (p. 34)
		
		 Establishing credibility and stating your position [argument] (6c)
		
		 Forming a working thesis [MLA] (56a)
		
		 Forming a working thesis [APA] (61a)
			Drafting an introduction for your thesis [MLA] (50d)
			
			 Forming a working thesis [APA] (p. 622)
			
			 Forming a working thesis [*Chicago*] (p. 686)
				T Composing and revising
				 Drafting
				   Drafting an introduction with thesis
				   Drafting a conclusion
				 Revising
				   Revising with comments
				 T Academic writing
				 Constructing reasonable arguments
				   Stating your position in your introduction
				 T MLA papers
				 Supporting a thesis
				   Forming a working thesis
				 T APA papers
				 Supporting a thesis
				   Forming a thesis
				 T *Chicago* (CMS) papers
				 Supporting a thesis
				   Forming a thesis
				 T Writing about literature
				 Planning an interpretation of literature
				   Drafting an interpretive thesis
				 Writing a literature paper
				   Drafting an introduction that announces your interpretation
				 S *introduction; conclusion; thesis*

T = *Writer's Help* table of contents
S = Search terms in *Writer's Help*

Practice, models, and more

hackerhandbooks.com/bedhandbook	hackerhandbooks.com/writersref	hackerhandbooks.com/rules	hackerhandbooks.com/pocket	*Writer's Help* (writershelp.com)
e **The writing process**	**Practice exercises**	**Practice exercises**	**Practice exercises**	**Exercises**
As you write	**Composing and revising**	**The writing process**	**MLA**	**Composing and revising**
Revising a thesis	C2–2 and C2–3 Thesis statements	2–2 and 2–3 Thesis statements	29–1 and 29–2 Thesis statements in MLA papers	Thesis statements 1 and 2
Revising an introduction	**MLA**	**MLA**	**APA**	**Academic writing**
Revising a conclusion	MLA 1–1 and MLA 1–2 Thesis statements in MLA papers	56–1 and 56–2 Thesis statements in MLA papers	35–1 and 35–2 Thesis statements in APA papers	Thesis statements in literature papers
Exercises	**APA**	**APA**	*Chicago*	**MLA papers**
1–5 and 1–6 Thesis statements	APA 1–1 and APA 1–2 Thesis statements in APA papers	61–1 and 61–2 Thesis statements in APA papers	40–1 and 40–2 Thesis statements in *Chicago* papers	Thesis statements in MLA papers 1 and 2
1–7 Introductions	**CMS (*Chicago*)**	**Model papers and other sample documents**	**Model papers and other sample documents**	**APA papers**
e **Academic reading and writing**	CMS 1–1 and CMS 1–2 Thesis statements in CMS (*Chicago*) papers	Jacobs, "From Lecture to Conversation: Redefining What's 'Fit to Print'" (argument)	Jacobs, "From Lecture to Conversation: Redefining What's 'Fit to Print'" (argument)	Thesis statements in APA papers 1 and 2
As you write	**Model papers and other sample documents**	Larson, "The Transformation of Mrs. Peters: An Analysis of 'A Jury of Her Peers'" (literary analysis)	Larson, "The Transformation of Mrs. Peters: An Analysis of 'A Jury of Her Peers'" (literary analysis)	*Chicago* (CMS) **papers**
Drafting your central claim and supporting claims	Jacobs, "From Lecture to Conversation: Redefining What's 'Fit to Print'" (argument)	Peel, "Opposing Voices in 'Ballad of the Landlord'" (literary analysis)	Peel, "Opposing Voices in 'Ballad of the Landlord'" (literary analysis)	Thesis statements in *Chicago* (CMS) papers 1 and 2
Exercises	Larson, "The Transformation of Mrs. Peters: An Analysis of 'A Jury of Her Peers'" (literary analysis)	Orlov, "Online Monitoring: A Threat to Employee Privacy in the Wired Workplace" (research; MLA)	Orlov, "Online Monitoring: A Threat to Employee Privacy in the Wired Workplace" (research; MLA)	T **MLA papers**
7–1 Thesis statements in literature papers	Peel, "Opposing Voices in 'Ballad of the Landlord'" (literary analysis)	Mirano, "Can Medication Cure Obesity in Children? A Review of the Literature" (literature review; APA)	Mirano, "Can Medication Cure Obesity in Children? A Review of the Literature" (literature review; APA)	**Directory to MLA model papers**
Sample student writing	Orlov, "Online Monitoring: A Threat to Employee Privacy in the Wired Workplace" (research; MLA)			Jacobs, "From Lecture to Conversation: Redefining What's 'Fit to Print'" (argument)
Jacobs, "From Lecture to Conversation: Redefining What's 'Fit to Print'" (argument)				Larson, "The Transformation of Mrs. Peters: An Analysis of 'A Jury of Her Peers'" (literary analysis)
Larson, "The Transformation of Mrs. Peters: An Analysis of 'A Jury of Her Peers'" (literary analysis)				Peel, "Opposing Voices in 'Ballad of the Landlord'" (literary analysis)
e **Researched writing**				Orlov, "Online Monitoring: A Threat to Employee Privacy in the Wired Workplace" (research; MLA)
Sample student writing				
Orlov, "Online Monitoring: A Threat to Employee Privacy in the Wired Workplace" (research; MLA)				

e Students can access integrated media with the purchase of a new handbook (or with standalone purchase online).
NOTE: Instructor registration grants you access to all media for your handbook.

Practice, models, and more *(continued)*

hackerhandbooks.com/bedhandbook	hackerhandbooks.com/writersref	hackerhandbooks.com/rules	hackerhandbooks.com/pocket	*Writer's Help* (writershelp.com)
Mirano, "Can Medication Cure Obesity in Children? A Review of the Literature" (literature review; APA) Bishop, "The Massacre at Fort Pillow: Holding Nathan Bedford Forrest Accountable" (research; *Chicago*)	Mirano, "Can Medication Cure Obesity in Children? A Review of the Literature" (literature review; APA) Bishop, "The Massacre at Fort Pillow: Holding Nathan Bedford Forrest Accountable" (research; *Chicago*)	Bishop, "The Massacre at Fort Pillow: Holding Nathan Bedford Forrest Accountable" (research; *Chicago*)	Bishop, "The Massacre at Fort Pillow: Holding Nathan Bedford Forrest Accountable" (research; *Chicago*)	**T APA papers** **Directory to APA model papers** Mirano, "Can Medication Cure Obesity in Children? A Review of the Literature" (literature review; APA) **T *Chicago* (CMS) papers** **Directory to *Chicago* (CMS) model papers** Bishop, "The Massacre at Fort Pillow: Holding Nathan Bedford Forrest Accountable" (research; *Chicago*) **S** *model papers*

T = *Writer's Help* table of contents
S = Search terms in *Writer's Help*

Print ancillaries

The Bedford Handbook, 9th ed.	*A Writer's Reference*, 7th ed.	*Rules for Writers,* 7th ed.	*A Pocket Style Manual,* 6th ed.	*Writer's Help* (writershelp.com)
	Writing about Literature, a Hacker Handbooks Supplement	*Writing about Literature,* a Hacker Handbooks Supplement	*Writing about Literature,* a Hacker Handbooks Supplement	

Module 8
Teaching argument and counterargument

by Nancy Sommers

Challenges

Learning to argue a thesis and support it with appropriate evidence requires students to establish a position, anticipate counterpositions, and persuade readers. If students don't understand the persuasive nature of academic writing, or if they think of argument as a debate with winners or losers, they may have difficulty grasping the conventions and expectations of academic argument. Some specific challenges you might encounter include the following:

● Students are reluctant to take a stance on an issue.

● Students confuse opinions with positions.

● Students are unfamiliar with the language of argument: thesis, claim, evidence, counterargument.

● Students are unfamiliar with strategies for developing an argumentative thesis.

● Students believe that one piece of evidence "proves" a writer's point of view.

● Students are inexperienced with summarizing, paraphrasing, quoting, and interpreting evidence.

● Students believe that introducing counterarguments will weaken their positions.

● Students come from cultures that value different modes of argumentation.

For further discussion of working with multilingual writers, see Topic 5.

Strategies

Help students become comfortable with academic arguments by providing models of student and professional arguments. Give them plenty of practice with the key elements of well-constructed arguments: a thesis stated as a clear position on a debatable issue; an examination of the issue's context; sufficient, representative, and relevant evidence to support claims; and opposing positions, summarized and countered. Provide students with clear guidelines for reading and interpreting the structure of arguments. Introduce students to the idea of constructing and evaluating their own arguments with the following strategies:

1. Conduct thesis workshops. Ask students to draft a working thesis. Then have them brainstorm counter thesis statements to illustrate that effective argumentative thesis statements can be opposed. Show students why addressing counterarguments strengthens their thesis statements.

2. Have students give two-minute oral arguments to support a stance they've taken. Ask peers to propose counterarguments. Give students practice using the language of counterargument: "But isn't it possible that . . . ?" or "Critics of this view might argue that. . . ." Help students understand that readers will make up their minds after listening to all sides of an argument.

3. Provide models of student and professional arguments to illustrate the elements of argumentation. Focus discussion on the questions each writer asks; the thesis being argued; the evidence each writer analyzes; and the counterarguments that are presented. See the sample lesson for this strategy.

Sample lesson for Strategy 3: Learning to analyze academic arguments

Lesson planning:	
Sequencing:	Use this lesson to introduce academic argument.
Student level:	This lesson targets students who are unfamiliar with the elements of academic argument. Students will need some prior experience identifying thesis statements, topic sentences, and evidence in written texts. They should also have had experience summarizing texts.
Learning objectives:	Students will be able to • read and evaluate an argument • identify the elements of an argument • question the assumptions of an argument • engage with the evidence of an argument • anticipate and address counterarguments
Time required:	Two sessions of at least fifty minutes
Materials/ resources:	The handbook (See the Resources chart at the end of this module.)

Lesson steps:	
Preparation for Session 1:	1. Ask students to read and annotate Sam Jacobs's argument "From Lecture to Conversation: Redefining What's 'Fit to Print'" if it appears in your handbook or on the handbook's companion Web site. (See "Guidelines for active reading" if your handbook includes it.) 2. Ask students to write a one-paragraph summary of Jacobs's argument. Explain that summarizing an argument helps the reader articulate an author's key points. 3. Ask students to e-mail their summaries to you before class and to bring a copy of their summaries to Session 1.
Session 1:	1. Point out that the class will be learning about argument by taking a close look at Jacobs's thesis, assumptions, and use of evidence and counterargument. With their summaries in hand, ask students to respond generally to the following questions: • What debate has Jacobs entered? • What is Jacobs's position in this debate? • What key claims does he make to support his position? 2. Look at Jacobs's essay with the class. Briefly review the purpose of thesis statements with students. Remind them that a thesis can be an answer to a question posed, the resolution of a problem identified, or a position taken in a debate. Point out how each sentence in Jacobs's introduction leads readers to his thesis. Focus students' attention on Jacobs's thesis by asking the following questions: • How does Jacobs's introduction identify a problem? • According to Jacobs, why should readers care about this problem? • What question is Jacobs asking about citizen journalism? • What are Jacobs's assumptions about the motto of the *New York Times*: "All the news that's fit to print"? How do these assumptions shape his argument? • How does his thesis show that he is taking a position in a debate? 3. Focus students' attention on Jacobs's use of counterargument. For a quick review, ask students to define *counterargument*. Point out to students that writers show themselves as more reasonable and credible thinkers if they acknowledge counterpositions. Then, ask students to evaluate Jacobs's counterargument. They should support their answers with specifics from Jacobs's essay. To aid them in their evaluation, have them address the following questions: • What language does Jacobs use to introduce a counterposition? • How does the inclusion of a counterargument strengthen his position? • How does mentioning the counterargument make him seem more reasonable and knowledgeable? • How does he respond to the counterposition? • How would Jacobs's argument have been weakened if he hadn't included a counterposition?

Session 1, *continued*:	4. Focus students' attention on Jacobs's evidence. First, ask students to name the types of evidence writers often use to support their arguments: facts, statistics, examples and illustrations, visuals, and expert opinions. Remind students of the importance of documenting sources to give credit to other authors. Then, ask students to evaluate the persuasiveness of Jacobs's support by answering the following questions about his use of evidence: • How does Jacobs use evidence to support his claims? • How does Jacobs interpret his evidence? Since evidence doesn't speak for itself, what would be missing if he presented evidence without interpretation? • Imagine removing one piece of evidence from Jacobs's essay. How would that absence weaken the essay? • Does Jacobs provide sufficient evidence? If not, what kind of evidence is missing?
Preparation for Session 2:	1. Ask students to enter the debate with Jacobs's argument by annotating his essay. 2. Based on the questioning they did in step 1, have students propose counter-arguments, thesis, evidence, reasoning, or assumptions. 3. Ask students to develop their counterpositions with these templates: "Some readers might point out . . ." "Critics of this view argue . . ." "Jacobs's argument fails to recognize . . ."
Session 2:	The goal of this exercise is to model for students how arguments grow out of lively conversations between writers and readers. 1. Begin the session by asking three or four students to write their counterarguments on the board. Remind students of the important role that counterargument plays in building strong argument essays. Some students will question Jacobs's assumptions about the limitations of print news. Other students will object to all or parts of his thesis that "online news provides unprecedented opportunities for readers to become more engaged with the news, to hold journalists accountable, and to participate as producers, not simply as consumers." 2. Put students into peer groups and assign some groups to support Jacobs's thesis and some to challenge it. With the group's assignment in mind, each student should first work alone to pose a question and write an argumentative thesis in response to that question. The group should then discuss these thesis statements and test them by thinking about objections readers might raise. Ask each group to appoint a spokesperson to record the group's thesis statements and possible challenges to those statements. The purpose of the peer group discussion is to help students learn the writerly habits of (a) developing a thesis in response to a question; (b) listening emphatically; (c) summarizing, fairly and credibly, the views of others; and (d) raising and responding to different sides of an argument. The peer discussion will also allow students to practice taking a stance, moving beyond opinion to argument, and learning how arguments evolve from lively conversations. Bring the class back together by asking each spokesperson to present the group's thesis statements and challenges to those statements. 3. Pull together the lessons of the two sessions by giving students five or ten minutes to write in response to this prompt: *What have you learned about argument and counterargument?* Collect the students' reflections and review them to see whether students have grasped the major concepts.

Follow-up:	1. Provide students with the following guidelines for constructing and strengthening their own arguments: • Identify a debatable issue. • Examine the issue's social and intellectual contexts. • Develop a thesis that clearly states your position on the issue. • Support your thesis with evidence and persuasive lines of reasoning. • View your audience as a panel of jurors. • Anticipate objections; counter opposing arguments. • Quote opposing views with fairness and accuracy. • Cite and document sources. 2. Use this lesson as groundwork for peer review of argument essays. Have students apply questions along these lines to each other's drafts: • What debate has the writer joined in this draft? What are the various positions in this debate? • How does the writer's thesis answer a question posed, resolve a problem, or take a position? • What assumptions is the writer making? • How has the writer anticipated and countered opposing arguments? • What two or three suggestions might you offer the writer to persuade readers and strengthen the argument?

Resources

Handbook coverage

The Bedford Handbook, 9th ed.	*A Writer's Reference,* 7th ed.	*Rules for Writers,* 7th ed.	*A Pocket Style Manual,* 6th ed.	*Writer's Help* (writershelp.com)
Reading actively (4a) Analyzing to demonstrate your critical reading (4d) Reading and writing arguments (6)	Reading actively: Annotating the text (A1-a) Analyzing to demonstrate your critical thinking (A1-d) Constructing reasonable arguments (A2) Evaluating arguments (A3)	Reading actively: Annotating the text (5a) Analyzing to demonstrate your critical thinking (5d) Constructing reasonable arguments (6) Evaluating arguments (7)		**T** **Academic writing** **Writing about texts** Active reading Analyzing a written or a visual text **Constructing reasonable arguments** **Evaluating arguments** **S** *argument; analysis*

T = *Writer's Help* table of contents
S = Search terms in *Writer's Help*

Practice, models, and more

hackerhandbooks.com/bedhandbook	hackerhandbooks.com/writersref	hackerhandbooks.com/rules	hackerhandbooks.com/pocket	*Writer's Help* (writershelp.com)
e Academic reading and writing	**Model papers and other sample documents**	**Model papers and other sample documents**	**Model papers and other sample documents**	**T MLA papers**
As you write	Jacobs, "From Lecture to Conversation: Redefining What's 'Fit to Print'" (argument)	Jacobs, "From Lecture to Conversation: Redefining What's 'Fit to Print'" (argument)	Jacobs, "From Lecture to Conversation: Redefining What's 'Fit to Print'" (argument)	**Directory to MLA model papers**
Reading actively				Jacobs, "From Lecture to Conversation: Redefining What's 'Fit to Print'" (argument)
Reading visual texts actively	Hammond, "Performance Enhancement through Biotechnology Has No Place in Sports" (argument)	Hammond, "Performance Enhancement through Biotechnology Has No Place in Sports" (argument)	Hammond, "Performance Enhancement through Biotechnology Has No Place in Sports" (argument)	
Evaluating ads for logic and fairness				Hammond, "Performance Enhancement through Biotechnology Has No Place in Sports" (argument)
Identifying appeals				
Evaluating an argument				S *model papers*
Appealing to your readers				
Drafting your central claim and supporting claims				
Practicing counterargument				
Exercises				
6–2 Evaluating arguments				
Sample student writing				
Jacobs, "From Lecture to Conversation: Redefining What's 'Fit to Print'" (argument)				

e Students can access integrated media with the purchase of a new handbook (or with standalone purchase online).
NOTE: Instructor registration grants you access to all media for your handbook.

T = *Writer's Help* table of contents
S = Search terms in *Writer's Help*

Module 9
Teaching students to conduct research and evaluate sources

Challenges

Many students enter college without experience in conducting research and working with sources at the college level. If they have written research papers in the past, the guidelines for these assignments were probably less rigorous than the demands of college research assignments, and students may not have ventured beyond a quick search on the Web. You will likely encounter the following challenges when you give research assignments:

- Students don't know how to pose a research question; research to them is an accumulation of information rather than evidence to support their own arguments.
- Students use only Internet search engines like Google to find sources for their projects.
- Students are unfamiliar with or even intimidated by the search tools and resources at the library, including online databases.
- Students don't have practice evaluating sources and thus are not able to distinguish between credible and unreliable sources.
- Students do not recognize bias in the sources they find.

Strategies

Students can benefit from guided exercises and tutorials that provide them with authentic, hands-on research experience. The following strategies can help you guide students through the process of finding, evaluating, and documenting sources:

1. Introduce students to the resources available at your school and show them how to search online databases. If possible, enlist the help of a reference librarian. Be willing to spend an entire class period to orient students.

2. Review the handbook's discussion of evaluating sources, including the checklists "Evaluating all sources" and "Evaluating Web sources." Using a common source, go through the appropriate checklist as a class.

3. Practice information gathering in a real-life scenario. For example, provide a sample thesis and ask students to locate a reliable electronic source. Have students explain how the source might support the sample thesis.

4. Practice creating sample works cited entries (or end citations) together. Help students navigate the handbook's citation directories and models.

5. Assign annotated bibliographies, which require students to find sources to support their argument, evaluate the sources in writing, and create an appropriate works cited list, references list, or bibliography. The sample lesson provides specific guidelines for applying this strategy.

Sample lesson for Strategy 5: Annotated bibliography

Lesson planning:	
Sequencing:	Use this lesson after students have learned about basic research strategies and have settled on a research question but before they complete any drafts.
Student level:	Students should have already had experience with writing thesis statements and paragraphs, writing about texts, and constructing arguments.
Learning objectives:	Students will be able to • evaluate sources using the guidelines in the handbook • navigate the appropriate documentation style section in the handbook to create end citations • begin an annotated bibliography
Time required:	Two sessions of at least fifty minutes
Materials/ resources:	Session 1 • The handbook • Source texts. Each student should bring three to five scholarly sources that fit his or her research project. Session 2 • The handbook • At least one sample annotated bibliography entry. Provide copies for each student, or create a transparency or an electronic copy to project on the board. • Ask students to bring bibliographic information for source texts.

Lesson steps:	
Preparation:	1. Guide students through the process of choosing a topic and a research question for your assignment. Assignments will vary depending on the goals of your course and department. The annotated bibliography can be used as a preliminary step toward a more extensive research paper, or it can serve as the final product of each student's research. 2. If possible, take a tour of your school's library or ask a librarian to introduce the search tools available on your campus. Many first-year and even second-year students will need help accessing academic articles through online databases. For background reading, assign your handbook's coverage of finding and evaluating sources. (See the Resources chart at the end of this module.) Let students know that they can turn to you, the librarian, and their handbook for help with understanding what constitutes a scholarly or an academic source. 3. After students have learned about your library system's search tools, ask them to bring three to five scholarly sources on their research topic to Session 1. In preparation, have them review your handbook's coverage of evaluating sources.
Session 1:	1. Discuss the handbook's coverage of evaluating sources, pointing out questions that students can ask to determine whether their sources are scholarly and credible. Focus on questions that can help students evaluate any source. Assessing an argument • What is the author's central claim or thesis? • How does the author support this claim — with relevant and sufficient evidence or only with anecdotes or emotional examples? • Are statistics consistent with those you encounter in other sources? Have they been used fairly? Does the author explain where the statistics come from? • Are any of the author's assumptions questionable? • Does the author consider opposing arguments and refute them persuasively? • Does the author fall prey to any logical fallacies? Checking for signs of bias • Does the author or publisher endorse political or religious views that could influence the argument? • Is the author or publisher associated with a special-interest group, such as Greenpeace or the National Rifle Association, that might present only one side of an issue? • Are alternative views presented and addressed? How fairly does the author treat opposing views? • Does the author's language show signs of bias? 2. If your students will be conducting research on the Web, guide them to specific questions they should ask to evaluate Web sources, including those about *authorship*, *sponsorship*, *purpose and audience*, and *currency* discussed in your handbook. Remind students that if an article's authorship and sponsorship are unknown, the source might not be credible or scholarly.

Session 1, *continued*:	2. If your students will be conducting research on the Web, guide them to specific questions they should ask to evaluate Web sources, including those about *authorship*, *sponsorship*, *purpose and audience*, and *currency* discussed in your handbook. Remind students that if an article's authorship and sponsorship are unknown, the source might not be credible or scholarly.
	3. Have a willing student share his or her research question and purpose and describe a sample source. Ask the student to provide basic information about the search process and source text:
	• How was the search performed (for example, with a Google search, with the library's online databases)?
	• What is the title of the text?
	• Who is the author? Does the author have any credentials?
	4. With the help of the class, discuss the credibility of the source. Even though students will not have read the source, they should still be able to determine whether the source warrants further reading or is unsuitable for inclusion in the research project. Consider discussing answers to the following questions:
	• Was the student's search process likely to turn up scholarly sources?
	• Does the title seem to be scholarly?
	• Do the author's credentials qualify him or her to write on the topic?
	5. Divide students into small groups (three or four students each) to evaluate the sources they have brought to class. Encourage them to follow the same process you used in evaluating the sample document and to use the handbook's guidelines for evaluating sources. Offer guidance to students who disagree about the credibility of a source or who have additional questions. If students discover that some of their sources are not credible or appropriate, let them know that they still have time to find other sources to include in their projects.
	6. For homework, ask students to replace any sources their group rejected as not credible or not scholarly. To begin working on their annotated bibliographies, students should bring to Session 2 the bibliographic information for all sources they are considering.
Session 2:	1. Begin this session by explaining the purpose of the annotated bibliography assignment: to provide students with authentic practice conducting college-level research, to help them learn about a topic of their choice, to give them practice summarizing sources, to help them figure out how sources relate to their topic and their own position, and to give them experience with evaluating and documenting the sources they find. If you plan to use the annotated bibliography as a preliminary step in a larger research project, you can also explain that this assignment will help them manage both their time and their information as they begin their research.
	2. Distribute or project a sample entry from an annotated bibliography and introduce its parts: the citation and the annotation. The annotation may take many forms, so you will need to specify what each entry should include. Usually three to seven sentences long, annotations often include one or more of the following points, depending on your course context and assignment goals: *For a list of sample annotated bibliographies on your handbook's companion Web site, see Resources at the end of this module.*
	• A brief summary of the source

Session 2, *continued*:	• An analysis or evaluation that identifies biases, explains how the source fits within the field, or compares the source to the others in the bibliography • An explanation of the source's function in the research project 3. Ask a willing student to share a sample source. Using the handbook as a guide, work with the class to create an end citation for the source. Students may need help navigating the MLA, APA, or *Chicago* style section of the handbook and identifying the source type and corresponding citation model. Many students won't recognize the difference between a Web site and an article posted on a Web site, for example, and will need specific guidance. 4. Work with students to write a sample annotation. Ask the student who contributed the source to provide general information about the text for the class to work from. 5. After the students have constructed a model citation and annotation, give them time to draft an annotated citation for one of their own sources. (Some students will finish more quickly than others; ask these students to continue drafting citations and annotations for their other sources.) 6. After about ten minutes, ask students to share one of their annotations with one or more peers and to note strengths in the samples of their peers. 7. Before the class period ends, ask a few students to comment on the strengths they noticed in their peers' work. With the writers' permission, share a few particularly strong annotations with the class. (Some writers may be shy about reading their own work. You can ask another student to read the entry aloud, or you can offer to read it to the class.) 8. Wrap up by summarizing the features of an annotated bibliography and the strengths of the samples noted in class. Assign a draft of the annotated bibliography for homework.
Follow-up:	Conduct peer reviews of full annotated bibliographies. You can devote an entire class period to the peer review, or you can ask students to share a few entries during one segment of the class period.
Variations:	If your school has such resources, consider reserving a computer classroom for Session 1 so that students have access to online sources and other materials in class.

Resources

Handbook coverage

The Bedford Handbook, 9th ed.	*A Writer's Reference,* 7th ed.	*Rules for Writers,* 7th ed.	*A Pocket Style Manual,* 6th ed.	*Writer's Help* (writershelp.com)
Thinking like a researcher; gathering sources (50) Managing information; taking notes responsibly (51) Evaluating sources (52) Writing guide: Annotated bibliography (p. 554) MLA list of works cited (56b) APA list of references (61b) *Chicago* documentation style (63d)	Conducting research (R1) Evaluating sources (R2) Managing information; avoiding plagiarism (R3) MLA list of works cited (MLA-4b) APA list of references (APA-4b) Model notes and bibliography entries (CMS-4c)	Conducting research (53) Evaluating sources (54) Managing information; avoiding plagiarism (55) MLA list of works cited (59b) APA list of references (64b)	Finding appropriate sources (26) Evaluating sources (27) Managing information; avoiding plagiarism (28) MLA list of works cited (33b) APA list of references (38b) Model notes and bibliography entries [*Chicago*] (43c)	**T Research** **Research strategy** **Evaluating sources** **T MLA papers** **MLA list of works cited** **T APA papers** **APA list of references** **T *Chicago* (CMS) papers** **Model notes and bibliography entries** **S** *research; evaluating sources; bibliography*

T = *Writer's Help* table of contents
S = Search terms in *Writer's Help*

Practice, models, and more

hackerhandbooks.com/bedhandbook	hackerhandbooks.com/writersref	hackerhandbooks.com/rules	hackerhandbooks.com/pocket	*Writer's Help* (writershelp.com)
e Researched writing	**Practice exercises**	**Practice exercises**	**Practice exercises**	**Exercises**
As you write Mapping out a search strategy Planning with sources Evaluating sources you find on the Web Developing an annotated bibiography **Finding research help** Locating sources using a variety of tools and databases **Exercises: MLA papers** 56–4 MLA documentation: identifying elements of sources 56–5 to 56–7 MLA documentation: works cited **Exercises: APA papers** 61–4 APA documentation: identifying elements of sources 61–5 to 61–7 APA documentation: reference list **Exercises:** *Chicago* **papers** 63–12 *Chicago* documentation: identifying elements of sources 63–16 to 63–18 *Chicago* documentation: bibliography	**MLA** MLA 4–4 MLA documentation: identifying elements of sources MLA 4–5 to 4–7 MLA documentation: works cited **APA** APA 4–4 APA documentation: identifying elements of sources APA 4–5 to 4–7 APA documentation: reference list **CMS (*Chicago*)** CMS 4–1 *Chicago* documentation: identifying elements of sources CMS 4–5 to 4–7 *Chicago* documentation: bibliography	**MLA** 59–4 MLA documentation: identifying elements of sources 59–5 to 59–7 MLA documentation: works cited **APA** 64–4 APA documentation: identifying elements of sources 64–5 to 64–7 APA documentation: reference list	**MLA** 33–4 MLA documentation: identifying elements of sources 33–5 to 33–7 MLA documentation: works cited **APA** 38–4 APA documentation: identifying elements of sources 38–5 to 38–7 APA documentation: reference list ***Chicago*** 43–1 *Chicago* documentation: identifying elements of sources 43–5 to 43–7 *Chicago* documentation: bibliography	**MLA papers** MLA documentation: identifying elements of sources MLA documentation: works cited 1, 2, 3 **APA papers** APA documentation: identifying elements of sources APA documentation: reference list 1, 2, 3 ***Chicago* (CMS) papers** *Chicago* (CMS) documentation: identifying elements of sources *Chicago* (CMS) documentation: bibliography 1, 2, 3

e Students can access integrated media with the purchase of a new handbook (or with standalone purchase online).
NOTE: Instructor registration grants you access to all media for your handbook.

Module 10
Teaching students to integrate sources

Challenges

The academic genres that your first- and second-year students are expected to read and write may be unfamiliar to them. While many students have had some exposure to fiction and nonfiction literature, they likely have not read many researched academic essays and journal articles. Because of their inexperience as both readers and writers of these types of texts, they can feel confused, ambivalent, and even frustrated when they are expected to use the conventions of researched writing that seasoned academics employ with ease.

The integration of sources is one such convention of academic writing. It is not the kind of skill that students encounter in any writing they do outside of school because most of their personal writing does not involve the use of source material.

Several issues commonly arise as students try to integrate sources into their own writing:

- Students do not know why they would need to integrate sources. When an assignment tells them to use a given number of sources, they locate and put that number of sources into an essay to fulfill the requirement, but they do not consider how the sources can inform or challenge their own ideas.

- Students do not introduce quotations with signal phrases, instead using "dropped" quotations.

- Students use inappropriate signal phrases (for example, writing "Smith quotes" rather than "Smith states" to introduce words written by Smith), or they use a limited number of signal phrases repetitively.

- Students do not use the technique of blending quotations into a sentence (for example, *Although Smith observes that the automobile "transformed the U.S. economy," he does not explore how it also transformed our nation culturally*).

- Students use quotations that are too long rather than using shorter passages.

- Students do not quote selectively; they may quote every time they want to bring in another writer's ideas rather than using an author's original words only when the writing is especially vivid or precise.

- Students do not have a sense of when to use paraphrase or summary rather than quotation.

- Students present a quotation that is not necessary to the essay.

- Students present a quotation without commenting on it or connecting the quotation to the argument or content of the essay.

Strategies

Exposure to and frequent practice with a variety of sources help students understand how to synthesize and integrate source material. To encourage students to become more confident and fluent in their use of outside sources, focus on strategies that expose them to models and then provide them with multiple opportunities for practice:

1. Have students thoroughly read and review the sections on integrating sources in their handbook and make sure they understand key terms such as *signal phrase* and *dropped quotation*.

2. Review a variety of models, including professional journal articles and student papers, that synthesize sources and integrate them smoothly and effectively.

3. Assign integration exercises from the handbook or companion Web site, as well as from ancillaries (such as the exercises in *Working with Sources*).

4. Make integrating sources a focus of peer review sessions by having students comment on how the sources in a draft are being introduced and used to inform, support, or challenge an argument.

To find coverage of and exercises for integrating sources in your handbook, see the Resources chart at the end of this module.

Sample lesson for Strategy 2: Using models to demonstrate synthesis and integration of sources

Lesson planning:	
Sequencing:	Use this lesson after students have gathered sources for their first source-based essay and have completed a draft.
Student level:	Novice writers with no experience integrating sources; intermediate writers who have some experience integrating sources. Because this lesson comes just before students submit the final draft of their first source-based essay, they will already have had some experience with college-level writing.
Learning objectives:	Students will be able to • define key terms: *integrating sources, synthesizing sources, signal phrases, dropped quotations* • identify dropped quotations and use a variety of signal phrases • demonstrate a novice-level ability to synthesize sources

Time:	One fifty-minute class period
Materials/ resources:	• The handbook (See the Resources chart at the end of this module.) • Sample student essay that includes well-integrated sources (see your handbook or companion Web site for models, or use one of your own) or professional article with sources

Lesson steps:

Preparation:	• Have your students review their handbook's synthesis coverage (see the Resources chart at the end of this module). • Ask your students to freewrite about a time when they made a purchase or a decision that required them to do some research and weigh options. Perhaps it was a decision to buy a car or to attend a particular college. Have them list the steps they took to gather information. What sources did they consult to help them make their decision and explain and defend their decision to others?

Session 1:	1. Invite volunteers to share the results of their freewriting. Point out any similarities. For example, the decision to attend a particular college or university may have involved consulting sources such as the institution's Web site, talking with high school guidance counselors, visiting campuses, and so forth. Discuss how involving sources in their decision making and using sources to help explain their choices to others would be called "synthesizing sources" and "integrating sources."
	
	 2. Review "Synthesizing Sources" in the handbook (see the Resources chart at the end of this module). Emphasize that synthesizing sources means connecting them to the argument, placing sources "in conversation" with each other, and deciding what function sources serve in the paper.
	
	 3. Remind students that integrating a quotation means that the source is not just added in. The source should be introduced, and it should advance the argument or subject in some way. Tell students the following:
	
	    • Use your sources for evidence to support your points or as ideas that you disagree with.
	
	    • Either way, don't just insert a quotation without context; discuss or interpret it.
	
	    • Sources that suddenly appear in an essay without any introduction or commentary are said to be "dropped" into the essay. They seem out of place and may leave readers wondering why they are there.
	
	 4. Give groups of students a brief passage from a professional journal article (or another student essay, such as one of the essays in the handbook or on the companion Web site). Ask the groups to respond to these questions:
	
	    a. Does the writer introduce sources with signal phrases to avoid dropped quotations?
	
	    b. Does the writer use a variety of signal phrases to indicate the role each source is playing in the paper or article?
	
	    c. How does the writer establish the authority of the sources he or she uses?
	
	    d. Why is the author using quotations? Does the author seem to have good reasons for quoting? Would summary or paraphrase be more effective in some cases?

Session 1, *continued*:	e. Do any quotations seem too long? f. How do quotations blend smoothly into the writer's sentences? g. How is the writer synthesizing sources (by commenting on them, interpreting them, agreeing or disagreeing with them, or otherwise using them to support the paper's argument)? Have groups share their responses with the whole class.
Follow-up:	• Conduct a peer review session focusing on the synthesis of sources. Have students exchange drafts and respond to the checklist of questions used in the class session. • Have students do some reflective writing when they submit drafts. As part of that writing, ask them to respond to the list of questions in the class session as an "integrating sources checklist" (for example, *Are you introducing sources with a variety of signal phrases? Are you establishing authority of your sources? Are you summarizing and paraphrasing as well as quoting?*)
Variations:	⊞ If you are using an online platform, you can ask students to find and post examples of effectively integrated sources and to explain their choices. They should note specific components of effective integration (labeling or highlighting signal phrases, using parenthetical citations, and so on). They should also document the source they draw on for examples. You might assign students to work in pairs, using e-mail, messaging, or a discussion space to work together. If students use an e-handbook, they can link to handbook coverage that supports their conclusions.

Resources

Handbook coverage

The Bedford Handbook, 9th ed.	*A Writer's Reference*, 7th ed.	*Rules for Writers*, 7th ed.	*A Pocket Style Manual*, 6th ed.	*Writer's Help* (writershelp.com)
Integrating quotations from the text [literature] (7f) Using quotations appropriately [MLA] (55a) Using signal phrases to integrate sources [MLA] (55b) Synthesizing sources [MLA] (55c) Using quotations appropriately [APA] (60a) Using signal phrases to integrate sources [APA] (60b) Synthesizing sources [APA] (60c) Integrating sources [*Chicago*] (63c)	Using quotations appropriately (MLA-3a) Using signal phrases to integrate sources (MLA-3b) Synthesizing sources (MLA-3c) Using quotations appropriately (APA-3a) Using signal phrases to integrate sources (APA-3b) Synthesizing sources (APA-3c) Using quotations appropriately (CMS-3a) Using signal phrases to integrate sources (CMS-3b)	Using quotations appropriately [MLA] (58a) Using signal phrases to integrate sources [MLA] (58b) Synthesizing sources [MLA] (58c) Using quotations appropriately [APA] (63a) Using signal phrases to integrate sources [APA] (63b) Synthesizing sources [APA] (63c)	Integrating nonfiction sources [MLA] (31) Integrating literary quotations [MLA] (32) Integrating sources [APA] (37) Integrating sources [*Chicago*] (42)	⊤ **MLA papers** **Integrating sources** ⊤ **APA papers** **Integrating sources** ⊤ ***Chicago* (CMS) papers** **Integrating sources** ⊤ **Writing about literature** **Integrating quotations from a literary work** ⑤ *integrating sources; synthesis; paraphrase; summary; quotation*

⊤ = *Writer's Help* table of contents
⑤ = Search terms in *Writer's Help*

Practice, models, and more

hackerhandbooks .com/bedhandbook	hackerhandbooks .com/writersref	hackerhandbooks .com/rules	hackerhandbooks .com/pocket	*Writer's Help* (writershelp.com)
e **Academic reading and writing**	**Practice exercises**	**Practice exercises**	**Practice exercises**	**Exercises**
As you write	**MLA**	**MLA**	**MLA**	**MLA papers**
Using quotations in literature papers	MLA 3-1 to 3-4 Integrating sources in MLA papers	58-1 to 58-4 Integrating sources in MLA papers	31-1 to 31-4 Integrating sources in MLA papers	Integrating sources in MLA papers 1, 2, 3, 4
e **Researched writing**	**APA**	**APA**	**APA**	**APA papers**
Exercises: MLA papers	APA 3-1 to 3-4 Integrating sources in APA papers	63-1 to 63-4 Integrating sources in APA papers	37-1 to 37-4 Integrating sources in APA papers	Integrating sources in APA papers 1, 2, 3, 4
55–1 to 55–4 Integrating sources in MLA papers	**CMS (*Chicago*)**	**Video tutorials***	***Chicago***	***Chicago* (CMS) papers**
Exercises: APA papers	CMS 3-1 to 3-4 Integrating sources in *Chicago* papers	Integrating sources [MLA]	42-1 to 42-4 Integrating sources in *Chicago* papers	Integrating sources in *Chicago* (CMS) papers 1, 2, 3, 4
60–1 to 60–4 Integrating sources in APA papers	**Video tutorials***	Summarizing and paraphrasing sources [MLA]	**Video tutorials***	
Exercises: *Chicago* papers	Integrating sources [MLA]		Integrating sources [MLA]	
63–8 to 63–11 Integrating sources in *Chicago* papers	Summarizing and paraphrasing sources [MLA]		Summarizing and paraphrasing sources [MLA]	

e Students can access integrated media with the purchase of a new handbook (or with standalone purchase online).
*Students and instructors can access these resources through the complete e-book.
NOTE: Instructor registration grants you access to all media for your handbook.

Print ancillaries

The Bedford Handbook, 9th ed.	*A Writer's Reference,* 7th ed.	*Rules for Writers,* 7th ed.	*A Pocket Style Manual,* 6th ed.	*Writer's Help* (writershelp.com)
Working with Sources: Exercises for The Bedford Handbook	*Working with Sources: Exercises for A Writer's Reference*	*Working with Sources: Exercises for Rules for Writers*		

Module 11
Teaching students to avoid plagiarism

Challenges

Teaching students to use sources responsibly and accurately is not as easy as telling them to avoid plagiarizing. The problem is not always academic dishonesty. Some students have difficulty understanding what plagiarism is and identifying it when it appears unintentionally in their own writing.

The concept of "intellectual property" is more challenging than ever for students to understand. Their use of the Internet and their daily interactions in social media include the frequent downloading and sharing of pictures, music, articles, and other material. The ease with which they copy and paste, alter, and forward copyrighted and noncopyrighted material has obscured the idea of ownership. Some materials, such as pictures, are forwarded and cross-posted so many times that the notions of authorship and ownership become lost.

Students often need help understanding that material they download to a laptop, electronic tablet, or smartphone belongs to and must be attributed to an author, composer, or artist. Students do not always realize that material they are using must be documented and cited.

When helping students avoid plagiarism, you may encounter these challenges:

- Students confuse the distinctions of quotation, summary, and paraphrase. For example, they might neglect to use quotation marks around borrowed language that includes a parenthetical citation.

- Students struggle with paraphrase, often swapping a few words with synonyms rather than using their own words and drawing on their own understanding to restate an author's ideas.

- Students misidentify sources and don't provide appropriate or complete source details in their citations.

- Students provide a citation in a works cited or reference list but forget to include in-text citations for the material they use from that source text.

- Students equate plagiarism with blatant cheating and thus don't guard against unintentional plagiarism.

- Students are unaware of resources such as their handbook that can help them properly identify and document various types of sources.

Strategies

Exposure to and repeated practice with a wide variety of sources and citations are the best strategies for helping students understand how to avoid plagiarism. To help students become more confident and accurate in their use of outside sources, focus on strategies that first expose students to models and then provide them with multiple opportunities for practice:

1. Have students thoroughly read and review the plagiarism sections in their handbook (see the Resources chart at the end of this module).

2. Review a variety of models, including professional journal articles and student papers, in which the authors document and cite sources correctly.

3. Assign citation and plagiarism exercises from the handbook or its companion Web site, as well as from ancillaries (such as the exercises in *Working with Sources*).

Sample lesson for Strategies 2 and 3: Identifying and eliminating plagiarism

Lesson planning:	
Sequencing:	Use this lesson before students submit the final draft of their first source-based essay. This lesson is most effective if students are writing about the same source or sources; if students are all familiar with the source(s), identifying plagiarism will be easier to do. (It may be helpful to work through Module 10 on integrating sources before conducting this lesson, so that students understand when summarizing, paraphrasing, and quoting are effective and how to use a variety of signal phrases.)
Student level:	Novice writers who have no experience with integrating sources; intermediate writers who have some experience using sources but continue to paraphrase inaccurately. Because this lesson falls just before students submit the final draft of their first source-based essay, they will already have had some experience with college-level writing.
Learning objectives:	Students will be able to • recognize plagiarism, including the inadvertent plagiarism that results from ineffective paraphrasing • apply key skills such as using in-text citations, quoting and paraphrasing, and avoiding plagiarism • revise citations in their own writing to eliminate plagiarism
Time required:	Three sessions of at least fifty minutes

Materials/ resources:	**Session 1**
	• An excerpt of a professional text, such as a journal article, that includes in-text citations in the target style (such as MLA, APA, or *Chicago*). Bring copies for each student, or create an electronic copy to project.
	• Student drafts of their source-based essay (Each student should bring a print copy of his or her paper.)
	• The handbook
	Session 2
	• Copies of the exercise on avoiding plagiarism for each student (p. 142)
	• The handbook
	Session 3
	• Revised source-based essay drafts (Each student should bring a revised version of his or her paper.)
	• Highlighting pens (Ask students to bring their own.)
	• The handbook

Lesson steps:

Session 1:	1. Introduce key terms and concepts that the students will need to know to cite sources effectively. You can do this by asking students to read about these topics in the handbook for homework and by eliciting definitions and examples from more experienced class members. Introduce the following topics, pointing to the coverage of each in the handbook:
	• Source text
	• In-text citation
	• Parenthetical reference
	• Quoting a source
	• Summarizing a source
	• Paraphrasing a source
	• Plagiarism
	• Managing information; avoiding plagiarism
	• "Recognizing intellectual property" chart, if your handbook includes it
	2. Distribute or project an excerpt of a professional text, such as a journal article, that includes in-text citations in the style you've assigned (such as MLA, APA, or *Chicago*).
	3. With help from the students, identify a few citations within the text. Draw students' attention to the parts of each citation: the quotation (or paraphrase) and the parenthetical reference.
	4. Ask students to identify a paraphrase and a direct quotation within the sample text and to explain how they are different. Remind students that quotations are words, phrases, or sentences taken word-for-word from the text *and* placed within quotation marks and that paraphrases are ideas from the text that writers put in their own words and sentence structure. Remind students that all language and ideas borrowed from a source must be cited.

Session 1, *continued*:	5. Turn the discussion to the students' papers. Ask students to highlight quotations and paraphrases that they have added (or attempted to add) to their own texts. Ask them to check for the parts of an in-text citation: borrowed ideas in the form of a quotation or paraphrase, and — in most cases — a parenthetical reference that includes a page number. Ask students to add any parts that are missing. (If your class is working with online sources, you will need to point out what type of information, if any, should be included in the parenthetical reference. Refer to the appropriate citation section in your handbook.)
	
	6. If time allows, ask students to exchange papers within a peer review group and respond to these questions:
	
	   • Is any information in the paper that would be considered intellectual property not being cited? Is any information that would not be considered intellectual property being cited unnecessarily? (If their handbook includes it, have students use the chart titled "Recognizing intellectual property" as their guide.)
	
	   • Are any citations incomplete? If so, give your peer concrete suggestions for improving them. (Have students use the appropriate section in their handbook as a guide. See the Resources chart at the end of this module for relevant handbook sections.)
	
	7. Ask students to continue revising their citations for homework and to bring new, clean drafts of their papers to Session 3.

Session 2:	1. Briefly review the key concepts listed in Session 1, step 1. You can do this by brainstorming with the class or dividing students into groups to generate a list of these key terms and to describe their functions, providing examples when possible. 2. Focus students' attention on paraphrasing and plagiarism. Spend some time discussing the features of an effective paraphrase. Students often know that paraphrases should be "in their own words," but they may not be aware that the sentence structure needs to be their own as well. Point out sample effective and ineffective paraphrases from the MLA (or APA or *Chicago*) section in the handbook. Note in particular how ineffective paraphrasing — repeated phrases or structures — can lead to inadvertent plagiarism. An effective paraphrase, remind them, starts with a solid understanding of what the source text is saying. 3. Distribute the exercise on integrating sources and avoiding plagiarism (p. 142), and guide students through the excerpt of a source text and several student samples with integrated sources. The directions ask students to determine whether each sample attempt to integrate sources is effective (correctly quoted or paraphrased) or ineffective (plagiarized). You can discuss each student sample in the exercise one by one, first giving students an opportunity to determine an answer on their own and then discussing the correct answer with the class. Alternatively, you can divide students into groups and ask them to negotiate answers together. After about ten minutes of group time, you can discuss the correct answers with the entire class and clear up any remaining points of confusion. When completing this exercise, students may be particularly surprised at what can be considered plagiarism, such as copying an author's sentence structure too closely. Use this opportunity to reinforce the definition of plagiarism and refer students to the plagiarism policies of your course and your school. 4. If you have remaining class time, move on to the activities in Session 3. If your class time is limited, ask students to complete the remaining questions for homework. 5. Remind students to bring revised, clean drafts of their essays and their highlighting pens to the next class session.

Session 3:	1. Begin this session by briefly reviewing key concepts. Ask students to contribute information about both direct quotations and paraphrases and to offer definitions of key concepts (such as *quotation* and *paraphrase*) while you jot their responses on the board. If your students struggle, review the answers to the exercise from Session 2.
	
	2. Have your students use the chart, "Integrating and Citing Sources to Avoid Plagiarism" as a guide. Ask students to highlight all the in-text citations in their drafts. Allow them five to ten minutes to check the effectiveness of their citations and to revise them, if necessary; encourage students to refer to their handbooks and the notes on the board.
	
	3. After they have checked their own citations, ask students to team up to review the citations in their peers' essays. (Students can work as partners or in small groups of up to four students.) Ask students to respond to the following questions in their groups:
	
	    • Does each citation include the necessary parts (source material and page number)?
	
	    • Is each citation accurate? Does it avoid plagiarism by fairly and accurately representing and citing the source? (Again, it's helpful if all students are working with the same source.) If not, make a concrete suggestion for improving the work.

Follow-up:	• Ask students to use the information from this lesson to revise their essays before they submit their final drafts. • Revisit this lesson throughout the term and assign practice exercises in your handbook or online to complete either at home or in class. Students often need repeated exposure to citation conventions.
Variations:	• Because your students will likely be using online sources (such as Web pages or online journal articles), point out how in-text citation guidelines differ for print and online sources. For example, students may not know how to work with unpaginated sources. Refer to "Managing information; avoiding plagiarism" and the citation coverage in your handbook for additional examples. • You can also have your students bring copies of their sources to class. Have them highlight sections they have used for their papers. The peer groups can compare the source to the paper to determine whether all source material used has been paraphrased, quoted, and cited completely and correctly.

Resources

Handbook coverage

The Bedford Handbook, 9th ed.	A Writer's Reference, 7th ed.	Rules for Writers, 7th ed.	A Pocket Style Manual, 6th ed.	Writer's Help (writershelp.com)
Managing information; taking notes responsibly (51) Citing sources; avoiding plagiarism [MLA] (54) Citing sources; avoiding plagiarism [APA] (59) Citing sources; avoiding plagiarism [*Chicago*] (63b)	Managing information; avoiding plagiarism (R3) Citing sources; avoiding plagiarism (MLA-2) Citing sources; avoiding plagiarism (APA-2) Citing sources; avoiding plagiarism (CMS-2)	Managing information; taking notes responsibly (55) Citing sources; avoiding plagiarism [MLA] (57) Citing sources; avoiding plagiarism [APA] (62)	Managing information; taking notes responsibly (51) Citing sources; avoiding plagiarism [MLA] (54) Citing sources; avoiding plagiarism [APA] (59) Citing sources; avoiding plagiarism [*Chicago*] (63b)	**⊤ Research** **Evaluating sources** Managing information; avoiding plagiarism Taking notes without plagiarizing **⊤ MLA papers** **Avoiding plagiarism** **⊤ APA papers** **Avoiding plagiarism** **⊤ *Chicago* (CMS) papers** **Avoiding plagiarism** **⊤ Writing about literature** **Avoiding plagiarism in literature papers** **Ⓢ** *plagiarism; intellectual property*

⊤ = *Writer's Help* table of contents
Ⓢ = Search terms in *Writer's Help*

Practice, models, and more

hackerhandbooks.com/bedhandbook	hackerhandbooks.com/writersref	hackerhandbooks.com/rules	hackerhandbooks.com/pocket	*Writer's Help* (writershelp.com)
e Academic reading and writing	**Practice exercises**	**Practice exercises**	**Practice exercises**	**Exercises**
As you write	**MLA**	**MLA**	**MLA**	**MLA papers**
Using quotations in literature papers	MLA 2-1 to 2-5 Avoiding plagiarism in MLA papers	57–1 to 57–5 Avoiding plagiarism in MLA papers	30-1 to 30-5 Avoiding plagiarism in MLA papers	Avoiding plagiarism in MLA papers 1, 2, 3, 4, 5
e Researched writing	MLA 2-6 Recognizing common knowledge in MLA papers	57–6 Recognizing common knowledge in MLA papers	MLA 20-6 Recognizing common knowledge in MLA papers	Recognizing common knowledge in MLA papers
As you write	**APA**	**APA**	**APA**	**APA papers**
Developing an annotated bibliography	APA 2-1 to 2-4 Avoiding plagiarism in APA papers	62–1 to 62–4 Avoiding plagiarism in APA papers	36-1 to 36-4 Avoiding plagiarism in APA papers	Avoiding plagiarism in APA papers 1, 2, 3, 4
Exercises: MLA papers	APA 2-5 Recognizing common knowledge in APA papers	62–5 Recognizing common knowledge in APA papers	APA 36-5 Recognizing common knowledge in APA papers	Recognizing common knowledge in APA papers
54–1 to 54–5 Avoiding plagiarism in MLA papers	**CMS (*Chicago*)**	**Video tutorials***	**Chicago**	***Chicago* (CMS) papers**
54–6 Recognizing common knowledge in MLA papers	CMS 2-1 to 2-4 Avoiding plagiarism in *Chicago* papers	Integrating sources [MLA]	41-1 to 41-4 Avoiding plagiarism in *Chicago* papers	Avoiding plagiarism in *Chicago* (CMS) papers 1, 2, 3, 4
Exercises: APA papers	CMS 2-5 Recognizing common knowledge in *Chicago* papers	Summarizing and paraphrasing sources [MLA]	41-5 Recognizing common knowledge in *Chicago* papers	Recognizing common knowledge in *Chicago* (CMS) papers
59–1 to 59–4 Avoiding plagiarism in APA papers	**Video tutorials***		**Video tutorials***	
59–5 Recognizing common knowledge in APA papers	Integrating sources [MLA]		Integrating sources [MLA]	
Exercises: *Chicago* papers	Summarizing and paraphrasing sources [MLA]		Summarizing and paraphrasing sources [MLA]	
63–3 to 63–6 Avoiding plagiarism in *Chicago* papers				
63–7 Recognizing common knowledge in *Chicago* papers				

e Students can access integrated media with the purchase of a new handbook (or with standalone purchase online).
*Students and instructors can access these resources through the complete e-book.
NOTE: Instructor registration grants you access to all media for your handbook.

Print ancillaries

The Bedford Handbook, 9th ed.	A Writer's Reference, 7th ed.	Rules for Writers, 7th ed.	A Pocket Style Manual, 6th ed.	Writer's Help (writershelp.com)
Working with Sources: Exercises for The Bedford Handbook	Working with Sources: Exercises for A Writer's Reference	Working with Sources: Exercises for Rules for Writers		

Exercise on avoiding plagiarism (MLA style)

Read the following passage and the information about its source. Then decide whether each student sample uses the source correctly. If the student has made an error in quoting, paraphrasing, or citing the source, revise the sample to avoid the error. If the student has used the source correctly, write "Correct."

ORIGINAL SOURCE

There are 385 units of the National Park System of the United States, and it is likely that some portion of every one is the result of private philanthropy. Whether the nucleus of an entire national park (as at Virgin Islands National Park on St. John) or the contents of a major interpretive center (as at Pecos National Historical Park) were a gift to the nation by a private individual or individuals, the art of giving to create or expand the parks, and through them benefit the American people and American wildlife, was well developed and widely practiced until World War II. This is not so much the case now, and one wonders why. It may also be that there is a resurgent interest in wildlands philanthropy these days, though largely from foundations rather than individuals. While public support and funding for protection of natural areas will continue to be fundamental, private conservation efforts are a necessary complement; without philanthropy, the national parks will not thrive.

The general public tends to believe that national parks consist of lands purchased by the United States government in places where a federal agency — the National Park Service — set out consciously to preserve a landscape, to protect a natural resource, to commemorate a historical event. This is far from the truth, even though some parks have been created in just this way. Parks are the product of a political process, and that process often gets its start from the dream of one person, or a small group of people, who put their minds, their energies, their time, and often their money into making a park happen.

From Winks, Robin W. "Philanthropy and National Parks." *Wild Earth: Wild Ideas for a World Out of Balance.* Ed. Tom Butler. Minneapolis: Milkweed, 2002. Print. The source passage is from pages 70–71.

Student samples with integrated source material

1. Winks acknowledges that although the donation of land from individuals to the National Park System is no longer typical, the preservation of wild areas by organizations is common (70).

2. According to Winks, private conservation efforts are just as important as public support and funding dedicated to protecting natural areas (70).

3. Winks notes that without philanthropy, the national parks will not thrive (70).

4. "Parks are the product of a political process," Winks writes, "and that process often gets its start from the dream of one person, or a small group of people" who dedicate themselves to "making a park happen" (70).

Answer key: Sample student attempts to integrate the source

1. **Correct**. This is an effective paraphrase. The sentence maintains the idea of the original source without using any unique language or sentence structure from the source.

2. **Incorrect**. This is an ineffective paraphrase, and it is unintentional plagiarism. The sentence includes several phrases that are lifted directly from the source (*private conservation efforts, public support and funding, and protect[ing] . . . natural areas*). Students should refer to the MLA section of the handbook that deals with paraphrases.

   Possible revision: Winks argues that public funding alone cannot save national parks. Individual support is key to the survival and growth of protected lands.

3. **Incorrect.** This sentence is plagiarized even though the writer gives the author's name and a page number. Except for the signal phrase, the sentence is lifted word-for-word from the source. Refer students to the MLA section of the handbook that deals with enclosing borrowed language in quotation marks.

   Possible revision: Winks notes that "without philanthropy, the national parks will not thrive" (70).

4. **Correct.** This is an effective quotation, properly cited. The sentence places all wording from the source within quotation marks.

Module 12
Teaching word choice and appropriate language

Challenges

The scene is familiar: On a student's draft an instructor circles a word with a note in the margin, "Best word?" or "Check word choice." In response, the student seems confused, asking "What's wrong with that word?" or "What word should I use?" Faced with a question about word choice, the student does not know what to do. The student may feel the safest and simplest response is to delete the sentence altogether, in which case the learning opportunity is lost.

Teaching students how to choose the most effective and appropriate word is not easy. You might encounter challenges like these:

● Students have limited understanding of what the "best" or "most appropriate" word might be in a writing situation because they may have limited experiences with academic vocabulary.

● Student vocabulary grows as students encounter unfamiliar words in a variety of settings, especially through reading—a process that can take several years.

● Students may not have a sense of connotations and may need help understanding that words have meanings beyond their dictionary definitions.

● Students may not have enough experience with purpose and audience to understand that a word that works effectively in one context could be out of place, or even offensive, in another context.

● Students might feel awkward or pretentious using academic or technical terms in fields in which they are not expert. Faced with this challenge, some students might avoid new words altogether.

● Other students, reaching for a sense of authority, might try to use new words, but their unfamiliarity with the context of those words results in their using the words awkwardly and even incorrectly.

Strategies

One semester or year of writing instruction is not enough time to give students all the experience they need to use words appropriately. However, it is enough time to make them aware that writers must choose and use words carefully. Using readings, you can guide students toward becoming aware that a writer's word choices can and should be informed by knowledge of the following:

- Exactness (denotation, connotation, concreteness, conciseness, active verbs, clichés, jargon, and so on)

- Appropriateness (pretentiousness, slang, regionalisms, nonstandard usages, formality, sexist and stereotypical terms, and the like)

- Effectiveness (such as purpose or audience in the context of using particular words)

Using their own writing, you can guide your students toward becoming aware of their own word choices as they write. Specifically, you can try these strategies:

1. Teach the concept of context by having students evaluate uses of words they are familiar with in texts that are accessible and familiar to them. A page from a popular magazine or the student newspaper could work for this objective. Are the word choices appropriate for the writer's purpose and audience? Does the writer use clichés or jargon? Do some modeling for the students. If a sentence from an article about college costs reads, "The spiraling cost of college tuition is taking a toll on middle-class families trying to educate their children," talk with students about the use of *spiraling* versus *rising* or *increasing*. Using an approachable text for such an exercise can help students build confidence with word choice skills.

2. Teach the concept of word choice by having students identify words they do not know in unfamiliar texts. A page from an article in a specialized or scholarly publication could work for this objective. Students can look up the definitions of the terms and consider why the author chose to use those words. Using a text students do not feel comfortable with can help them identify the effects of a writer's word choices.

3. Teach the concepts of effectiveness and appropriateness by having students analyze word choices from two articles arguing opposite sides of a controversial issue (or from two debaters on an issues-oriented television show). Do they use the same words differently? Do the opposing writers/speakers mean different things by the same words? Does one use seem more accurate or effective than the other?

4. Have students keep a word journal for a day, listing any words they hear that seem new, unusual, unique, or interesting in any way. The words could emerge from conversations; television, radio, or Internet news; or social media communications. As a follow-up exercise, students can write about and discuss how they heard these terms, describing the writer's (or speaker's) purpose and audience and commenting on the appropriateness of the word for the particular context.

5. Conduct a peer review session on drafts in which the only element under consideration will be the exactness, appropriateness, and effectiveness of the writers' word choices. In workshops, word choice often receives less attention than "larger" matters of development, organization, and integration of sources. A workshop narrowly focused on word choice will isolate this specific element.

Lesson planning:	
Sequencing:	Use this lesson to introduce the idea that word choices can be more or less effective and appropriate in writing that seeks to persuade.
Student level:	This lesson targets writers with little or no college-level writing experience.
Learning objectives:	Students will be able to • define and explain the importance of word effectiveness and appropriateness • identify words according to categories such as cliché, jargon, pretentiousness, regionalism, slang, formality, and bias
Time required:	One fifty-minute class session with follow-up in later class sessions
Materials/ resources:	• Handbook coverage of word choice and appropriate language (See the Resources chart at the end of this module.) • A video clip of debaters presenting two opposing sides of a controversial contemporary issue

Lesson steps:	
Preparation:	Before the class session, have students read the section on appropriate language in their handbook. Ask students to focus on key terms as they read (cliché, jargon, and so on).
Session 1:	As a class, discuss the coverage of appropriate language that your students read for homework. Review the major terms of appropriateness. Show the class a brief video clip from a recent issues-oriented news program that presents commentators debating a controversial issue from opposing sides. 1. Ask the students to freewrite briefly their own opinions on the topic (not on the video clip). This will focus their attention on the issue. 2. Explain that you are going to show the video clip again, but this time the students should listen for any words they hear from each side that could be considered off-putting, unfair, loaded, biased, or otherwise inappropriate. Students also should list any words that seem especially effective. For this purpose, have each student fill out a chart like the one at the end of this module. Ask the students to list the words from each speaker in the appropriate columns. 3. When the clip has concluded, ask the students to share words from their lists. Students should specify whether the word they're sharing seemed effective and appropriate to them or ineffective and inappropriate. Ask them to explain their decisions. Did the word make the speaker more persuasive or less? Using a clean copy of the chart, you or a volunteer can record responses where the whole class can see them.

Session 1, *continued*:	4. Ask others to respond with agreement or disagreement. Especially worthy of discussion would be any words that are marked both appropriate and inappropriate by different members of the class.
	5. Use this discussion to point out that word choice affects how listeners and readers perceive speakers and their arguments; what may be appropriate and effective to some may be inappropriate and ineffective to others. As a result, if the objective is to be persuasive, every speaker or writer must choose words carefully to build common ground with the reader.
Follow-up:	This in-class activity can be followed with an assignment. Assign students to read two opposing articles on a single issue. Ask them to summarize each article's argument and create a similar list of the most effective/appropriate or ineffective/inappropriate terms. Direct them to select two words as they did in class and describe the effects of each word.
	This activity can be followed up with a peer review workshop for position papers or other kinds of persuasive writing. Each peer reviewer can identify words that seem especially effective and words the reviewer might be unsure about.
Variations:	This classroom activity may be done with articles rather than video. The follow-up could invite students to locate and write about debates in other formats (television, newspaper, blogs, and so on).

Resources

Handbook coverage

The Bedford Handbook, 9th ed.	*A Writer's Reference*, 7th ed.	*Rules for Writers*, 7th ed.	*A Pocket Style Manual*, 6th ed.	*Writer's Help* (writershelp.com)
Preferring active verbs (8) Tightening wordy sentences (16) Choosing appropriate language (17) Finding the exact words (18) The dictionary (43b)	Active verbs (W3) Wordy sentences (W2) Appropriate language (W4) Exact language (W5) The dictionary and thesaurus (W6)	Preferring active verbs (8) Tightening wordy sentences (16) Choosing appropriate language (17) Finding the exact words (18) Using the dictionary (43b)	Tightening wordy sentences (1) Preferring active verbs (2) Finding an appropriate voice (9) Finding the exact words (18)	**⊤ Word choice** **Concise language** **Strong, active verbs** **Appropriate language** **Exact language** **The dictionary** **⑤** *word choice; appropriate language; concise language; exact language*

⊤ = *Writer's Help* table of contents
⑤ = Search terms in *Writer's Help*

Practice, models, and more

hackerhandbooks.com/bedhandbook	hackerhandbooks.com/writersref	hackerhandbooks.com/rules	hackerhandbooks.com/pocket	*Writer's Help* (writershelp.com)
e **Clear sentences** **Exercises** 8–5 Active vs. be verbs 8–6 Active verbs e **Word choice** **Exercises** 16–3 to 16–7 Wordy sentences 17–3 and 17–4 Jargon 17–8 to 17–10 Sexist language 18–3 and 18–4 Misused words 18–6 and 18–7 Standard idioms 18–9 and 18–10 Clichés and figures of speech ✓ **LearningCurve** Word choice and appropriate language	**Practice exercises** **Word choice** W2–3 to W2–6 Wordy sentences W3–4 Active vs. be verbs W3–5 Active verbs W4–5 Jargon W4–6 and W4–7 Sexist language W5–5 Misused words W5–6 Standard idioms W5–7 Clichés and mixed metaphors ✓ **LearningCurve** Word choice and appropriate language	**Practice exercises** **Clarity** 8–4 Active vs. be verbs 8–5 Active verbs 16–3 to 16–6 Wordy sentences 17–6 Jargon 17–7 and 17–8 Sexist language 18–5 Misused words 18–6 Standard idioms 18–7 Clichés and mixed metaphors ✓ **LearningCurve** Word choice and appropriate language	**Practice exercises** **Clarity** 1–1 to 1–4 Wordy sentences 2–3 Active vs. be verbs 2–4 Active verbs 9–1 Jargon 9–2 Clichés and mixed metaphors 9–3 and 9–4 Sexist language ✓ **LearningCurve** Word choice and appropriate language	**Exercises** **Word choice** Recognizing wordiness 1, 2 Revising for conciseness 1, 2 Active vs. be verbs Jargon Sexist language 1, 2 Misused words Standard idioms Clichés and mixed metaphors

e Students can access integrated media with the purchase of a new handbook (or with standalone purchase online).
✓ Students can access LearningCurve (game-like, adaptive exercises) with the purchase of a new handbook (or with standalone purchase online).
NOTE: Instructor registration grants you access to all media for your handbook.

Word Choice Chart

Student Name				
Source (Article or Video)				

Speaker/Writer	Words	Check One		Reasoning
		Appropriate Effective	Inappropriate Ineffective	
Name of speaker/writer 1:				
Name of speaker/writer 2:				

Module 13
Teaching grammar and punctuation

Challenges

When you assess the first batch of papers for a given class, you'll likely discover that not all students know how to edit their work effectively for an academic audience. Specifically, one or more of the following issues might surface:

- Students use spoken, regional, or cultural varieties of English where academic (standard) forms are expected.

- Students rely on their *sense* of what is correct rather than on a formal understanding of English sentence structure.

- While students understand grammar instruction and can recognize forms in sample sentences, they still have difficulty applying the rules in their own writing.

- Students don't use the handbook or other reference tools as they write; they instead expect the instructor to correct grammar and punctuation errors for them.

- Not all students have the same needs, so instructors may have a difficult time designing activities that can be adapted to the students' varying skill levels.

Strategies

To help students learn to edit effectively, use strategies such as the following that heighten their understanding of standard English patterns and require them to revisit their own writing:

1. Use grammar and punctuation exercises, such as those in the handbook (if available) or on the companion Web site, as a first step in teaching a pattern.

2. Require students to correct errors you have identified on drafts before they submit their final papers.

3. Require students to maintain editing logs (lists of their own errors with examples and with corrections). The sample lesson provides specific guidelines for applying this strategy.

Sample lesson for Strategy 3: Using an editing log

Lesson planning:	
Sequencing:	Prepare for this lesson from the beginning of the term; use this lesson after one or more essays have been assessed and returned to students.
Student level:	Novice to advanced; any students who have one or more grammar or punctuation errors in their work
Learning objectives:	Students will be able to • correct grammar and punctuation mistakes in their work • identify or explain the rule or pattern used to correct their errors
Time required:	One session of at least fifty minutes to introduce and begin the log
Materials/ resources:	• The handbook • Completed essays or drafts with errors that you have identified but not corrected • Paper for each student (Ask students to bring their own notebook paper.) Optional: • A copy of the editing log for each student (See p. 158.) • An electronic copy or a transparency of the editing log and a projector

Lesson steps:	
Preparation:	1. From the beginning of the term, introduce students to grammar and punctuation rules in mini-lessons or homework assignments. A simple way to preview grammar topics is to ask students to read the appropriate pages in the handbook, complete the related exercises for homework, and review some or all of the answers in class. Focus on those errors that occur most frequently or that seem to cause the most confusion for your students. (Comma splices, fragments, and missing commas after introductory elements are common errors and thus are good topics to begin with.) 2. When you assess students' papers during the term, identify grammar and punctuation problems by circling, highlighting, underlining, or placing a check mark next to errors. Alternatively, you can code each error with a handbook section number. Do not correct the errors; simply point them out. *For examples of comments on student papers, see Topic 4.* When you mark errors, you can choose to identify only those related to grammar topics you have already covered in class, or you can identify any errors that are addressed in the handbook. Use your judgment to determine which method will best suit your students' needs and abilities.

Lesson steps:	
Preparation, *continued*:	How many errors you mark also depends on your assessment of your students' needs. For example, you might mark only the errors in one paragraph, only the errors on one page, or only the first ten errors in the paper. Choose a number that is manageable for both you and your students. *See "Managing the paper load" in Topic 4.* 3. When you return papers to students, alert them that they will need to use your feedback to complete their editing logs. Remind them to keep their papers in a safe place, preferably a folder or binder designated just for your class. Ask them to bring these papers to class on the day you plan to introduce the log.
Session 1:	1. Explain to students the rationale of revisiting their own work to edit mistakes. • Explain that while there are many varieties of English, students are expected to use academic (standard written) English in most college classes and professional settings. • Acknowledge that not everyone speaks standard English all the time (in fact, very few people do), so their own usage might contain a few patterns that are considered "errors" in standard English. • Acknowledge that although exercises are a starting point, students can become good editors only by continuing to polish their own work. 2. Introduce the class to the format of the editing log by projecting a sample grid or sketching it on the board. Original sentence: Edited sentence: Rule or pattern applied: 3. Hand out an editing log page to each student, or ask students to copy the grid onto their own paper. 4. Using some examples that the students volunteer, play the part of the student and model the process of completing an entry in the log: • Look over the feedback on an essay and find a sentence that contains an error. • Copy the original sentence to the log. Circle, underline, highlight, or in some way mark the error in the original sentence.

Session 1, *continued*:	• Using your handbook as necessary, write an edited version of the sentence below the original. Circle, underline, highlight, or in some way mark the correction in the edited sentence. • Write the grammar rule or pattern from the handbook that you used to edit the error. Rather than describing the error (such as "missing comma"), explain how to fix the mistake ("add a comma after an introductory element"). **Sample** **Original sentence:** Air pollution poses risks to all <u>humans it</u> can be deadly for asthma sufferers. **Edited sentence:** Air pollution poses risks to all humans, <u>but</u> it can be deadly for asthma sufferers. **Rule or pattern applied:** To edit a run-on sentence, use a comma and a coordinating conjunction (*and, but, or*). (Handbook section 20) 5. Encourage students to begin their own logs in class. Allow time for students to complete at least two entries so that they can address concerns or seek help from you.
Follow-up:	• Collect the editing logs periodically or at the midpoint and end of the term to assign credit for the work completed. Provide students with additional feedback if necessary. • Encourage students to refer to their logs during the editing stage of any essay project so that they can find and correct similar mistakes.
Variations:	• Assign the editing log as a take-home quiz after each essay is returned or as a midterm exam after two or more essays have been returned. If some students have few or no errors to correct, you can assign automatic credit for these quizzes as a reward for their effort. • Require the editing log as part of a writing portfolio. Ask students to write a reflection or cover letter for the log explaining how their editing skills have improved during the semester. 🖥 If you are teaching online, introduce students to the editing log with the tools you use to present other lectures or lessons. When you assess students' papers, use the highlight, underline, or font color function in your word processing program to identify errors in students' work.

Resources

Handbook coverage

The Bedford Handbook, 9th ed.	A Writer's Reference, 7th ed.	Rules for Writers, 7th ed.	A Pocket Style Manual, 6th ed.	Writer's Help (writershelp.com)

Revising and editing sentences; proofreading a final draft (2c)
 	
Clear sentences (8 to 15)
 	
Word choice (16 to 18)
 	
Grammatical sentences (19 to 27)
 	
Multilingual writers and ESL challenges (28 to 31)
 	
Punctuation (32 to 39)
 	
Mechanics (40 to 45)
 	
Grammar basics (46 to 49)
	Revising and editing sentences (C3-b)
	
	Revising with comments (C3-c)
	
	Proofreading (C3-d)
	
	Sentence style (S1 to S7)
	
	Word choice (W1 to W6)
	
	Grammatical sentences (G1 to G6)
	
	Multilingual writers and ESL challenges (M1 to M5)
	
	Punctuation and mechanics (P1 to P10)
	
	Basic grammar (B1 to B4)
		Revising and editing sentences (3b)
		
		Proofreading the manuscript (3c)
		
		Clarity (8 to 18)
		
		Grammar (19 to 27)
		
		Multilingual writers and ESL challenges (28 to 31)
		
		Punctuation (32 to 39)
		
		Mechanics (40 to 45)
		
		Grammar basics (46 to 49)
			Clarity (1 to 9)
			
			Grammar (10 to 16)
			
			Punctuation (17 to 21)
			
			Mechanics (22 to 24)
				T Composing and revising
				  Revising
				    Editing sentences and paragraphs
				    Proofreading
				    Revising with comments
				T Style
				T Word choice
				T Grammatical sentences
				T Multilingual writers and ESL challenges
				T Punctuation
				T Mechanics
				T Basic grammar
				S *revising; quick help; grammar; multilingual; punctuation*

T = *Writer's Help* table of contents
S = Search terms in *Writer's Help*

Practice, models, and more

hackerhandbooks .com/bedhandbook	hackerhandbooks .com/writersref	hackerhandbooks .com/rules	hackerhandbooks .com/pocket	*Writer's Help* (writershelp.com)
e **The writing process**	**Practice exercises**	**Practice exercises**	**Practice exercises**	**Exercises**
As you write	Sentence style	Clarity	Clarity	Style
Using reviewers' comments	Word choice	Grammar	Grammar	Word choice
Proofreading your work	Grammatical sentences	Multilingual writers and ESL challenges	Punctuation	Grammatical sentences
e **Clear sentences**	Multilingual writers and ESL challenges	Punctuation	Mechanics	ESL challenges
Exercises	Punctuation and mechanics	Mechanics	✓ LearningCurve	Punctuation
✓ LearningCurve	Basic grammar	Grammar basics		Mechanics
e **Word choice**	✓ **LearningCurve**	✓ LearningCurve		Basic grammar
Exercises				
✓ LearningCurve				
e **Grammatical sentences**				
Exercises				
✓ LearningCurve				
e **Multilingual writers and ESL challenges**				
Exercises				
✓ LearningCurve				
e **Punctuation**				
Exercises				
✓ LearningCurve				
e **Mechanics**				
Exercises				
✓ LearningCurve				
e **Grammar basics**				
Exercises				
✓ LearningCurve				

e Students can access integrated media with the purchase of a new handbook (or with standalone purchase online).
✓ Students can access LearningCurve (game-like, adaptive exercises) with the purchase of a new handbook (or with standalone purchase online).
NOTE: Instructor registration grants you access to all media for your handbook.

Print ancillaries

The Bedford Handbook, 9th ed.	A Writer's Reference, 7th ed.	Rules for Writers, 7th ed.	A Pocket Style Manual, 6th ed.	Writer's Help (writershelp.com)
	Resources for Multilingual Writers and ESL, a Hacker Handbooks Supplement *Exercises for A Writer's Reference, 7th Edition*	*Resources for Multilingual Writers and ESL,* a Hacker Handbooks Supplement	*Resources for Multilingual Writers and ESL,* a Hacker Handbooks Supplement	

Editing log

Original sentence:

Edited sentence:

Rule or pattern applied:

Original sentence:

Edited sentence:

Rule or pattern applied:

Original sentence:

Edited sentence:

Rule or pattern applied:

Module 14
Teaching with peer review

Challenges

When orchestrated effectively, peer review can provide students with critical feedback and an authentic collaborative writing experience before their final drafts are completed. If, however, students don't trust the process or don't feel that they have adequate preparation, they may see peer review as a fruitless exercise. Some specific challenges you might encounter include the following:

- Students don't take the process seriously. They think that the instructor's opinion is the only one that counts and don't value the feedback of their peers.

- Students resist constructively criticizing their peers' work because they don't want to hurt feelings.

- Students don't feel that their knowledge of writing or grammar qualifies them to critique another student's work.

- Students are not invested in the process and therefore provide only vague responses.

- Students think of peer review as editing; they attempt to correct surface errors and neglect global issues.

- Students don't understand that responding to writing in a peer review can help them become better critical readers.

Strategies

Make peer review more effective for students by building their trust in the process and giving them an opportunity to show their strengths and opinions as readers rather than editors. You can do so by using the following strategies:

1. Work with students to develop guidelines and a rubric for evaluating the quality of feedback that reviewers provide.

2. Provide clear guidelines to avoid turning peer review sessions into editing workshops. Ask students to focus their comments on the effectiveness of the paper's argument, organization, or support, for example, rather than on punctuation or grammar.

3. Model the types of questions that good reviewers ask throughout the peer review process, such as "What is the writer's main idea?" and "Does the paper have enough appropriate support for the thesis?"

4. Train students to provide effective feedback using sample papers. Model the peer review process for the class. The sample lesson offers step-by-step suggestions for using this strategy.

Sample lesson for Strategy 4: Guided peer review

Lesson planning:	
Sequencing:	Use this lesson during the drafting stage of any writing assignment, preferably early in the term.
Student level:	Both novice and experienced writers
Learning objectives:	Students will be able to • identify the features of a high-quality peer review session • effectively review a peer's work by pointing out strengths, areas in need of improvement, or both
Time required:	Two sessions of at least fifty minutes
Materials/ resources:	• For Session 1, at least three sample papers to review. The papers can be models that you have written or anonymous student papers from previous terms. For this guided review, it's best if the papers are brief — between 500 and 750 words. (To save paper, produce a photocopy for every two or three students, and collect the sample papers at the end of the period to use with other sections of your class. Students should be able to read the samples without straining, but they don't need individual copies.) • For Session 2, one sample paper for the whole class to review and students' own essay drafts for peer review in groups
Lesson steps:	
Session 1:	1. Open class by discussing the rationale for using peer review, covering any or all of the following ideas: • Writing does not take place in a vacuum. • Meaning is created when readers engage with a piece of writing. • A peer's feedback provides perspectives that the author might not consider when working alone. • All professional writing is to some extent collaborative. 2. Give students an opportunity to share what they found most and least valuable about their past peer review experiences. As they offer their ideas, jot their responses on the board.

Session 1, *continued*:	3. Encouraging students to draw from the ideas on the board, work together as a class to develop a set of guidelines for high-quality peer reviews. Remind students that they can avoid negative experiences with peer review by clearly asserting their expectations at this point. Students will most likely need specific direction in this step to think of peer review as more than proofreading. Guide them to consider all the salient features of a paper that peers can comment on, including the thesis, organization, style, voice, and support. **Sample peer review guidelines** A high-quality peer review • comments on the effectiveness of the thesis • describes at least two specific strengths in the paper • offers one specific suggestion for improvement 4. Distribute copies of the first sample paper or project it on the board. (Remember, to save paper, you don't need to provide a separate copy for each student.) Work with students to conduct a review that adheres to all of the students' guidelines for a high-quality peer review. Students often see the flaws in other works and tend to ignore the strengths. In this step, encourage them to provide well-rounded feedback. 5. Revisit the guidelines the class has established, and ask students to reflect on their role as reviewers. Did the guidelines feel restrictive? Did reviewers withhold comments that they felt might have been helpful? Or were students uncomfortable providing some of the feedback the guidelines required? Allow the students to suggest revisions to the guidelines if necessary; record their suggestions. 6. After class, type up the peer review guidelines that your class has created. Make photocopies or prepare an electronic copy to distribute or post online and to project in class. **Note:** To ensure that your students can comment on the models with confidence, you may want to spend more time modeling the process and working through sample papers as a class. Many students begin to feel comfortable after two or three sample reviews, though you can, of course, revisit these steps as many times and at as many points in the semester as needed.
Session 2:	1. Warm up by reviewing a sample paper with the whole class. Distribute or project the guidelines that your class developed during Session 1. Allow students to ask questions about the sample paper, guidelines, or peer review process in general. 2. Divide students into groups of three or four. 3. Ask students to pass their papers clockwise or counterclockwise within each group and begin to read *without* pens in hand. Students will be tempted to mark on their peers' papers, but encourage them to read without marking so that they avoid simply proofreading the paper. If they would like to write, ask them to take notes on separate sheets of paper, not on the peer's work. Ask students to continue reading and passing the papers for an amount of time that you determine. Choose an amount of time that fits the assignment and your class period. (If students are working on a very long paper, consider asking them to exchange with only one peer, not several.)

Session 2, *continued*:	4. After the reading period, encourage students to discuss each paper with their group, sticking to the guidelines the class has established for reviewers. Early in the semester, while students are just getting to know one another, you can ask them to focus only on the strengths of the papers they review. As they begin to feel more comfortable with one another, you can ask them to also look at areas in need of improvement. During the discussion period, each writer should feel free to ask questions of the reviewers and take notes or make corrections on his or her own paper. Encourage students to be active in this process. You may need to visit each group to provide additional modeling until the students feel comfortable. 5. Near the end of the session, give students a few minutes to begin revising on their own. They may want to start making changes to their work while the ideas and suggestions are still fresh. 6. Optional: At the end of the class period or at the beginning of the next class, ask students to rate the quality of their peers' reviews. They can use symbols — such as a plus (+), check mark (✓), and minus (–) — or single words — such as *thorough*, *average*, and *vague* — to denote the grade categories. Take these ratings into consideration as you calculate the students' participation grades at the end of the term.
Follow-up:	• Ask students to revise their drafts using the comments from the peer review sessions. Remind your students that they don't have to take their peers' advice if they have a clear reason for rejecting it; the comments of peers are suggestions, not commands. You might ask students to write about their application or rejection of their peers' suggestions and to submit those comments with their revised papers. • Conduct additional peer review sessions for new drafts of the same assignment or for different assignments. Students' reviewing abilities will grow with each opportunity to practice the process. • Model the peer review process several times during the term. (See the final note in Session 1.)
Variations:	• Create guidelines for different purposes: reviewing thesis statements, reviewing organization, reviewing citations, and so forth. • If the assignment has very specific instructions, such as a requirement for a certain number of outside sources, draw up those guidelines ahead of time and develop further guidelines with the class. • 🖥 If you are working in an online platform, consider using the discussion board for peer reviews. Students can follow the guidelines that the class has established for reviewers.

Resources

Handbook coverage

The Bedford Handbook, 9th ed.	A Writer's Reference, 7th ed.	Rules for Writers, 7th ed.	A Pocket Style Manual, 6th ed.	Writer's Help (writershelp.com)

Revising with comments (2a)
 	
Approaching global revision in cycles (2b)
 	
Revising and editing sentences; proofreading a final draft (2c)
 	
Guidelines for peer reviewers (p. 58)
 	
Guidelines for using reviewers' comments (p. 59)
 	
Checklist for global revision (p. 64)
	Making global revisions (C3-a)
	
	Revising and editing sentences (C3-b)
	
	Revising with comments (C3-c)
	
	Proofreading (C3-d)
	
	Checklist for global revision (p. 21)
	
	Checklist for peer reviewers (p. 22)
		Making global revisions: Thinking big (2a)
		
		Revising and editing sentences (2b)
		
		Proofreading the manuscript (2c)
		
		Checklist for global revision (p. 36)
		
		Checklist for peer reviewers (p. 38)
			Checklist for global revision	**T Composing and revising**
				  Revising
				    Making global revisions
				    Editing sentences and paragraphs
				    Proofreading
				    Revising with comments
				  S *revising*; *peer review*

T = *Writer's Help* table of contents
S = Search terms in *Writer's Help*

Practice, models, and more

hackerhandbooks .com/bedhandbook	hackerhandbooks .com/writersref	hackerhandbooks .com/rules	hackerhandbooks .com/pocket	Writer's Help (writershelp.com)

e The writing process
  As you write
    Using reviewers' comments
    Proofreading your work
    Learning from other writers
  Exercises
    2–1 Conducting a peer review
	Practice exercises
	  Composing and revising
	    C3–1 Conducting a peer review
	Video tutorial*
	  Revising with peer comments
		Practice exercises
		  The writing process
		    3–1 Conducting a peer review
		Video tutorial*
		  Revising with peer comments
				Exercises
				  Composing and revising
				    Conducting a peer review

e Students can access integrated media with the purchase of a new handbook (or with standalone purchase online).
*Students can access this video tutorial through the complete e-book.
NOTE: Instructor registration grants you access to all media for your handbook.

Module 15
Teaching multimodal projects

by Dànielle Nicole DeVoss

Challenges

Students often enter our classrooms expecting to write traditional essays and anticipating that their ideas will be confined to written words on standard, letter-sized paper with one-inch margins. Some of your students will have composed with multiple modes, such as written words, audio, static images, and moving images, but those with prior experience may not necessarily have been instructed to think about audience, purpose, and context when creating multimodal projects. Asking students to analyze multimodal compositions such as videos, slide presentations, or photo essays before inviting them to craft multimodal work prepares them to make deliberate decisions about modes, purpose, audience, and context in their own work.

Addressing multimodal projects in your classroom may pose some of the following challenges:

- Although students are daily consumers of multimodal texts, such as advertisements or Web sites, they may not be used to thinking critically about them.

- Students are often treated, by default, as "digital natives" and assumed to be savvy consumers and producers of digital media, even though this isn't necessarily the case. Students may be intimidated by the term *multimodal*. Student familiarity and comfort with multimodal analysis and composition may vary widely, and you may find it difficult to gauge the right level of instruction and support for the whole class.

- Students will likely require time to experiment as they adjust to both the concepts and the tools of multimodal composing.

- Although students might have analyzed visuals previously, they don't know how to communicate their understanding of visual rhetoric in an essay.

Strategies

1. Ask students to keep a journal in which they list and discuss multimodal texts they encounter every day and identify the different modes at work in these texts.

2. Ask students to think about a monomodal, or single-mode, assignment they recently completed (a written essay or a podcast, for example). Have them freewrite about how they might express that information or argument multimodally.

3. Provide low-stakes opportunities for students to experiment with the concepts and tools of multimodal composing. Ask students to take a monomodal composition (an essay they wrote or a podcast they recorded) and translate aspects of it to at least one other mode. The content they submit does not need to be polished or even coherent; the project is an opportunity to experiment with different modes.

4. Share a multimodal composition with the class. Ask students to analyze the modes (written words, sound, static images, moving images) individually and to think about how they work together to convey meaning.

5. Have students work in groups to plan their own multimodal project. They should describe how they will integrate various modes to achieve their purpose and reach their audience. Asking them to consider what kinds of time and tools they might need would also be useful.

Direct students to chapters MM2–MM6 in Understanding and Composing Multimodal Projects *(a Hacker Handbooks Supplement) for help analyzing individual modes and multimodal projects.*

Sample lesson for Strategies 4 and 5: Analyzing and planning a public service announcement (PSA) video

Lesson planning:	
Sequencing:	Use this lesson before students begin composing multimodal projects of their own. Students should have had some experience analyzing a monomodal text — examining the ways in which authors make and support arguments or convey information.
Student level:	Varied; this lesson can be integrated in writing classes ranging from basic composition to upper-level technical and professional communication.
Learning objectives:	Students will be able to • view a multimodal composition as both consumers and producers • identify the different modes being used in a multimodal composition (words, sounds, static images, moving images) • analyze the "work" that each mode is doing — how each mode functions on its own • understand how the modes work together to convey meaning • use storyboards to plan a multimodal project

Time required:	Two class sessions of fifty minutes each. If time is tight, some of the Session 1 work might be done out of class; for instance, you might ask students to review the multimodal compositions before class and to come ready for discussion.
Materials/ resources:	• Two or three video public service announcements (PSAs). Consider using PSAs about national, state, local, or campus issues that show a range of technical and aesthetic approaches. • Projection and sound system technology or at least one laptop or computer workstation per group of students. If viewing the PSAs as a class is not an option or if viewing in groups will be too noisy, you may want to ask students to view the PSAs before class and take good notes. If students do not have access to the PSAs in class, their responses may be less detailed. Providing the chart on page 172 for note taking outside of class may help. • Questions and prompts for discussion

Lesson steps:

| Session 1: Analyzing a multimodal work (PSA) | 1. Initiate a discussion about PSAs so that everyone shares an understanding of what PSAs are, who produces them and why, and how they typically work. Students should understand that a PSA is an advertisement meant to inform viewers about a cause, rally support for an issue, raise funds for an organization, and so on. Ask students to explain what modes are and how they can be used. Students may find it helpful to think about PSAs that they have seen before, or even ads for commercial products on TV. Have students talk about how such pieces use the different modes (words, sounds, static images, and moving images) to communicate their message. Place students into small groups. Have each group choose one PSA to view together. (If you cannot view PSAs in small groups or in class at all, see Variations on p. 169.)

2. Provide each group with a set of questions to consider. The chart on page 172 gives a grid with sample questions you can use. Each student should record his or her own observations during viewing.

3. Have students share their notes within their groups. Each group should assign a note taker to record the group's observations and conclusions in a fresh grid.

4. Gather as a class and have each group present its PSA and its group's comments. If class time allows, the class can discuss each group's comments as they are presented. If possible, project each group's grid or create one for each group on a chalk- or whiteboard.

5. After discussing the modes at work in the PSAs as a class, discuss the rhetorical effectiveness of each of the modes. To guide the discussion, ask students to respond to the following questions and to justify their claims based on the specific work the modes are doing in the PSA:

   a. What are the target audiences of the PSAs (young or old, rural or urban, working-class or wealthy, for example)? How can you tell? How do the modes seem designed to reach each audience? Are they effective for reaching that audience?

   b. What do you think is the purpose of each PSA? Who made the PSA and why? What effect do you think the PSA is meant to have (increase awareness, change behavior, solicit donations, and so on)? How do the modes encourage that response?

   c. How would you judge the argument of each PSA? Are the claims made in the PSA strong, clear, and reasonable? Is there evidence offered for the claims? How do the modes themselves support or weaken those claims? |

Session 2: Planning a multimodal project	After the analysis discussion in Session 1, students should be prepared to plan their own multimodal project—a video PSA.
	1. Review the key concepts from the previous session: Discuss what PSAs are and what they are designed to do, and discuss how composers can use a combination of modes to reach their audience and achieve their purpose. It may be helpful to briefly return to a PSA that particularly resonated with students in the previous session to review some key points.
	2. Ask the class to brainstorm four or five local or campus issues of concern to students.
	3. Have students divide into groups of three or four to work collaboratively on planning a multimodal project. Each group should select one of the issues identified in step 2. (If you want groups to work on different topics, you may want to assign topics or ask students to group themselves by topic of interest. Alternatively, you may also want to highlight different approaches by asking all students to work on the same topic.)
	4. Once students are in their project groups, ask each group to think about what sort of video PSA they might create to raise awareness or inspire action. Prompt them to first discuss who their target audience is. Then ask them to think about the modes they would use and how they would use them to reach their target audience and serve their purpose. You might pose questions like these about specific modes:
	a. What written text would members of your audience likely respond to? Would they react to a warning, or would they respond better to a gentle suggestion? Will they engage in longer passages of text or prefer just a quick phrase or two?
	b. What sound would members of your audience likely respond to? Do you think your message will stick if they hear the voice of an older person? Of a peer? If they hear a dramatic piece of piano music or perhaps a current, upbeat guitar riff?
	c. What static images might best convey your purpose? If you decide to cover traffic-related hazards on campus, for instance, will it encourage your audience members to drive more carefully if you include photos of car accident scenes? If your purpose is to encourage students to contribute to the local food bank, will it inspire them to see photos of children eating healthy meals?
	5. Once students have addressed some of these questions and wrestled with the different opportunities the modes offer, encourage them to think about how they might organize their multimodal project. (Letting students know at this stage roughly how long you think the PSA should be will help them stick to a reasonable scope.) Provide student groups with storyboarding sheets (see p. 171 for an example) that they can use to sketch out their PSAs. The following questions can help guide students as they storyboard:
	a. How will you start your PSA? What sort of introduction is best? What modes will you use?
	b. How will you transition if you have multiple scenes or sequences in the PSA? What mode or modes will help you create effective transitions?
	c. How will the PSA end? With a phone number or URL for more information? With a call to action? With a recommendation? What mode or modes will signal the end of the PSA?
	6. After students have storyboarded their PSA, they should identify what content they will need to gather and what content they will need to create. The following questions can help them think through this planning stage:

Session 2, *continued*:	a. What written text will you need to produce? Will you need to research and gather quotes? Statistics? Other types of writing to support your purpose? b. What sounds will you have to find or record? c. What static images might you need to find or create? d. What moving images or video clips will you need to find or shoot and edit? 7. Invite each project group to report to the class on the following points. Consider taking notes on the board or screen as each group reports. a. the issue to be covered and point to be made in the PSA b. the text to be produced c. the sound to be gathered or recorded d. the images to be gathered or created e. the video to be gathered or shot f. the kinds of research, equipment, and other resources needed to complete the project
Follow-up:	Each group should leave Session 2 with a specific plan in place for how to organize the PSA, write the text, produce the sound, gather images, and capture video. Then you can assign students to compose the PSAs they have planned. Make sure that group plans developed in class conform to any specific parameters you've established for the project, such as length, number of modes, and number of sources. Having students submit a revised storyboard along the way may be helpful.
Variations:	• For step 1 in Session 1, if you cannot view PSAs in small groups, you can show two or three PSAs to the whole class and assign each group to take notes on one PSA. • If you cannot view PSAs in class at all, you can assign students to view PSAs for homework before Session 1.

Resources

Handbook coverage

The Bedford Handbook, 9th ed.	*A Writer's Reference*, 7th ed.	*Rules for Writers*, 7th ed.	*A Pocket Style Manual*, 6th ed.	*Writer's Help* (writershelp.com)
Reading and writing about images and multimodal texts (5)	Writing about texts (A1)	Writing about texts (5)		T **Academic writing** Writing about texts T **Understanding and composing multimodal projects** S *multimedia; visuals; analyze; sound; image; moving image; written words*

T = *Writer's Help* table of contents
S = Search terms in *Writer's Help*

Practice, models, and more

hackerhandbooks .com/bedhandbook	hackerhandbooks .com/writersref	hackerhandbooks .com/rules	hackerhandbooks .com/pocket	*Writer's Help* (writershelp.com)
e **Academic reading and writing** **As you write** Reading visual texts actively Analyzing an image or a multimodal text **Sample student writing** Yoshida, "Sometimes a Cup of Coffee Is Just a Cup of Coffee" (analysis of an advertisement) **hackerhandbooks .com/multimodal** Resources for understanding and composing multimodal projects	**Model papers and other sample documents** Lee, "The Golden Arches Go Green: McDonald's and Real Lettuce" (analysis) **hackerhandbooks .com/multimodal** Resources for understanding and composing multimodal projects	**Model papers and other sample documents** Lee, "The Golden Arches Go Green: McDonald's and Real Lettuce" (analysis) **hackerhandbooks .com/multimodal** Resources for understanding and composing multimodal projects	**Model papers and other sample documents** Lee, "The Golden Arches Go Green: McDonald's and Real Lettuce" (analysis) **hackerhandbooks .com/multimodal** Resources for understanding and composing multimodal projects	**Model papers** Yoshida, "Sometimes a Cup of Coffee Is Just a Cup of Coffee" (analysis of an advertisement) **hackerhandbooks .com/multimodal** Resources for understanding and composing multimodal projects

e Students can access integrated media with the purchase of a new handbook (or with standalone purchase online).
NOTE: Instructor registration grants you access to all media for your handbook.

Print ancillaries

The Bedford Handbook, 9th ed.	*A Writer's Reference*, 7th ed.	*Rules for Writers*, 7th ed.	*A Pocket Style Manual*, 6th ed.	*Writer's Help* (writershelp.com)
Understanding and Composing Multimodal Projects, a Hacker Handbooks Supplement	*Understanding and Composing Multimodal Projects*, a Hacker Handbooks Supplement	*Understanding and Composing Multimodal Projects*, a Hacker Handbooks Supplement	*Understanding and Composing Multimodal Projects*, a Hacker Handbooks Supplement	

Sample storyboard

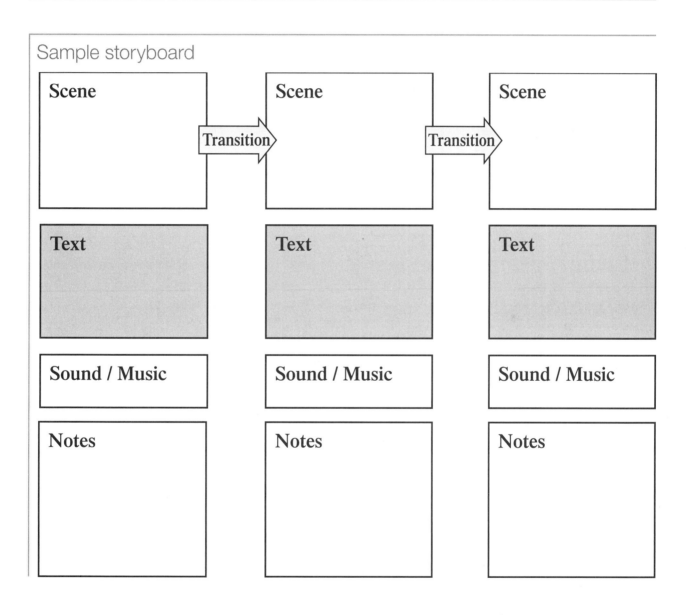

Observation chart for PSAs

Mode	PSA: _____	PSA: _____
What **written words** appear in the PSA? What are the words doing, showing, or telling?		
What **sound** is included in the PSA? Does the sound change at all during the PSA? What is the sound doing or enhancing?		
What **static images** appear in the PSA? Are the images of people? Animals? Places? Things? What are the images doing or showing?		
What **moving images** appear in the PSA? What do the images show? What is their role in the PSA?		

Module 16
Addressing writing in the disciplines

by Terry Myers Zawacki

Challenges

Students traveling from course to course across the curriculum encounter such a wide variety of writing assignments and teacher expectations that they may not understand how writing skills transfer from one setting to another. They may need you to clarify the relevance of your assignments for writing tasks in other courses. Varying expectations and grading policies can make even the most competent writers question their ability to write well in college. As a writing teacher, you may face some of the following related challenges:

- Students lack confidence as writers because they don't understand why they encounter varying assignments and expectations in different courses.

- Teachers and students alike sometimes assume that "good" academic writing means the same thing from one teacher and course to the next across the curriculum, even though formats, conventions, and individual teacher preferences may differ.

- Students become frustrated when they find out that genres with the same name (a book review, for example) may carry different meanings, depending on the course and the discipline.

- Students don't understand how the writing and rhetorical skills they learn in a composition class can be applied to writing assignments in other academic contexts.

- Students are unaccustomed to reflecting on their own writing and have trouble adapting their writing to suit courses and teachers across disciplines.

Strategies

Working with the following strategies can help your students recognize the foundation elements of strong academic writing and understand the roots and value of varying requirements and expectations across disciplines.

For specific instructor and student self-reflection prompts, see "Helping students become rhetorically aware writers" in Topic 6 (p. 53).

1. Think about your academic writing experiences and practices and model self-reflection for students. Give students opportunities to reflect on their own experiences and practices as writers.

2. Discuss with students your goals and expectations for them as writers. Explain how these goals and expectations are related to your academic background and the requirements of your department and school.

3. Introduce students to rhetorical features that are common to academic writing across disciplines (reasoned analysis and claims supported by evidence, for example) and those that are discipline specific (such as conventions for genres, formatting, use of evidence, and structure and style).

4. Work with students to examine assignments they receive in other courses. Help students analyze varying expectations in courses across the curriculum.

5. Help students analyze one of your assignments, including your goals and expectations for them as writers, the context those goals and expectations reflect, the genre and rhetorical strategies you are asking students to practice, and the rhetorical knowledge that will transfer to other courses across the curriculum. Ask students to suggest ways that you can clarify your goals and expectations. The sample lesson provides specific guidelines for applying this strategy.

Sample lesson for Strategy 5: Analyzing an assignment

Lesson planning:	
Sequencing:	Use this lesson when you hand out the first major writing assignment. You may want to use variations of this lesson for subsequent assignments you give and for assignments students encounter in other courses.
Student level:	This activity will work best if students can draw on previous writing assignments in other disciplines. Late high school or early college writing experience is sufficient.
Learning objectives:	Students will be able to • identify and draw on what they know about genres and rhetorical strategies to help them understand writing assignments • recognize the contexts for their teachers' assignments and expectations • identify similarities and differences between your assignments and expectations and those of other teachers in your discipline and other disciplines • identify conventions of academic writing that cut across disciplines and those that are specific to particular disciplines

Time required:	Two sessions of at least fifty minutes; some outside preparation
Materials/ resources:	• Blackboard or computer and projector (or overhead projector with transparencies) • Copies of essay assignment and chart (see pp. 181–83)

Lesson steps:

Preparation for Session 1:	For homework, give students a draft of your first essay assignment prompt and ask them to write in response to the following set of prompts (you may find it useful to review the assignment prompt yourself and write out your own responses):
	• Think about the papers you've written for your courses in college or in the last two years of high school. Make a list of the kinds of papers you were asked to write. Include the name of the course for which you completed each assignment.
	• Turn to the writing assignment you've been given for this course. Based on the name of the assignment (such as essay, argument, analysis, narrative), describe the kind of writing you think is expected. What features (tone, support, format, for example) do you associate with this type of writing? Are those associations based on assignments of the same category from other courses you've taken? Which courses?
	• Read and annotate the prompt. Underline the key words in the assignment that help you understand the writing task, the form and structure you should use (for example, whether you need a thesis and where it should be placed or whether to use headings and subheadings), what kind of information to include and how much, how formal or informal you should sound, and so on.
	• Consider whether this assignment is similar to or different from the kinds of papers you've written in other courses. Does this assignment seem to be typical of a particular type of course (literature, history, or creative writing, for example)? Or does the paper you're being asked to write seem to be different in almost every way from papers you've written in other classes? Be sure to explain your response.
	• Why do you think you have been given this writing assignment? As far as you can tell from the description, what are the teacher's goals and expectations? How do you know? Are some things not spelled out but rather written "between the lines"? If so, what is implied rather than explicitly stated?
	• What standards or criteria will be applied in the evaluation of this assignment? Which of them are similar to those that other teachers have applied, and which are different?
Session 1:	1. Begin by making sure students understand the terms *discipline*, *genre*, and *rhetorical strategy*. You can use their responses to the prep work to illustrate each of these terms.
	2. In class, explain to students that the names teachers give to the types of writing they assign (genres such as argument essay or lab report) often reflect preferences and conventions specific to their discipline. Key words in the assignment (*narration*, *description*, and *contrast*, for example) specify the rhetorical strategies to be used in responding to the assignment prompt. (To provide a concrete example, you can ask students when they might use narration. Their answers might include *personal essays*, *autobiographies*, *case studies*, or *crime reports*.)
	3. Put students into groups of four to share and expand the ideas they began forming with their homework responses. One student in each group should take notes. To keep the discussion focused, provide specific guidelines:

Session 1, continued:	• Ask students to list the names teachers have given to the papers they've assigned. They should consider how assignments of the same name have differed from one teacher or course to the next (for example, how an "essay" they've written for an English course might be different from an essay they've written for a history course).
	
	• Ask students to discuss and note the rhetorical, structural, and textual features they associate with the genres they've listed.
	
	    They can consider, for example, how different genres might use narration or description or the kinds of things they've been asked to compare and contrast for different courses.
	
	    They can discuss the different ways teachers have expected them to structure their papers and differences they've noticed in teachers' preferences for textual features such as introductions, the placement of a thesis sentence, the use of headings and subheadings, using and citing sources, and stylistic features such as length of paragraphs and sentences, use of figurative language, and so on.
	
	• Ask the groups to fill in a chart (see p. 181 for a sample) listing the genres they've discussed, their rhetorical and/or disciplinary purposes, and the structures and other textual features that seem to be most typical of each. They should note which genres and textual features seem to apply across disciplines and which seem to be particular to courses in specific disciplines. (If you teach in a networked classroom or an online space, provide this chart electronically so that groups can share their work. If not, provide each group with a transparency of the chart.)
	
	• Finally, ask the groups to turn their attention back to your assignment and to discuss the genre knowledge they will draw on to respond to the assignment. Ask them to make a list of the key words and descriptions they've used as cues to figure out your expectations.
	
	4. Ask students to present the results of their group's discussion to the class. Give each group no more than fifteen minutes to present, as there will no doubt be considerable overlap. (Consider asking each group if they can think of another, more effective way of conveying this information, such as a diagram or list. Explain to them that writers should always make decisions about appropriate genres, formats, structures, and conventions based on the rhetorical situation — that is, the purpose, the audience, and the task.)
	
	5. At the end of the class, ask students to do a little reflective writing on their own. They should write a few paragraphs about how this analysis has changed their understanding of expectations for academic writing in general and the features of writing that are specific to disciplines. What writing skills and genre knowledge can they apply to your assignment that they might also apply to assignments in other courses and disciplines?
	
	Note: This reflective writing can occur in the last ten minutes of class, after class in a journal, online on a class discussion board, or in an informal homework assignment to be turned in for the next class. You might choose not to collect this writing.

Session 2:	1. In a large group discussion, ask students what questions they still have about how to accomplish your assignment successfully. Do students understand the goals and requirements of the assignment? Are any guidelines missing or vague? Are objectives clearly stated? 2. Following this discussion, ask students to work together to make revisions to the assignment, clarifying the language, refining or adding guidelines or objectives, or inserting more detailed explanations. Encourage them to draft anything they feel is missing. They should provide concrete solutions for any problems. (As an incentive, you may decide to give extra credit or points to the groups whose revisions become part of the final version of your assignment.)

Follow-up:	• To extend the benefits of this assignment, you may want to ask students to bring in copies of assignments from other courses and work through a similar set of prompts. Call on volunteers to explain how their assignments fit into the course, what the teacher seems to expect, and the contexts (general academic, disciplinary, institutional, and personal) for the teacher's expectations. Working from a few such assignments, the class can list the key terms teachers use to describe assignments, as well as the formats, structures, kinds of evidence, and stylistic conventions they expect.
	• To encourage further reflection on this activity, you might ask students to write a letter of advice to first-year students about how to successfully respond to assignments and meet expectations across disciplines.
	• Reflecting on learning helps students transfer knowledge and skills from one context to another. Give your students frequent opportunities to reflect on what they have learned in your course about academic writing and themselves as academic writers and on what skills and abilities they still need to learn to become confident, flexible writers capable of meeting expectations across the curriculum.

Resources

Handbook coverage

The Bedford Handbook, 9th ed.	A Writer's Reference, 7th ed.	Rules for Writers, 7th ed.	A Pocket Style Manual, 6th ed.	Writer's Help (writershelp.com)
Reading and writing about literature (7)	Writing in the disciplines (A4)	Writing papers in MLA style (56 to 60)	MLA papers (29 to 34)	⊡ **Academic writing**
Learning to write in a discipline (64)	MLA papers (MLA-1 to MLA-5)	Writing papers in APA style (61 to 65)	APA papers (35 to 39)	**Writing in the disciplines**
Approaching writing assignments in the disciplines (65)	APA papers (APA-1 to APA-5)		*Chicago* papers (40 to 44)	⊡ **Writing in the disciplines**
Writing MLA papers (53 to 57)	CMS papers (CMS-1 to CMS-5)		CSE papers (45 and 46)	⊡ **Writing about literature**
Writing APA papers (58 to 62)				⊡ *disciplines; model papers*
Writing *Chicago* papers (63)				

⊡ = *Writer's Help* table of contents
⊡ = Search terms in *Writer's Help*

Practice, models, and more

hackerhandbooks .com/bedhandbook	hackerhandbooks .com/writersref	hackerhandbooks .com/rules	hackerhandbooks .com/pocket	*Writer's Help* (writershelp.com)
e Academic reading and writing	**Practice exercises**	**Practice exercises**	**Practice exercises**	**Exercises**
As you write	**MLA**	**MLA**	**MLA**	**MLA papers**
Asking questions about literature	MLA 1–1 to MLA 4–8 MLA papers	56–1 to 59–8 MLA papers	29–1 to 33–8 MLA papers	**APA papers**
Using quotations in literature papers	LIT 1–1 Thesis statements in literature papers	67–1 Thesis statements in literature papers	**APA**	*Chicago* (CMS) papers
Sample student writing	**APA**	**APA**	35–1 to 38–8 APA papers	**T MLA papers**
Jacobs, "From Lecture to Conversation: Redefining What's 'Fit to Print'" (composition; MLA)	APA 1–1 to APA 4–8 APA papers	61–1 to 64–8 APA papers	*Chicago*	**Directory to MLA model papers**
Larson, "The Transformation of Mrs. Peters: An Analysis of 'A Jury of Her Peers'" (literature; MLA)	**CMS (*Chicago*) papers**	**Model papers and other sample documents**	40–1 to 43–8 *Chicago* papers	**T APA papers**
	CMS 1–1 to CMS 4–8 CMS papers	[38 model papers in 15 disciplines]	**Model papers and other sample documents**	**Directory to APA model papers**
Exercises	**Model papers and other sample documents**		[38 model papers in 15 disciplines]	**T *Chicago* (CMS) papers**
7–1 Thesis statements in literature papers	[38 model papers in 15 disciplines]			**Directory to *Chicago* (CMS) model papers**
e Researched writing				
As you write				
Writing a working thesis for a research paper				
Sample student writing				
Orlov, "Online Monitoring: A Threat to Employee Privacy in the Wired Workplace" (composition; MLA)				
Mirano. "Can Medication Cure Obesity in Children? A Review of the Literature" (psychology; APA)				

e Students can access integrated media with the purchase of a new handbook (or with standalone purchase online).
T = *Writer's Help* table of contents
NOTE: Instructor registration grants you access to all media for your handbook.

Practice, models, and more (*continued*)

hackerhandbooks .com/bedhandbook	hackerhandbooks .com/writersref	hackerhandbooks .com/rules	hackerhandbooks .com/pocket	*Writer's Help* (writershelp.com)
Bishop, "The Massacre at Fort Pillow: Holding Nathan Bedford Forrest Accountable" (history; *Chicago*) **Exercises: MLA papers** 53–1 to 56–8 MLA papers **Exercises: APA papers** 58–1 to 61–8 APA papers **Exercises: *Chicago* papers** 631 to 63–19 e **Writing in the disciplines** **As you write** Examining the writing in a particular field Examining a writing assignment from one of your courses				

Print ancillaries

The Bedford Handbook, 9th ed.	A Writer's Reference, 7th ed.	Rules for Writers, 7th ed.	A Pocket Style Manual, 6th ed.	Writer's Help (writershelp.com)
Writing in the Disciplines: Advice and Models, a Hacker Handbooks Supplement	*Writing in the Disciplines: Advice and Models,* a Hacker Handbooks Supplement *Writing about Literature,* a Hacker Handbooks Supplement *Exercises for A Writer's Reference,* 7th Edition	*Writing in the Disciplines: Advice and Models,* a Hacker Handbooks Supplement *Writing about Literature,* a Hacker Handbooks Supplement	*Writing in the Disciplines: Advice and Models,* a Hacker Handbooks Supplement *Writing about Literature,* a Hacker Handbooks Supplement	

Sample chart for lesson on writing in the disciplines, Session 1 (See p. 175.)

Type of writing assignment (genre)	Course/discipline	Task, purpose, and rhetorical strategies	Kinds of evidence required	Most prominent textual features called for	Other teacher directives and advice
Personal essay	Composition	Describe a turning point in your life. Narrate the event with lots of specific description.	Personal experience	First person; chronological order; vivid details; dialogue and other story devices	Craft a thesis that explains the point of the narrative and the larger meaning. Use active voice. Don't just summarize in the conclusion. Explain why the story matters.
Argument essay	History	Compare political power in ancient and medieval times. Describe power, and compare it on several points. Argue which is better.	Specific explanations and examples from the textbook and lectures	Develop a thesis that states the purpose and takes a position. Provide a brief description of the historical context. Compare and contrast three or four main points about each system with evidence.	Don't use first person or offer personal opinion. Avoid passive voice. Do not use contractions. Use past tense. Use *Chicago* style.
Argument essay	English	Take a position for or against a topical issue. Describe reasons for and against your position. Explain why your reasons are better.	Personal knowledge backed up with other sources as needed	Start with the context for your argument. State the thesis at the end of the introduction in one sentence, which may also include the points you'll make. In the conclusion, restate the argument and explain why the issue matters.	You may use first person. Give the strongest points first. Give opposing views either point by point or in one paragraph. Quote or paraphrase opinions from other sources if used.

Type of writing assignment (genre)	Course/ discipline	Task, purpose, and rhetorical strategies	Kinds of evidence required	Most prominent textual features called for	Other teacher directives and advice
Research paper	Psychology	Research and report on studies exploring the causes of autism. Describe studies that have been done and synthesize research findings around your main points.	Experiments; systematic observations; case studies	Develop a thesis that states the purpose of the paper. In your introduction, give definitions and other necessary background. Include descriptions of methods, findings, and conclusions.	Do not use first person or include personal opinions. Summarize the studies. Paraphrase sources. Do not quote. Use APA style. Do not use contractions.
Lab report	Biology	Report on an experiment. Organize the paper with subheads for review of other experiments ("literature review"), hypothesis, methods, results, and conclusions.	Systematic, objective descriptions of methods and results; other researchers' experiments, results, and conclusions	Place the hypothesis after the review of literature. Summarize the studies. Paraphrase specific points. Use quotes only rarely.	Use CSE documentation style. Do not use *I*. Leave out personal opinions. Do not use contractions. (Note: Some teachers require APA style.)
Literary analysis essay	English	Analyze a character in a novel. Explain how the character is developed and why — for example, how the character fits into the plot and theme of the novel.	Character description with details from novel (not opinion); textual examples of the character's actions, thoughts, relationship to other characters, and so on	Briefly summarize the plot. Develop a thesis that makes an argument about the character's role in the context of the theme and plot. Support your points with specific examples and details from the novel. Quotes from the text are expected.	Analyze. Don't just summarize story passages. Support your interpretations with textual evidence. Avoid personal opinions about your likes and dislikes. Don't use *I* or passive voice. Use present tense. Use MLA style.

List similarities among assignments					
List differences among assignments					

Part III

Sample Course Materials

As you build your own syllabi, assignments, and rubrics, you might consult these samples in Part III. Find more models and fresh ideas at hackerhandbooks.com/teaching.

Notes

ENGLISH COMPOSITION 1010

COURSE SYLLABUS

TERM: Spring 2014
PREREQUISITE: Completion of DSPW 0800 or acceptable placement scores
INSTRUCTOR: Bobbie Kilbane
PHONE: xxx-xxx-xxxx
OFFICE HOURS: Mon., Wed., Fri.: 10:10 a.m.–11:00 a.m. and 12:00 p.m.–3:00 p.m.
Tues.: Language Center 9:00 a.m.–10:30 a.m.; Office 10:30 a.m.–11:00 a.m.
Thurs.: 9:00 a.m.–10:00 a.m.
E-MAIL: x@volstate.edu
TEXTBOOKS: *The Bedford Handbook,* 9th edition, Diana Hacker and Nancy Sommers. Bedford/ St. Martin's, 2014.
The Longman Writer, 7th edition, Nadall, Langan, and Comodromos, eds. Pearson, 2009.

Overarching Goals

In English Composition 1010, students will develop and organize ideas, learn an effective writing process, and acquire mastery of composition fundamentals that will apply to a variety of writing situations throughout their academic and professional careers. English Composition 1010 will provide opportunities for students to discuss writing with instructors and peers in a safe and respectful learning environment.

Learning Objectives

Upon completing English Composition 1010, the student will be able to

- Organize essays that explain or describe a topic, narrate a personal experience, reflect on observations, and write an analysis
- Follow a process for writing an effective essay, apply invention strategies, revise drafts, and incorporate peer feedback
- Read and respond to different types of essays, observing rhetorical structure (reading as a writer)
- Identify and correct mechanical errors as part of the revision/editing process
- Analyze and comment on in-process writing, recognizing elements of strength and areas for improvement in written drafts
- Incorporate self-assessment and reflection into the writing process
- Integrate quotations, paraphrases, and summaries into his or her own writing and document them appropriately

Course Requirements

- Complete reading assignments before class (expect daily quizzes).
- Following a systematic writing process, compose four essays, two to four pages long, typed and double-spaced. Types of essays include personal narrative or description, comparison-contrast, cause-and-effect analysis, classification-division, and a research essay.
- Have a rough draft on the due date for a peer review (draft exchange).
- Maintain a course folder that includes all drafts of each essay.
- Attend at least one scheduled conference with instructor; you must bring an in-process draft of an essay.
- Avoid plagiarism—that is, using someone else's writing without acknowledging the source (see handout on plagiarism).

Bobbie Kilbane, Volunteer State Community College

Attendance and Participation

On the negative side:
- More than three absences require written evidence (such as a doctor's excuse) that the student is unable to attend class. Each unexcused absence over four is figured into the student's average as a zero.
- Coming in late three times will lower your grade.
- Missing a scheduled conference will drop your grade one letter.
- Turning in late assignments must be arranged in advance with the instructor.
- Using any electronic devices or cell phones in class or leaving class to answer a call is not allowed.
- Coming to class without an assigned rough draft when we are working with the draft in class will be counted as a zero for the day.
- Behavior that suggests that the class is not important (sleeping, eating, chewing tobacco, leaving early) is not acceptable, and you will be asked to leave.

On the positive side:
- Be on time.
- Bring materials to class (use a dictionary for reading and writing assignments).
- Prepare for each class (READ ASSIGNMENTS).
- Participate in class and small-group discussions.
- Ask your instructor for help or clarification; schedule a conference if necessary.
- Communicate with your instructor by e-mail.

Instructional Methods

- Small group discussions of written in-process drafts
- Class activities with full-class participation expected
- Mini-workshops on mechanics (troubleshooting)
- Conferences
- Brief lectures
- In-class writing

Evaluation

The final course grade will be based on the following:
- A course folder containing class notes, reflections on the readings and related topics, in-process drafts, daily quizzes, and other assignments = 20%
- Four essays at 15% each + writing sample essay = 60%
- Final portfolio (containing a final revision of each essay) and final essay = 20%

The course folder and daily quizzes (20% of final grade) will include
- All rough drafts of each essay numbered to correspond to the final draft
- The graded final draft of each essay
- Rules Lists for each graded assignment
- Quizzes and reflections on readings

The final portfolio (20% of final grade):
- The final portfolio should contain final, revised drafts of all four essays and your final examination essay, which is written in class.
- The final portfolio will be graded on improvement of writing from the beginning to the end of English Composition 1010.
- The final portfolio is a pocket folder with the four final drafts on one side and the final examination paper on the other side.
- The final portfolio is worth 20% of the final grade.

Bobbie Kilbane, Volunteer State Community College

Conferences

Conferences are meant to help students work on their own drafts. The instructor will not edit the draft and will only suggest revisions or improvements to the student. In the conference, the instructor will serve as an informed member of the student's audience. Students will answer the following questions:

- What pleases you the most about this draft?
- What areas need more work?
- What changes are you considering?
- What questions would you like to ask me about the draft?

At the end of the course, students are required to meet with the instructor to review the course folder and discuss the scope, improvement, and quality of their writing for the whole semester.

ADA and Equal Opportunity Statement

In compliance with the Americans with Disabilities Act, it is the student's responsibility to disclose any disability to the Office of Disability Services to receive assistance with accommodations. It is the intent of VSCC to be free of discrimination or harassment on the basis of sex, race, color, religion, age, disability, political affiliation, sexual orientation, veteran status, or physical appearance.

Plagiarism Statement

According to the *Volunteer State Community College Student Handbook,* "Plagiarism is using other people's ideas as your own, copying all or parts of someone else's work, having another person write the assignment, getting too much assistance in writing, or failing to document accurately the use of source material" (14). Plagiarism is punishable by possible failure in the course, to be judged by the teacher, and a definite zero on the project. Students are responsible for seeking help if they are unsure about how or when to cite sources; ignorance of the rules is not a justification for plagiarism.

Financial Aid Statement

Students who are receiving Title IV financial assistance (Pell Grant, Student Loan, or SEOG Grant) must regularly attend class (a minimum of the first full week) or be subject to repay PART or ALL of the Federal Financial Aid received for the semester.

Bobbie Kilbane, Volunteer State Community College

Assignment Schedule

English Composition 1010, Section 23

From Feb. 11, 2014 through May 6, 2014

Tues. Feb. 11:
- Essay 1 due
- Sentence Patterns Workshop (based on *The Bedford Handbook*)
- Assignment Guidelines Narrative Essay (2)

Thurs. Feb. 13:
- "4th of July" LW pp. 208-211
- "Charity Display" LW pp. 220-222

Tues. Feb. 18:
- "Shooting an Elephant" LW 213-218
- Mechanics Workshop (based on *The Bedford Handbook*)
- Return Essay 1

Thurs. Feb. 20:
- Chapter 8 LW "Revising Sentences and Words" pp. 110-135
- Activities 1 through 5 pp. 135-137

Tues. Feb. 25:
- Rules List on Essay 1 due (based on *The Bedford Handbook*)
- Student Models
- Mechanics Workshop (based on *The Bedford Handbook*)

Thurs. Feb. 27:
- No Class – Department Meeting

Tues. Mar. 4:
- Rough Draft Exchange – Narrative Essay (bring *The Bedford Handbook*)

Thurs. Mar. 6:
- Essay 2 (Narrative) due
- Chapter 15 "Writing Comparison-Contrast" LW pp. 346-362
- Assignment Guidelines – Comparison-Contrast

Spring Break March 10 through March 14

Tues. Mar. 18:
- "Slow Walk of Trees" LW pp. 362-364
- Return Graded Essay 2

Bobbie Kilbane, Volunteer State Community College

Thurs. Mar. 20:
- "Reality TV" LW pp. 370-372
- "Euromail and Amerimail" LW pp. 374-377

Tues. Mar. 25:
- Class Canceled – Conference

Thurs. Mar. 27:
- Rough Draft Exchange Essay 3 Comparison-Contrast (bring *The Bedford Handbook*)
- Rules List on Essay 2 due (based on *The Bedford Handbook*)
- Assignment Guidelines – Research Project

Tues. Apr. 1:
- Meet in Library to Begin Research
- **Final Draft of Essay 3 due**

Thurs. Apr. 3:
- Meet in Library – Database Exercise/Group Members Assigned
- Chapter 16 "Cause and Effect" LW pp. 382-400 (quiz)

Tues. Apr. 8:
- Meet in Library – Problem Selection/Group Work on Research
- Return Graded Essay 3

Thurs. Apr. 10:
- Meet in Library – Groups Work on Research
- Documenting a Research Paper/*The Bedford Handbook* Section 56 MLA

Tues. Apr. 15:
- "Why We Crave Horror Movies" LW pp. 402-405
- Documenting a Research Paper/*The Bedford Handbook* Section 56 MLA
- Rules List on Essay 3 due

Thurs. Apr. 17:
- "Innocents Afield" LW pp. 407-409 and "Black Men and Public Space" LW pp. 412-414
- Exchange Rough Drafts of Individual Research Essays (bring *The Bedford Handbook*)

Tues. Apr. 22:
- **Individual Research Essays due**
- **Start Group Presentations**

Thurs. Apr. 24:
- Group Presentations

Tues. Apr. 29 and Thurs. May 1:
- Conferences (individuals to be scheduled)
- Return Graded Essay 4

Bobbie Kilbane, Volunteer State Community College

Tues. May 6:

- **Final Exam – 10:30–12:30**
- **Final Portfolios due (include four revised essays)**

Bobbie Kilbane, Volunteer State Community College

ENGL 1A: College Composition and Reading (4 Units, Section 6441)
Course Syllabus, Fall 2013

Instructor:	Kevin Ferns
E-mail:	x@yccd.edu
Voicemail:	xxx-xxx-xxxx
Class Time and Location:	Monday and Wednesday, 9:00–10:50 a.m., Room 801
	(Writing Lab: Wednesday, 10:00–10:50 a.m., Room 845)
Office Hours and Location:	M/W, 11:00 a.m.–12:50 p.m. and 3:00–4:00 p.m.; T/Th,
	9:00–10:20 a.m. and 3:00–4:00 p.m.; or by appointment, Room 853C

REQUIRED MATERIALS

- Hacker, Diana, and Nancy Sommers. *Rules for Writers*, 7th ed. Boston: Bedford/St. Martin's, 2012. ISBN 0-312-64736-0.
- Muller, Gilbert. *The McGraw-Hill Reader*, 10th ed. Boston: McGraw-Hill, 2008. ISBN 978-0-07-353313-1.
- A good dictionary. You might try *Merriam Webster's Collegiate Dictionary*, 11th ed., although this one can be hefty. A lighter and cheaper model is the pocket *American Heritage Dictionary* (less than $10 in our bookstore).
- A notebook or binder for recording notes, ideas, and freewrites (and to hold this syllabus).

Be sure to purchase the updated editions listed and bring all course materials to each class. If you need to make copies of assigned pages until you obtain your own copies of each text, these texts are on reserve in the library (for library use only).

COURSE PREREQUISITE

Satisfactory score on the Placement Examination and appropriate skills and knowledge or a grade of C or better in English 51.

COURSE OVERVIEW

> "I write to find out what I'm thinking. I write to find out who I am.
> I write to understand things." —Julia Alvarez

> "Writing and rewriting are a constant search for what one is saying." —John Updike

English 1A is dedicated to reading, writing, and discussion to improve critical thinking and writing skills. You will explore the craft and process of writing and produce several original essays that demonstrate excellence in critical analysis, organization, and development. This course will emphasize critical thinking skills, and our primary focus will fall on skills required across disciplines (namely, the ability to understand and respond to a text, to develop and defend your own ideas, and to integrate sources with your own thinking). We will also consider mechanical and grammatical issues, and you will be responsible for observing the rules of Standard English in all of the coursework you do. When you have completed this course, you will have written more than 5,000 words of formal writing and more than 20,000 words online, and you will be comfortable using formal research techniques to synthesize ideas from various sources to inform your opinion on a topic.

→

Kevin Ferns, Woodland Community College (Yuba Community College District)

GRADES

Your final grade will be assessed based on your performance in four areas:

1. Quizzes, 10%   Quizzes on assigned readings may be administered at the beginning of class.

2. Responses, 20%   This includes in-class assignments and discussions on WebCT.

3. Exams, 30%   Two midterm essay exams and a final in-class essay exam are required.

4. Essays, 40%   Four draft and final essays are required.

A final grade of 90 percent or higher earns an A; 80 to 89 percent earns a B; 70 to 79 percent earns a C; and 60 to 69 percent earns a D. All grades are non-negotiable. If you are concerned about your progress in this class or would like to know your status, please e-mail me or see me during office hours, and we can discuss what you can do to improve your writing. We will be meeting during the writing labs to discuss your writing as well.

Quizzes (10%): Thoughtful critical reading is essential to your development as a writer, and you must make an effort to understand assigned readings before coming to class. At the beginning of class, a quiz may be given to assess your understanding of or engagement with assigned readings or lessons. I will use quizzes as a means to assess your progress and understanding of course material throughout the semester. If you miss a class or are late on the day a quiz is given, you will receive a zero for that quiz. You cannot make it up at a later date. Quizzes will be periodically returned to you with minimal comments and will be assessed on a check plus (outstanding response)/check (average response)/check minus (more effort needed) basis. This assessment will be converted to a percentage of your grade at the end of the semester. If you do not miss any quizzes and consistently earn check plus or check marks, you will receive an A or a B for this segment of your grade.

Responses and replies on WebCT and in-class writing assignments (20%): Prior to most class days, I will provide on WebCT a question or questions in the Discussions area related to the assigned readings. Your responses represent your initial informal thoughts, and this informal writing will help prepare you for the class discussion on the readings. In the response, you are writing to learn, so you can take chances, push yourself in new directions, and be creative with this writing. Your response will be viewed by your classmates; therefore, I expect you to maintain the attention to grammar, spelling, and critical thought (not to mention respect for fellow classmates) that you would show in essays and in class discussion. Before each class period, you will be required to log on to WebCT and post one response to this prompt (250-word minimum; type in the word count at the end of the post) and two paragraph-long replies to your classmates. Your responses and replies will be assessed on a credit or no-credit basis and converted to a percentage of your grade at the end of the semester. All response questions will be posted at least two days in advance of the due date, so you will have ample time to post your responses and replies. I will read your responses and reply privately at my discretion. Responses will not be accepted more than one week after the due date, so it is imperative that you keep up with the readings and responses. If you submit complete responses and replies on time, you will receive an A for this segment of your grade. Late or short responses are worth half credit, and failure to submit a response or replies to other students earns you a zero for that response. If you consistently fail to submit responses on time, you will not pass the class.

Exams (30%): You will write two in-class essays (10% each) in preparation for the English department final exam (10%). On both midterms and on the final, you will be asked to respond to a prompt in essay format. Each exam will be rated according to the rubric in this syllabus based on content, structure, organization, development of ideas, and mechanics: a 4+ is 100%, a 4 is 95%, a 4– is 90%, a 3+ is 85%, a 3 is 80%, a 3– is 75%, a 2+ is 70%, a 2 is 65%, and a 2– is 60%. Failure to complete a midterm or the final exam will result in a final grade of F for the course. I will be grading the midterm essays, but the final in-class essay will be graded by a team of professors from the WCC English department. You must maintain at least a C average (2+ or above) on this portion of your grade to pass the course.

Kevin Ferns, Woodland Community College (Yuba Community College District)

Essays (40%): You must type and submit four draft and final essays by the beginning of class on the due dates listed. I will not grade your draft essays, but I will be offering advice and comments for revision, as will your peers. The essay-writing and revision process is essential to producing a successful final draft; therefore, your essay grade will be reduced if you fail to do the following:

1. Submit drafts on time.

2. Meet the minimum word count.

3. Format according to MLA guidelines.

4. Participate actively in the peer review sessions.

5. Offer written feedback for each group member during the peer reviews (and submit a copy to me via e-mail).

6. Significantly revise your essays and submit a revision summary with each final essay detailing the changes made. Each revised essay should include a one-page revision summary cover sheet. Your revision summary is an analysis of how you revised your essay based on the information you received from your peers and/or instructor. In the revision summary, you should reflect on your writing process by identifying at least one writing problem you needed to solve as you revised (other than grammar and spelling) and explaining in detail how you solved it. In addition, you should discuss your revisions in the context of your essay's supporting points and organization. With your essay's purpose and audience in mind, discuss how you improved your writing. Your revision summary is your final essay's cover letter to me explaining how and why your essay is stronger based on the revisions made.

You will receive a grade (based on the rubric in this syllabus) on each revised essay, which will be due approximately one week after each peer review workshop. Revised essays should be submitted both in hard copy on the due date and electronically via www.turnitin.com (Class ID is xxxxxxx; enrollment password is xxxxx) before class on the assigned due date. Essays are always due at the beginning of class. Essays submitted late will be penalized up to half of the total essay grade. If you fail to turn in an essay or submit an essay more than one week late, you will receive an F grade for the course.

Some advice on grades: Keep in mind that your final letter grade will not have a plus or minus after it. Therefore, when it comes to borderline grades, the difference between rounding up to an A or down to a B may depend on whether you made a noticeable effort to improve in this class. I do notice such things as perfect attendance, thoughtful and enthusiastic participation in class discussions, careful attention to revisions in your writing, and a willingness to work hard consistently, and these qualities could make the difference between a passing grade and a failing one.

COURSE EXPECTATIONS

Attendance: The class experience is an essential component of your education, and your participation is vital to successful class discussions and activities. Therefore, attendance is required. I understand that emergencies sometimes occur, and you will be allowed three absences over the course of the semester. (I make no distinction between excused and unexcused absences, so please use your absences wisely.) Please arrive before the beginning of class and remain in class until you are dismissed. If you arrive excessively late or depart before the end of class, you will be considered absent for the day. If you are late or absent, you will be expected to follow up with a trusted classmate to determine what you have missed. If you miss more than three classes, your grade will drop one letter grade for each additional missed class (thus, an A student would earn a D on a sixth absence).

Academic integrity: As a student at Woodland Community College, you join a community of scholars committed to excellence in the teaching and learning process. I assume that you will pursue your studies with integrity and honesty, meaning you will never appropriate another person's words, thoughts, ideas, or data as your own. Plagiarism includes the following:

Kevin Ferns, Woodland Community College (Yuba Community College District)

- Failure to properly cite the source of any material borrowed from an outside source (such as books, periodicals, and the Internet), including failure to use quotation marks to distinguish another author's exact words from your own, failure to give credit for the paraphrased ideas of others, and failure to include bibliographic information for all secondary sources used.
- Submitting any assignment not written by you for this class (such as an essay written by a friend or purchased from an online source, an essay written by you for another class, or an essay copied from a book, magazine, or other media source).

If you violate this policy, I am obligated under the Woodland Community College Student Honor Code to take disciplinary action that may include assigning an F grade for the assignment or an F grade for the course. Depending on the severity of the infraction, you may also be placed on disciplinary probation. If you have any questions or concerns regarding how to incorporate sources correctly or avoid plagiarism, please see me for assistance.

ADDITIONAL WRITING ASSISTANCE

Your success in this class depends on your commitment to improvement. I recommend that you take advantage of the opportunities available on the WCC campus at the Tutoring Center (Room 809). You can sign up for free peer tutoring to help you identify and prioritize your goals to improve your writing. You can also visit the English Writing Lab (Room 850) to work individually on your essays with the instructional assistant to improve your writing. I recommend that you sign up for these services early in the semester for maximum benefit. The longer you wait, the more difficult it is to make significant progress with your writing.

ACCOMMODATIONS

If you have a learning disability, please provide the appropriate documentation as soon as possible to ensure that you receive the necessary accommodations. This information will be kept confidential.

ELECTRONIC DEVICES

Please turn off and put away your phone, iPod, laptop computer, and any other electronic devices before entering the classroom.

FOOD

Please do not bring food into the classroom. Bottled beverages and coffee with a secure cap are permissible. Food and drink are not allowed in the computer labs.

GUESTS

Please do not bring your friends, pets, or children to class.

COMMITMENT

Whether you are reading, writing, or discussing your thoughts, your development as a writer depends on your commitment to each class activity. This course will demand a great deal of your time and effort over the next 16 weeks, and you will need to prioritize this class to make measurable progress. If you come to class every day prepared to participate and contribute, turn in assignments on time, and take an obvious interest in your work and in improving your writing ability, you will most likely succeed in this course.

OUT-OF-CLASS ESSAY SCORING RUBRIC

C = **Content, 25%**
O = **Organization, 25%**
M = **Mechanics and Punctuation, 25%**
P = **Process, 25%**

Kevin Ferns, Woodland Community College (Yuba Community College District)

A = A superior essay (90–100 total; 23–25 per category) is fresh, personal, and engaging and includes the following:

C: A well-chosen thesis clearly controls the direction of the paper; supporting points are thoroughly developed with clear, well-chosen, vivid examples; analysis of the subject is clear, thorough, and logical; the intended audience's needs are fulfilled.

O: Paragraphs exhibit unity and coherence; organization is smooth and logical.

M: Diction and tone are appropriate and exhibit flair and demonstrate superior control; sentence structure is varied and superbly managed; few, if any, errors in mechanics exist.

P: Essay has correct formatting; all drafts, revisions, revision summary, and peer review materials are submitted on time with word count met; workshops are attended; significant revisions are made successfully.

B = A strong essay (80–89 total; 20–22 per category) is above average and succeeds at most of the following:

C: Thesis is clear and worthwhile, and it controls the essay's direction; analysis is clear and logical, with only rare lapses; examples are well chosen but may occasionally be lacking in specificity or vividness.

O: Organization is generally clear and logical; paragraphs support the thesis and are generally unified and coherent.

M: Essay may contain a few errors or some ineffective sentences, but other sentences will show flair; essay generally shows evidence of careful proofreading (overall freedom from mechanical errors).

P: Essay has decent formatting; all drafts, revisions, revision summary, and peer review materials are submitted on time; workshops are attended; most revisions are made successfully.

C = An adequate essay (70–79 total; 18–19 per category) is average and includes the following:

C: The topic is worthy of development in a college essay; essay generally features an appropriate tone for the assignment and intended audience; examples might be sparse and/or occasionally not quite to the point; the essay is primarily analytical, but the writer might depend at some points on narration where analysis is required.

O: Organization is generally clear but sometimes formulaic; paragraphs support the thesis, but some might lack unity or coherence.

M: Sentence structure might be choppy or lack variety; essay is generally free of errors in spelling, punctuation, and capitalization; occasional errors don't impede understanding.

P: Essay has some formatting errors; most drafts, revisions, and peer review materials/workshops are submitted on time; word count may not be met; revision summary is too brief/lacks specificity, or not all revisions are made successfully.

D = A marginal essay (60–69 total; 15–17 per category) is below average and does the following:

C: Essay responds simplistically to prompt; thesis is not clearly stated.

O: Paragraphs may lack focus and wander from the point or not advance the thesis, mostly summarize, lack a controlling idea, have little or no analysis, or have little development.

M: Sentences lack variety; significant proofreading, mechanical, and spelling errors are present.

P: Essay has formatting errors; drafts, revisions, revision summary, and/or peer review materials are submitted late; workshops are not attended, or revisions are not made successfully; word counts are not met.

Kevin Ferns, Woodland Community College (Yuba Community College District)

F = **A failing essay** (0–59 total; less than 15 per category)

The F essay is a clear fail that misunderstands the point of the assignment; lacks direction; is unduly brief; lacks development and coherence; or contains numerous spelling, punctuation, or grammar errors. Late submission or a lack of emphasis on the revision process and peer reviews can lead to an F paper as well.

IN-CLASS ESSAY SCORING RUBRIC

4 to 4+ (95–100%): A superior essay demonstrates a clear ability to go beyond the basics of the assignment and shows mastery of the critical thinking abilities that are required to understand, interpret, and argue the topic. In addition, it has only minor flaws. An essay in this category does the following:

- It addresses the topic clearly and responds effectively to all aspects of the task.
- It states or clearly implies the writer's position or thesis and provides in-depth analysis of the source essay.
- The response is clearly and logically organized with ideas supported by relevant reasons, well-chosen examples, strong transitions, and concrete details.
- The essay explores the issues thoughtfully and in depth without redundancy.
- Quoted passages or references to a source text are explained and credited to the author.
- Word choice is appropriate to the essay's audience and purpose and may show some flair.

3+ to 4– (85–90%): A strong essay demonstrates clear competence in writing by going beyond just the basic requirements of the assignment and demonstrating an ability to critically understand, interpret, and argue the topic. It may have some errors, but they are not serious enough to distract or confuse the reader. An essay in this category does the following:

- Clearly addresses the topic but may respond to some aspects of the task more effectively than others
- States or clearly implies the writer's position or thesis with strong analysis of the source essay's appeals
- Is clearly and logically organized and developed with relevant reasons and examples
- Shows some depth and complexity by explaining thoroughly while avoiding redundancy
- Displays syntactic variety and maintains appropriate vocabulary
- Credits to the author any quoted passages or references
- May have a few errors in grammar, mechanics, or usage

3– to 3 (75–80%): An adequate essay completes the basic requirements of the assignment. It may have some errors that distract the reader, but these errors do not significantly impede understanding. An essay in this category does the following:

- Addresses the topic but may slight some aspects of the task
- States or implies the writer's position or thesis with average analysis of the source text
- Is adequately organized and developed, generally supporting ideas with reasons, examples, and details
- Treats the topic simplistically or superficially and without depth, or may repeat ideas
- Displays some syntactic variety and maintains appropriate vocabulary
- May have some errors in grammar, mechanics, and/or usage

2 to 2+ (65–70%): A marginal essay demonstrates developing competence but may lack analytical insight into the topic or appropriate development, given the purpose of the essay. An essay in this category does the following:

- Distorts, neglects, or ignores aspects of the task and may confuse some aspects of the source essay
- Announces the topic but lacks a stated or implied position or thesis
- Lacks focus and demonstrates confused or illogical thinking
- Is poorly organized or developed, has weak or irrelevant details, and may contain factual errors
- Has problems with syntactic variety, simplistic or inappropriate vocabulary, and an accumulation of errors in grammar, mechanics, and usage that impede understanding

Kevin Ferns, Woodland Community College (Yuba Community College District)

1 to 2– (50–60%): A weak essay suggests possible difficulties in reading and writing and may have one or more of the following weaknesses:

- The essay displays confusion about the topic or ignores important aspects of the task; it lacks a thesis.
- It provides simplistic generalizations without support and has weak organization.
- Errors in grammar, mechanics, and usage impede reader understanding.

ENGLISH 1A COURSE SCHEDULE

The course schedule is designed to be flexible to meet your needs. The following assignments will be modified and detailed as we progress, and I will notify you as we make updates and changes to this schedule throughout the semester. I will list specific homework and reading response assignments on the board at the beginning of each class session and on WebCT. Page numbers refer to *The McGraw-Hill Reader* unless *Rules for Writers* is specified.

Date	Class Topic	Essays and Workshops
Mon., 8/12	Course Introduction	Writing history essay
Wed., 8/14	"Critical Thinking, Reading, and Writing" (2–11); Adler, "How to Mark a Book" (57–61); Elbow, "Freewriting" (68–71)	Writing Lab; Introduction to WebCT
Mon., 8/19	"Critical Thinking, Reading, and Writing" (11–27)	Essay 1 assigned: Evaluation and Response
Wed., 8/21	*Rules for Writers*, Chapter 5 (70–83); "Critical Thinking, Reading, and Writing" (32–54)	Writing Lab
Mon., 8/26	"Reading and Writing Effective Arguments" (104–114 and 126–129); *Rules for Writers*, Chapter 7 (102–110)	Writing Lab
Wed., 8/28	"The Penalty of Death" and "The Death Penalty Is a Step Back" (145–150)	
Mon., 9/2	Labor Day (No Class)	
Wed., 9/4	"Debate: Animal Research" (154–158)	Writing Lab
Mon., 9/9	"Debate: The Patriot Act" (160–170)	
Wed., 9/11	"Debate: The Patriot Act" (171–175)	Writing Lab; Essay 1 draft due (4 copies)
Mon., 9/16	"Critical Thinking, Reading, and Writing" (54–56)	Peer review workshop; peer essay evaluations due
Wed., 9/18	"Reading and Writing Effective Arguments" (117–126 and 129–143); *Rules for Writers*, Chapter 6 (84–101)	Writing Lab; Essay 2 assigned: Health and Medicine
Mon., 9/23	Midterm Exam 1: Evaluation and Response	Essay 1 final due with revision summary; submit to www.turnitin.com
Wed., 9/25	"Writing a Research Paper" (178–232); *Rules for Writers*, Chapters 53–60 (420–532)	Writing Lab
Mon., 9/30	"This Is the End of the World" (733–741)	

Kevin Ferns, Woodland Community College (Yuba Community College District)

Date	Class Topic	Essays and Workshops
Wed., 10/2	"We Are Not Immune" (742–751)	Writing Lab
Mon., 10/7	"The Terrifying Normalcy of AIDS" (760–763); "The Globalization of Eating Disorders" (787–790)	
Wed., 10/9	"The Man Who Couldn't Stop Eating" (764–777)	Writing Lab; Essay 2 draft due (4 copies)
Mon., 10/14		Peer review workshop; peer essay evaluations due
Wed., 10/16	"Why Are We Fascinated by Gangsters?" (558–575)	Essay 3 assigned: Media and Popular Culture
Mon., 10/21	Midterm Exam 2: Evaluation and Response	Essay 2 final due with revision summary; submit to www.turnitin.com
Wed., 10/23	"My Creature from the Black Lagoon" (582–589)	Writing Lab
Mon., 10/28	"Wonder Woman" (593–601)	
Wed., 10/30	"Escape from Wonderland" (610–622)	Writing Lab
Mon., 11/4	"Loose Ends" (577–578); "Supersaturation" (602–608)	
Wed., 11/6	"Red, White, and Beer" (590–592); "Analyzing Visual Texts" (28–32) and "An Album of Advertisements: Images of Culture"	Writing Lab; Essay 3 draft due (4 copies)
Mon., 11/11	Veterans Day (No Class)	
Wed., 11/13		Peer review workshop; peer essay evaluations due
Mon., 11/18	"Superstition" (676–686)	Essay 4 assigned: Philosophy, Ethics, and Religion
Wed., 11/20	"I Listen to My Parents and I Wonder What They Believe" (688–692); "Salvation" (693–695)	Essay 3 final due with revision summary; submit to www.turnitin.com
Mon., 11/25	"The Allegory of the Cave" (704–707)	
Wed., 11/27	Thanksgiving (No Class)	
Mon., 12/2	"The Culture of Disbelief" (716–724); "Not about Islam?" (709–711)	Essay 4 draft due (4 copies)
Wed., 12/4		Peer review workshop; peer essay evaluations due
Mon., 12/9	Final Exam Review	
Wed., 12/11	Final Exam, Evaluation and Response, 8:00–11:00 a.m., Room TBA	Essay 4 final due with revision summary; submit to www.turnitin.com

Kevin Ferns, Woodland Community College (Yuba Community College District)

English 101: Syllabus

Instructor: Sheena Denney Boran
E-mail: x@olemiss.edu
Office: Somerville x
Office hours: MW 3-4, and by appointment

Course Texts

Bullock, Richard, and Maureen Daly Goggin, eds. *The Norton Field Guide to Writing, with Readings.* 2nd ed. New York: W. W. Norton, 2009.

Hacker, Diana, and Nancy Sommers. *A Writer's Reference.* 7th ed. Boston: Bedford/St. Martin's, 2011.

Note: Readings outside the texts will be posted on Blackboard under Readings. You will be required to print out copies of the materials and bring them to class on the assigned dates. More information will be given in class.

Course Description

This course will assist students in recognizing and understanding different audiences and rhetorical purposes for reaching those audiences. Throughout the course, students will be assigned readings and participate in class discussions that serve to illuminate potential rhetorical purposes. In addition, students will regularly use a writing process that nurtures ideas and develops texts over time; the semester will feature major assignments from five different genres culminating in a portfolio project that serves to highlight this writing process. The assigned work in English 101 should prove simultaneously challenging and interesting and encourage students to work with their peers and their instructor in better understanding how the written language functions academically, professionally, and privately. To that end, students will examine ideas (both their own and those of others) critically, engage in reflective practices, begin to interact with and document secondary source material in anticipation of English 102, and learn to better understand and navigate the standard conventions of academic English.

Student Learning Outcomes

1. Students will demonstrate writing as a process that requires brainstorming, drafting, revising, editing, and proofreading.

2. Students will use writing to respond to readings, to explore unfamiliar ideas, to question thinking different from their own, to reflect on personal experiences, and to develop sound arguments.

3. Students will produce writing suitable for a variety of purposes, with an emphasis on academic purposes.

4. Students will integrate primary sources with their own ideas through summary, paraphrase, and quotation, and document those sources properly.

5. Students will produce writing that is free of serious grammatical and mechanical errors.

Grading

Memoir	10%
In-Class Essay	5%
Advertisement Analysis	15%

Sheena Denney Boran, University of Mississippi

Position Argument	20%
Photo/Image Essay	15%
Homework/Class Participation	10%
Portfolio	25%

Major Due Dates

Monday, February 10 – Memoir Due

Wednesday, February 19 – In-class Essay

Monday, March 17 – Advertisement Analysis Due

Monday, March 31 – Position Argument Due

Monday, April 14 – Photo/Image Essay Due

Monday, April 28 – Portfolio Due

Attendance Policy

Students are expected to attend all class meetings; improving writing skills takes time and is a process unlike learning content alone. Because students may experience some circumstances which prevent complete attendance, the following policy is in effect:

MWF Courses

1 day missed: no penalty

2 days missed: no penalty

3 days missed: no penalty

4 days missed: no penalty

5 days missed: final course grade lowered by one letter grade

6 days missed: final course grade lowered by two letter grades

7 days missed: final course grade lowered by three letter grades

8 days missed: failure

There will be no excused or unexcused absences.

Late Work Policy

Due to the structured nature of this class, late work is unacceptable. If you are aware that you will be unable to meet a deadline, contact the instructor prior to the assignment due date.

Classroom Decorum

The classroom is a place of learning; others are paying to be here too. Please make sure not to distract others from learning and to respect the opinions of others. From time to time we will review each other's writing in peer review sessions. Please follow the guideline of being a "critical friend" in all of your responses to classmates' work. Students who cannot adhere to these behavioral expectations are subject to discipline in accordance with the procedures described in the M Book.

Disabilities

If you have a documented disability as described by the Rehabilitation Act of 1973 (P.L. 933-112 Section 504) or the Americans with Disabilities Act (ADA) and would like to request academic and/or physical accommodations, please contact Student Disability Services at 234 Martindale Center,

Sheena Denney Boran, University of Mississippi

xxx-xxx-xxxx. Course requirements will not be waived but reasonable accommodations may be provided as appropriate.

Plagiarism

All work that you submit under your name for credit at UM is assumed to be your original work. While teachers hope and expect that you will incorporate the thinking of others in your work, you must credit others' work when you rely upon it. In your written assignments, there are only three methods for properly integrating the work of others: quotation, paraphrase, and summary (see pp. 361-365, 376-379, 448-451, and 502-504 in *A Writer's Reference*).

The penalty for plagiarism in English 101 is failure of the course. Additional penalties are possible.

Policies Subject to Change

All information in this syllabus is subject to change at any time, especially during the first weeks of the semester. I will announce changes to our schedule during class time and also via Blackboard. You are responsible for changes to the schedule as they arise, regardless of whether or not you attend class.

DAILY SCHEDULE OF ACTIVITIES

Week One	
Wed., Jan. 22	Class introductions, Bios *HW: Read Robert Atwan on Opinion and Participating in Class Discussion (Blackboard)*
Fri., Jan. 24	Opinion Exercise, How to Talk in Class *HW: Discussion prompt response: "How I Write Papers." Bring to Monday's class.* *HW: Read pp. 153-160 in* Norton.
Week Two	
Mon., Jan. 27	Introduction to Memoir, Brainstorming *HW: Choose the central event for your memoir, and write down everything you can remember about it. Read pp. 343-349 and pp. 826-830 in* Norton *and section C1-b in* A Writer's Reference.
Wed., Jan. 29	Drafting the Memoir, Narrating *HW: Select a narrative strategy for your memoir, and produce a rough draft that conforms to that narrative strategy, making appropriate use of time markers and transitions. Read pp. 324-332 and pp. 802-808 in* Norton *and p. 35 in* A Writer's Reference.
Fri., Jan. 31	Revising the Memoir, Describing *HW: Examine your own memoir and add sensory details. Read pp. 261-270 and pp. 819-824 in* Norton *and p. 36 in* A Writer's Reference.

Week Three	
Mon., Feb. 3	Revising the Memoir, Beginning and Ending *HW: Select appropriate beginning and ending strategies for your memoir. Revise accordingly. Be sure to revise transitions throughout your memoir so that it flows smoothly from beginning to end. Read sections C2 and C3 and pp. 32-33 in* A Writer's Reference.
Wed., Feb. 5	Memoir Peer Review *HW: Read pp. 367-372 in* Norton *and p. 22, Guidelines for peer reviewers, in* A Writer's Reference.
Fri., Feb. 7	**Class Canceled – Conferences**
Week Four	
Mon., Feb. 10	**Paper One Due (Memoir)** Introduction to In-Class Essay, The Writing Process *HW: Read sample in-class essays (Blackboard)*
Wed., Feb. 12	Reading Questions & Outlining *HW: Read pp. 272-277 in* Norton *and section C1-d in* A Writer's Reference.
Fri., Feb. 14	In-Class Essay, Guiding the Reader *HW: Read pp. 653-657 in* Norton.
Week Five	
Mon., Feb. 17	Practice In-Class Essay *HW: Reading TBA*
Wed., Feb. 19	**Paper Two Due (in class essay)** *HW: Read pp. 38 and 43-58 in* Norton.
Fri., Feb. 21	Introduction to Advertisement Analysis *HW: Read pp. 325-366 and 604-608 in* Norton *and pp. 68, 70, and 77 in* A Writer's Reference. *Begin searching for an advertisement to analyze in your essay.*
Week Six	
Mon., Feb. 24	Practice Advertisement Analysis *HW: Choose an advertisement (or group of advertisements) to analyze in your essay. Summarize the content of the advertisement in a brief paragraph. Read Rebecca Hollingsworth's "An Imperfect Reality" (Blackboard).*
Wed., Feb. 26	Drafting the Advertisement Analysis *HW: Read p. 70 and the outline on p. 72 in* A Writer's Reference. *Begin drafting analysis of your advertisement, making use of image analysis terms.*
Fri., Feb. 28	Drafting the Advertisement Analysis *HW: Read section A3-a in* A Writer's Reference. *Examine your advertisement for each of the appeals, as well as logical fallacies and underlying cultural assumptions. Revise your analysis to include this new information.*

Week Seven	
Mon., Mar. 3	**Class Canceled – Conferences**
Wed., Mar. 5	**Class Canceled – Conferences**
Fri., Mar. 7	Advertisement Analysis Peer Review *Bring to class two hard copies of your Advertisement Analysis and two copies of the peer review sheet (Blackboard).* *HW: Read pp. 83-110 in* Norton.
Week Eight	
Mon., Mar. 10	**Spring break, no class**
Wed., Mar. 12	**Spring break, no class**
Fri., Mar. 14	**Spring break, no class**
Week Nine	
Mon., Mar. 17	**Paper Three Due (Advertisement Analysis)** Introduction to Position Argument *HW: Read pp. 283-299 and pp. 666-676 in* Norton. *Brainstorm at least three possible issues about which to write.*
Wed., Mar. 19	Drafting the Position Argument: Logos, Ethos, Pathos *HW: Read pp. 408-419 and pp. 684-695 in* Norton. *Choose the issue for your argument essay and generate a position statement.*
Fri., Mar. 21	Drafting the Position Argument: Quotation, Paraphrase, Summary *HW: Read pp. 67-85 in* A Writer's Reference *and Ann Marie Paulin's "Cruelty, Civility, and Other Weighty Matters" (Blackboard). Begin drafting Position Argument, focusing on what others say.*
Week Ten	
Mon., Mar. 24	Drafting the Position Argument: Responding to Others *HW: Read pp. 697-716 in* Norton *and section A2-f in* A Writer's Reference. *Continue drafting Position Argument, focusing on your own position.*
Wed., Mar. 26	Revising the Position Argument *HW: Read chapter C3 in* A Writer's Reference. *Revise Position Argument.*
Fri., Mar. 28	Position Argument Peer Review *Bring to class two hard copies of your Position Argument and two copies of the peer review sheet (Blackboard).*
Week Eleven	
Mon., Mar. 31	**Paper Four Due (Position Argument)** Introduction to Photo/Image Essay *HW: Read pp. 528-532 in* Norton. *Write a one-paragraph summary of the essay you want to adapt for this project.*
Wed., Apr. 2	Finding, Creating, and Using Photos and Images
Fri., Apr. 4	**Virtual Class Meeting** *HW: Collect or create at least 15 images for your essay. Read Simon Benlow's "An Apology to Future Generations" (Blackboard).*

Sheena Denney Boran, University of Mississippi

Week Twelve	
Mon., Apr. 7	Drafting the Photo/Image Essay *HW: Create a storyboard for your essay.*
Wed., Apr. 9	Revising the Photo/Image Essay *HW: Review chapter C3 in* A Writer's Reference.
Fri., Apr. 11	Photo/Image Essay Peer Review *Bring to class two hard copies of your Photo/Image Essay and two copies of the peer review sheet (Blackboard).*
Week Thirteen	
Mon., Apr. 14	**Photo/Image Essay Due** Photo/Image Essay Presentations
Wed., Apr. 16	Photo/Image Essay Presentations
Fri., Apr. 18	Photo/Image Essay Presentations/Portfolio preparation *HW: Read section C3-e in* A Writer's Reference.
Week Fourteen	
Mon., Apr. 21	Portfolio preparation
Wed., Apr. 23	Portfolio preparation
Fri., Apr. 25	Portfolio preparation
Week Fifteen	
Mon., Apr. 28	Final tweaks/revision to portfolio **Portfolio Due by 5:00 PM**
Wed., Apr. 30	Portfolio presentations
Fri., May 2	Portfolio presentations **Last day of class**

English 200: ADVANCED COMPOSITION
Three Credits

Meeting Days/Times:	(88545) Tuesdays and Thursdays, 7:30 a.m. to 8:45 a.m. – HOLM 248
	(88546) Tuesdays and Thursdays, 9:00 a.m. to 10:15 a.m. – SAKAM B308
Instructor:	Jill Dahlman; x@hawaii.edu
Office:	KUY XXX
Effective Date:	Spring 2012 (January 9, 2012, through May 11, 2012)

University of Hawaii at Manoa
College of Languages, Linguistics, and Literature

MISSION STATEMENT

The College of Languages, Linguistics, and Literature (LLL) places the study of language in its many manifestations at the center of its students' education. Through small classes and close student-faculty interchange, the College prepares students for lifelong learning in English studies, Hawaiian and foreign languages, and applied and theoretical linguistics. While taking a global view of language, literature, and linguistics, LLL offers a special focus on Asia-Pacific-Hawaii.

LLL faculty conduct research and produce scholarship according to the highest standards of inquiry and creativity in the liberal arts tradition. The range of faculty interests—from the analysis of language structure, acquisition, history, and use to the creation of teaching materials for familiar as well as less commonly taught languages; from the study of classic and contemporary texts of world literatures to the production of new literatures—reflects its commitment to innovation and excellence.

CATALOG DESCRIPTION

Further study of rhetorical, conceptual, and stylistic demands of writing; instruction develops the writing and research skills covered in Composition I. Pre: 100, 100A, 101/101L, or ELI 100.

Activities Required at Scheduled Times Other Than Class Times

- Homework, including but not limited to CompClass discussion board postings, quizzes, reading of short essays, and other homework that may be noted in class
- Compilation of portfolio
- Writing assignments
- Research Unit to be completed independent of class
- Frequent checking of e-mail and CompClass discussion board

Jill Dahlman, University of Hawaii at Manoa, College of Languages, Linguistics, and Literature

STUDENT LEARNING OUTCOMES

Upon successful completion of English 200, students should be able to complete the following as independent learners. The student learning outcomes for the course are:

00. Write well-reasoned compositions that reveal the complexity of the topic students have chosen to explore or argue.

01. Read for main points, perspective, and purpose; evaluate the quality of evidence, negotiate conflicting positions, and analyze the effectiveness of a text's approach to integrate that knowledge into their writing.

02. Choose language, style, and organization appropriate to particular purposes and audiences.

03. Synthesize previous experience and knowledge with the ideas and information students discover as they read and write.

04. Use sources such as libraries and the Internet to enhance students' understanding of the ideas they explore or argue in their writing; analyze and evaluate their research for reliability, bias, and relevance.

05. Use readers' responses as one source for revising writing.

06. Use standard disciplinary conventions to integrate and document sources.

07. Edit and proofread in the later stages of the writing process, especially when writing for public audiences; control such surface features as syntax, grammar, punctuation, and spelling.

COURSE CONTENT

- **Discussion board postings** will satisfy learning outcomes 01, 03, 04, 05, and 06.
- Essays found in *Writing and Revising* and essay readings and discussions in *From Critical Thinking to Argument* will satisfy learning outcome 02.
- *A Pocket Style Manual*, **6th Edition**, will aid in satisfying learning outcomes 03, 04, 06, and 07.
- **Writing assignments**, most of which are to be completed outside of class (see course schedule for specific details), will satisfy learning outcomes 01, 03, 04, 05, 06, and 07.
- **Homework**, including quizzes, will work toward all learning outcomes.

Concepts or Topics

- Ethos, pathos, logos (and other rhetorical skills)
- Rhetoric/rhetorical situation
- The differences among audiences; how to write to be effective for each audience
- The ability to write for specific purposes and to identify purpose in the writing of others
- Learning to dig deeply into outside material, unpack the material, and understand its deeper meaning
- Understand the difference between summarizing, paraphrasing, and plagiarism

Skills or Competencies

1. Work independently to accomplish specific tasks, such as homework, research, and writing
2. Successfully manage time in order to complete all tasks
3. Follow directions
4. Ask questions to clear up misunderstandings, clarify directions, or seek assistance on papers (if needed)
5. Understand that writing is a process that takes time in order to produce excellent work
6. Understand the importance and necessity of mastering multiple proofreading and revision techniques
7. Demonstrate respect toward the professor and classmates at all times

Jill Dahlman, University of Hawaii at Manoa, College of Languages, Linguistics, and Literature

SCORING BREAKDOWN—KEEPING TRACK OF SCORES

Assignment	Grade	Out of Possible	Total
Discussion forum postings Need a total of 30 (x 3 points)		90	
Summary-Responses Need a total of 9 (x 5 points)		45	
Attendance/class participation		50	
Open-book quizzes		70	
Identity Unit • Major paper (mandatory) • Paper option(s)		40 20	
Music Unit • Major paper (mandatory) • Paper option(s)		40 20	
Star Trek Unit • Major paper (mandatory) • Paper option(s)		40 20	
Comic Book Unit • Paper option(s)		30	
Science Fiction Unit • Major paper (mandatory) • Paper option(s)		40 20	
Research Paper (all components mandatory) • Project proposal • Annotated bibliography (5 entries x 10 points) • Drafts and peer review • Project presentation • Research paper		25 50 10 50 90	
Portfolio		250	

COURSE TASKS

1. Attend each class meeting.

2. Complete all assigned readings on time.

3. Complete all assignments on time.

4. Use library resources for scholarly credibility.

5. Take the initiative to ask the instructor relevant questions both inside and outside of class.

6. Contribute to class discussions.

Jill Dahlman, University of Hawaii at Manoa, College of Languages, Linguistics, and Literature

ASSIGNMENTS

Discussion Board Postings: 90 points (10%)

To become great writers, we need practice. To that end, we will be using discussion board postings in this class. Thirty (30) discussion board postings will be required (two will be due each week). There should be no concern for grammar, punctuation, paragraphs, and so on, as the purpose of these entries is to provide you with practice writing and debating with your fellow classmates. The most important part of an entry is the content. If you choose to respond to another student's posting, you must be respectful in your response. There is no tolerance for name-calling, degradation, or any other form of slander against another student. In other words, attack the issue or argument, not the person. A discussion board posting must be 250 words (with a word count noted at the end of each posting) in order to qualify for full points. Each additional posting will earn you 3 points extra credit (up to 15 points extra credit).

The first two postings have been chosen for you. For the first 250-word posting, introduce yourself and tell your classmates something about yourself. What interests you? Why are you in school? What accomplishment are you most proud of? What do you hope to get out of this class (other than an A!)?

In the second posting, elaborate on why you are in this class, in this university, or in your major. How did you arrive at the conclusion to take this course, enroll at UH, or choose your major?

Note: Although there is no "definitive" due date for each discussion board posting, do yourself a favor and keep current with these! The *last thing* you want to be doing the week of finals is writing thirty-three discussion board postings. And as an added incentive, I award 10 points extra credit at the end of the semester if you have kept current.

Summary-Responses: 45 points (4.5%)

Effective summarizing of articles, papers, and books (among other things) is important for writing good research papers. You will be required to write nine summary-responses to *Worlds of Exile and Illusion* by Ursula K. LeGuin. From the following reading schedule, you will need to choose nine sections to write a 500-word summary-response. The first 250 words should be a brief summary of the section you have read. The second 250 words should be your response to the section or the story itself. Consider the following questions when responding (however, you are not limited to these questions):

- Did you like or dislike this section? Why? What was appealing? What made you dislike the story? (Consider setting, character, plot, or other literary elements.) Would you recommend this story?
- What message (implicit or explicit) do you think the author is trying to offer about the present or the future?
- What character did you connect with the most? The least? Why did you make such a connection?
- Can you see parallels between today's society and society of the future?

Due Date: There is no specific due date for these postings; however, like the discussion board postings, you will want to keep current with the suggested due dates (noted in the chart) to ensure that you are not scrambling the week of finals to get these summary-responses in and, more important, that you are prepared to write the final major assignment: the argument paper. Should you choose to write additional postings, you will earn extra credit points (5 points per posting). *Please be sure to post under the appropriate heading!*

Posting due dates

Page	Due Date
3–28	January 20
28–57	January 27
57–82	February 3
83–115	February 10
115–139	February 17
139–166	February 24
166–190	March 2
190–215	March 9
215–247	March 16
248–276	March 23
276–307	April 6
307–338	April 13
339–370 (end)	April 20

Jill Dahlman, University of Hawaii at Manoa, College of Languages, Linguistics, and Literature

Integrating Sources Quizzes (2): 70 points (7%)

Two online, do-at-home, open-book quizzes covering sources, plagiarism, MLA in-text citations, integration of sources, and MLA works cited and APA references lists will be covered. To successfully complete these quizzes, you will need to review these sections in *A Pocket Style Manual*. You may take each quiz *once* at any time *before February 28, 2012*. After February 28, the quizzes will no longer be available, and you will have lost 70 points.

Attendance: 50 points (5%)

In-class assignments are required. Time will be provided to work on these assignments. It is very difficult to work on in-class assignments if you are not in class. Please make every effort to be present in class. Points will be added for each class attended with participation. If you fall asleep, you will lose points. If you are habitually late or leave habitually early, your points will reflect this. If you are text messaging, disruptive, or otherwise not acting as a fully functioning member of this class at any time or in any way violate the University of Hawaii Student Conduct Code, you may be asked to leave, and you will incur an unexcused absence for each occurrence.

Unless you are able to provide written documentation as to why you were not in class (an excused absence, such as a doctor's/employer's note), your absence will be considered unexcused. Four unexcused absences will result in a one-letter reduction in your grade. Please note that if you are not in class for a scheduled peer review, it will be considered a double unexcused absence. Each additional absence (over three) will cost you 10 points. *If you miss six or more classes, you will fail the class—no matter how good your scores are.*

Tardiness in any way, shape, or form is not tolerated. You are expected to be at your job on time. This is your job. Your job is to be in the classroom before the start of class. **Being tardy two times will be considered an unexcused absence.** Because this class uses discussion as one of its methods of teaching, you cannot expect to learn something unless you are sitting in the classroom discussing the material. You are responsible for all missed assignments. And as an added incentive for perfect attendance, I award 10 points extra credit at the end of the semester if you have no absences—excused or unexcused.

Writing Assignments: 270 points (27%)

Assignments are described below. Four major assignments are required. You will determine the remainder of your points for each unit. Drafts and peer reviews are mandatory and are worth points. Without these drafts and peer reviews, you will lose 10% of your grade on each assignment. If you do not attend a peer review session, *you will be docked two unexcused absences*. Be present at these peer reviews!

Good writing takes time and multiple revisions. The schedule provides you with an opportunity to hand in a draft early in the process, so you will be able to easily complete the assignment. Not only does this method help you understand the process it takes to turn in a good paper, but it also provides you with ample time to complete and revise the assignment. All papers and all drafts must be turned in through the Writing Tab found on CompClass. Each draft that you are turning in for a grade must be submitted through the Writing Tab under the appropriate heading. If, for whatever reason, you cannot upload your document by the due date and time, e-mail the paper to me that night and turn in the paper copy at the beginning of the next regularly scheduled class meeting. If it isn't there before the class starts, it is late and definitely not eligible for full points.

The paper is due on the date indicated. Unless you are dead or in a documented coma, there will be NO EXCEPTIONS. Papers more than two class meeting days late are not eligible for points.

Jill Dahlman, University of Hawaii at Manoa, College of Languages, Linguistics, and Literature

BASIC GUIDELINES FOR WRITTEN ASSIGNMENTS

If you follow all of these guidelines, you will earn 2 points extra credit on each major paper and 1 point extra credit on each minor or optional assignment. If you don't follow instructions, you will be docked points as noted.

> Surname, First Name
> English 100/Dahlman
> Topic of/Title of Assignment
> Due Date: Day Year Month

Place your name in the *top left corner* of the first page as noted.

1. Highlight your thesis (worth 4 points on the major paper/1 point on the minor/option paper) in one color.

2. Highlight each in-text citation in another color (worth 2 points on the major paper/1 point on the minor/option paper).

3. Place a word count at the end of the document (worth 4 points on the major paper/1 point on the minor/option paper).

4. For major papers only: Post your own paper and read postings from the members of this class on Comment.

5. **A bibliography or works cited page** must be attached to each paper (if not attached, a 4-point deduction on the major paper/1-point deduction on the minor/option paper will occur).

6. If you want to know what grade you would have received on any paper, attach a copy of the "general rubric" found at the end of this syllabus. You can print these out from the syllabus that has been posted on CompClass.

7. OPTIONAL (worth 5 points extra credit): Post constructive comments to someone's paper (not necessarily in your peer review group) during the week of peer review (up to two days before the due date). Comments should include the following: a general statement of your impressions after your first quick reading; a specific statement covering what you particularly like and what you see as problematic; and finally, a question that you feel will help the writer in his or her writing process.

8. **Reminder:** ALL FINAL PAPERS ARE DUE ON THE DATE INDICATED — NO EXCEPTIONS!

LEARNING RESOURCES

Students are expected to obtain and bring with them to each class meeting their Working Folder for portfolio workshops (announced and unannounced) and the following books: *A Pocket Style Manual* by Diana Hacker and Nancy Sommers and *Portfolio Keeping*, 2nd Edition, by Nedra Reynolds and Rich Rice. Additionally, students will be required to have an active hawaii.edu account in order to complete the Library Resource Unit and an Internet account to gain access to the discussion board on CompClass. Although you are not required to own a computer, access to both a computer and the Internet is a "must" for this class.

ADDITIONAL INFORMATION

A **"University Performance" Standard:** Students are expected to make a serious academic commitment to their success in this course. You must at least keep up with the syllabus schedule. Whenever possible, however, it is a good idea to work slightly ahead of the syllabus to compensate for the unexpected.

Jill Dahlman, University of Hawaii at Manoa, College of Languages, Linguistics, and Literature

Plagiarism Policy: The University of Hawaii system defines plagiarism as follows:

> Plagiarism includes, but is not limited to, submitting, to satisfy an academic requirement, any document that has been copied in whole or in part from another individual's work without identifying that individual; neglecting to identify as a quotation a documented idea that has not been assimilated into the student's language and style; paraphrasing a passage so closely that the reader is misled as to the source; *submitting the same written or oral material in more than one course without obtaining authorization from the instructors involved*; and "dry-labbing," which includes obtaining and using experimental data from other students without the express consent of the instructor, utilizing experimental data and laboratory write-ups from other sections of the course or from previous terms, and fabricating data to fit the expected results (emphasis mine).

If you are caught plagiarizing in any manner that even remotely resembles the UH-system policy, you will be dealt with severely. This could include punishment ranging from a zero on the assignment to expulsion from the class or university. If plagiarism is suspected, the student will be expected to conference with me, to produce every single piece of documentation used in the assignment, and to orally defend his or her paper. If concern is still raised, or if the student requests independent assessment, the student shall be expected to appear before a panel of three professors with all evidence of documented sources and to orally defend his or her paper. In short, don't do it.

Incomplete: An Incomplete is not automatically given. An Incomplete is considered only when less than 10% of all coursework is left to complete and only under extreme circumstances. In short, don't expect it.

Grading

A = 900–1,000 points

B = 800–899 points

C = 700–799 points

D = 600–699 points

F = 599 or below

Drop Dates

January 13, 2012 – No record; 100% refund

January 30, 2012 – No record; 50% refund

March 19, 2012 – Drop with a W on your record. Please note: It is far better to receive a W and repeat the course than to receive a D or an F. If you think that you are not going to pass, talk to me before the drop date.

PROPOSED SCHEDULE (NOTE: THIS IS NOT ETCHED IN STONE!)

Key: *WR = Writing and Revising*   *CTA = From Critical Thinking to Argument*

Date	To Be Covered in Class	Homework
WEEK ONE Tuesday 1/10	• Syllabus and expectations	• Post discussion board (DB) postings: 1. Welcome & Introductions 2. "Learning to Read"

Jill Dahlman, University of Hawaii at Manoa, College of Languages, Linguistics, and Literature

Thursday 1/12	• General overview of CompClass • Drop date 1/13 with no record and 100% refund	• Post draft of Reflecting paper by midnight Tuesday 1/17 in the Writing Tab • Option paper 1 (Identity) due Tuesday • Read Ch. 1 in *WR*
WEEK TWO Tuesday 1/17	• Draft 1 of Reflecting paper due by midnight • Choose DB topics • Review Ch. 1 in *WR*	• Post DB postings 3 and 4 • Read Ch. 7 in *WR*
Thursday 1/19	• Review Ch. 7 in *WR* • **Option paper 1 (Identity) due**	• Post draft 2 of Reflecting paper in the Writing Tab by midnight Tuesday 1/24 for peer review on Thursday • Complete Summary-Response 1 by Friday 1/20
WEEK THREE Tuesday 1/24	• Peer review of draft 2 of Reflecting paper (due by 1/29) • LIBRARY FIELD TRIP: Class held in Hamilton 113 with Ross Christensen (Head toward the back!)	• Post DB postings 5 and 6 • Option paper 2 (Identity) due Tuesday • Read Ch. 5 in *WR*
Thursday 1/26	• **Option paper 2 (Identity) due** • Choose DB topics • Review Ch. 5 in *WR* • Drop date 1/30 with no record	• Turn in final Reflecting paper and ALL IDENTITY ASSIGNMENTS on Tuesday • Bring in lyrics to song • Complete Summary-Response 2 by Friday 1/27
WEEK FOUR Tuesday 1/31	• **Final Reflecting paper due** • **All Identity Unit assignments due** • Choose DB topics • Rhetoric of music	• Post DB postings 7 and 8 • Read Ch. 5 in *CTA*
Thursday 2/2	• Research proposal due • Rhetoric of music • Review Ch. 5 in *CTA*	• Complete Summary-Response 3 by Friday 2/3 • Option paper 1 (Music) due Tuesday • Post draft 1 of Analysis paper in Writing Tab by midnight on Tuesday • Read Ch. 3 in *CTA*
WEEK FIVE Tuesday 2/7	• Draft 1 of Analysis paper due by midnight • Choose DB topics • Review Ch. 3 in *CTA*	• Post DB postings 9 and 10 • Complete Summary-Response 4 by Friday 2/10 • Read Ch. 4 in *WR*

Jill Dahlman, University of Hawaii at Manoa, College of Languages, Linguistics, and Literature

Thursday 2/9	• **Option paper 1 (Music) due** • Review Ch. 4 in *WR*	• Turn in Option paper 2 (Music) on Tuesday • Post draft 2 of Analysis paper in the Writing Tab by midnight on Monday for peer review on Tuesday • Read Ch. 2 in *WR*
WEEK SIX Tuesday 2/14	• Peer review of draft 2 of Analysis paper (due by 2/19) • Choose DB topics • Review Ch. 2 in *WR*	• Post DB postings 11 and 12
Thursday 2/16	• **Option paper 2 (Music) due** • Watch *Star Trek*	• Complete Summary-Response 5 by Friday 2/17 • Turn in final Analysis paper on Tuesday • **All assignments (Music) due Tuesday**
WEEK SEVEN Tuesday 2/21	• **Final Analysis paper due** • **All Music Unit assignments due** • Choose DB topics • Watch *Star Trek: The Next Generation*	• Post DB postings 13 and 14
Thursday 2/23	• Watch *How William Shatner Changed the World*	• Option paper 1 (*Star Trek*) due Tuesday in class • Complete Summary-Response 6 by Friday 2/24 • Post draft 1 of Explaining paper in the Writing Tab by midnight on Tuesday • Read Ch. 11 in *WR*
WEEK EIGHT Tuesday 2/28	• Draft 1 of Explaining paper due by midnight • Choose DB topics • Discussion of annotations • Review Ch. 11 in *WR*	• Annotated Bibliography 1 due Thursday • Read Ch. 2 in *CTA*
Thursday 3/1	• **Option paper 1 (*Star Trek*) due** • Annotated Bibliography 1 due • Review Ch. 2 in *CTA*	• Post DB postings 15 and 16 • Option paper 2 (*Star Trek*) due Tuesday in class • Annotated Bibliography 2 due Tuesday • Complete Summary-Response 7 by Friday 3/2 • Post draft 2 of Explaining paper in the Writing Tab by Monday at midnight for peer review on Tuesday

Jill Dahlman, University of Hawaii at Manoa, College of Languages, Linguistics, and Literature

WEEK NINE Tuesday 3/6	• **Class ONLINE!** • Peer review of Explaining paper (due by 3/11) • Annotated Bibliography 2 due	• Complete Summary-Response 8 by Friday 3/9 • Annotated Bibliography 3 due Thursday
Thursday 3/8	• **Class ONLINE!** • **Option paper 2 (*Star Trek*) due** • Annotated Bibliography 3 due	• Post DB postings 17 and 18 • Turn in final Explaining paper on Tuesday • **All Option papers (*Star Trek*) due Tuesday** • Read Ch. 7 in *CTA*

WEEK TEN Tuesday 3/13	• **Final Explaining paper due** • **All *Star Trek* Unit assignments due** • Choose DB topics • Review Ch. 7 in *CTA* • MLA Workshop	• Complete Summary-Response 9 by Friday 3/16 • Annotated Bibliography 4 due Thursday • Read Ch. 4 in *CTA*
Thursday 3/15	• Annotated Bibliography 4 due • Discussion of comic books (in general) • Review Ch. 4 in *CTA* • Final drop date 3/19 with a W on your record	• Post DB postings 19 and 20 • Option paper 1 (Comics) due Tuesday 3/20 • Annotated Bibliography 5 due Tuesday 3/20 • **Mandatory! Integrating Sources Quizzes (2) due Thursday 3/22**

WEEK ELEVEN Tuesday 3/20	• Annotated Bibliography 5 due • **Option paper 1 (Comics) due** • Choose DB topics	• Post DB postings 21 and 22 • Read Ch. 3 in *WR*
Thursday 3/22	• **Integrating Sources Quizzes (2) due TODAY** • Review Ch. 3 in *WR* • Portfolio/Research Paper Workshop	• Option paper 2 (Comics) due Tuesday • **All Comics papers due Tuesday 4/3** • Read Ch. 1 in *CTA*

WEEK TWELVE Tuesday 3/27	• No school: Spring break	
Thursday 3/29	• No school: Spring break	

WEEK THIRTEEN Tuesday 4/3	• **Option paper 2 (Comics) due** • **All Comics papers due TODAY** • Choose DB topics • Review Ch. 1 in *CTA* • Portfolio/Research Paper Workshop	• Post DB postings 23 and 24 • Rough draft 1 of Argumentation paper due Thursday • Read Ch. 10 in *WR*

Jill Dahlman, University of Hawaii at Manoa, College of Languages, Linguistics, and Literature

Thursday 4/5	• **Rough draft 1 of Argumentation paper due** • Review Ch. 10 in *WR* • Portfolio/Research Paper Workshop	• Option paper 1 (SF) due Tuesday • Read Ch. 6 in *CTA*
WEEK FOURTEEN Tuesday 4/10	• **Option paper 1 (SF) due** • Choose DB topics • Review Ch. 6 in *CTA* • Portfolio/Research Paper Workshop	• Post DB posting 25 and 26 • Post draft 2 of Argumentation paper in the Writing Tab by Wednesday at midnight for peer review on Thursday • Read Ch. 6 in *WR*
Thursday 4/12	• **Peer review of Argumentation paper (due by 4/21)** • Review Ch. 6 in *WR* • Portfolio/Research Paper Workshop	• Option paper 2 (SF) due Tuesday • Post draft 1 of Research paper in the Writing Tab by Tuesday at midnight
WEEK FIFTEEN Tuesday 4/17	• Draft 1 of Research paper due by midnight • **Option paper 2 (SF) due** • Choose DB topics • Portfolio/Research Paper Workshop	• Post DB posting 27 and 28 • Final Argumentation paper due Tuesday • **All SF papers due Thursday** • Read Ch. 8 in *WR*
Thursday 4/19	• **Final Argumentation paper due** • **All SF papers due TODAY** • Review Ch. 8 in *WR* • Portfolio/Research Paper Workshop	• Post draft 2 of Research paper in the Writing Tab by Sunday at midnight for peer review on Tuesday • Read Ch. 9 in *WR*
WEEK SIXTEEN Tuesday 4/24	• Draft 2 of Research paper due by midnight • Peer review of Research paper due by 4/30 • Choose DB topics • Review Ch. 9 in *WR* • Presentations!	• Post DB postings 29 and 30
Thursday 4/26	• Presentations!	• Turn in final Research paper and portfolio Tuesday 5/1
WEEK SEVENTEEN Tuesday 5/1	• Presentations! • Portfolio/Research paper due	

Jill Dahlman, University of Hawaii at Manoa, College of Languages, Linguistics, and Literature

GENERAL RUBRIC FOR ALL PAPERS
(include with your paper if you want specific feedback)

Item	A–B (✓+)	B–C (✓)	C–D (✓–)
Argument _____	The argument is superior in content.	The argument is average in content.	The argument is below average in content.
Thesis _____	Your thesis is excellent, and your paper follows the thesis.	Your thesis is average, and your paper somewhat follows the thesis.	Your thesis is below average, and your paper does not follow the thesis.
Introduction and conclusion _____	Your introduction and conclusion are on point, and the reader can easily follow your line of reasoning from start to finish.	Your introduction OR conclusion are on point, and the reader can somewhat follow your line of reasoning from start to finish.	Your introduction and conclusion are not on point, and the reader cannot easily follow your line of reasoning from start to finish.
Support _____	Your argument relied on established facts rather than on emotion (no name calling; sticking to the objective facts).	Your argument relied on some established facts rather than on emotion.	Your argument relied heavily on emotion rather than on fact; you often leave your reader wondering what is going on.
Counterargument _____	You took another side into account (acknowledged counterarguments; possibly even refuted a few).	You may not have explicitly taken another side into account, but the viewpoint conveyed in the paper is objective.	You took no other side into account.
Accuracy _____	Your facts were accurate and indicated that you read outside sources for clarity (i.e., you did the homework).	Most of your facts were accurate and indicated that you read some outside sources for clarity (i.e., you did the homework).	Your facts were not accurate and indicated that you had not read outside sources for clarity (i.e., you did not do the homework).
Grammar and punctuation _____	Your grammar and punctuation were excellent, with minimal errors.	Your grammar and punctuation were average, with errors that did not get in the way of the meaning of your paper.	Your grammar and punctuation were below average, with errors that got in the way of the meaning of your paper.
In-text citations _____	Your in-text citations and works cited/bibliography are excellent.	Your in-text citations and works cited/bibliography are average.	Your in-text citations and works cited/bibliography are below average — you need help.
Proofreading _____	You have few, if any, corrections to make.	You have a few corrections to make if you want to make this a stellar paper.	You have many corrections to make.

Jill Dahlman, University of Hawaii at Manoa, College of Languages, Linguistics, and Literature

Critical Reading and Writing
(ENGL110, Fall 2013)
MWF 1:25 PM–2:15 PM GORE 218

Prof. Stephen A. Bernhardt
Department of English
Kirkpatrick Chair in Writing
Office XXX Memorial Hall
Phone XXX-XXX-XXXX
Office Hours: MW 2:30–3:30

Use Sakai e-mail to contact

REQUIRED BOOKS

Hacker, Bernhardt, Sommers. *Writer's Help*. Boston: Bedford/St. Martin's. Purchase either a 2-year or 4-year subscription at writershelp.com.
The UD Bookstore will also sell you an access card. If you are buying your books with financial aid/grants, you need to purchase at the UD Bookstore, not online. **Use the following information for "instructor e-mail address" during registration at writershelp.com: xxx@udel.edu.**
Ramage, Bean, Johnson. *The Allyn & Bacon Guide to Writing.* Concise 6th ed. New York: Pearson, 2012.
The Arak Anthology. University of Delaware, 2010–2011. Award-winning writing from students in Engl110 from Fall 2012. Available at the bookstore.

Please bring your laptop to class. We have a wireless building and a newly designed classroom that supports group interaction through technology. We will want to work in groups and look at our writing in class. We will also be using *Writer's Help*, an online handbook, so you need to be connected.

LEARNING OBJECTIVES

By the end of this course, you should be able to do the following:

Underlined terms are links to relevant pages in Writer's Help.

- Read and write with attention to <u>purpose, audience, situation,</u> <u>tone,</u> <u>argument,</u> and <u>style</u>
- Write well in a variety of academic genres: summary, exposition, response, research report, critical analysis
- Find, <u>assess,</u> and document sources, using research to strengthen your arguments
- Manage your writing well, with good control of the process
- Make good use of writing technologies
- Work well as a <u>peer reviewer</u> and <u>collaborator</u> with other writers
- Follow a citation style for in-text and end-of-text documentation (e.g., <u>MLA</u>, <u>APA</u>, *<u>Chicago</u>*, <u>CSE</u>)
- Identify your weaknesses and learn to control <u>grammar</u>, <u>punctuation</u>, and <u>style</u>

Stephen A. Bernhardt, University of Delaware

ATTENDANCE

You need to be in class on time, having read the work, having done the exercises, having prepared your draft, and being ready to work. If you miss a class, talk to someone first and then see me if necessary to be sure you don't miss important information about assignments. If you are absent, you are still responsible for getting the assignments turned in on time via Sakai.

Two or three excused absences are ok. I can excuse absences for good reasons (sickness) or special events (such as athletic competitions), as long as you explain to me in an e-mail or in person the reason for your absence. You should do this before the absence, if possible. If the event is documented (like a team meet), show me the documentation.

Emergency Absences: If serious illnesses, family emergencies, or other crises occur during the term, you must contact the Assistant Dean of your College as soon as possible. This office can assist you in notifying faculty and in validating for your teachers what has happened. Such validation will be necessary for you to make up missed classwork and assignments. Emergencies include deaths in the family, accidents or illness that puts you in the hospital, and so on.

If you observe religious holidays and need to adjust your schedule, let me know and we can work it out.

COMMUNICATION

You should take advantage of my office hours for one-on-one conferences. You can either schedule an appointment or drop in during my hours. I am always free after class and will be in my office before class. You should visit my office at least twice.

You will need to check Sakai frequently, at least once between classes. Check mail, notice the announcements, check the discussion forum. It will help you keep up and do well. I check my Sakai mail almost every day and always between classes.

I will use Sakai Messages (NOT my UD e-mail) to communicate with you and post advice and announcements in Announcements (top left of home screen).

We will discuss issues as a group on our class Sakai Forum. You will also be able to ask the group through e-mail for information about assignments, strategies, or requirements via the list. We will also post ideas for writing, drafts for review, and other useful information at the Forum.

If you have a question about how to do an assignment or want help, post your question to the Forum, so everyone benefits from your question. If you are not sure about something, there will be other people in class with the same question.

The chat room is open in Sakai. Use it to consult with your peers as you work on assignments. Be careful what you post — everyone, including me, can see everything.

Please limit in-class communication to work related to this class. Limit your Web browsing, Facebooking, texting, tweeting, and phone use when we are in session. Mute the phone! Courtesy involves being attentive, limiting noncourse-related communication, and being an active listener.

GRADING

Specific points for assignments are below. In the Sakai gradebook, you will be able to see the overall total points and what you have so far, so you know where you stand.

Class participation, leadership, teamwork, and work habits all influence your grade. Talk in class about what you are learning. Help others be successful.

Grade Calculation

letter to professor	✓
profile draft	2
profile final	8
college finance draft	2
college finance final	8
reverse outline *Arak*	5
source analysis *Arak*	5
exploratory essay draft	5
exploratory essay final	5
annotated bibliography	10
research paper nutshell	5
research paper draft	5
research paper final	15
fixing your own problems	10
in-class essay exam	5
class participation	10
Total	100

A = 92–100
A– = 90–91
B+ = 88–89
B = 82–87
B– = 80–81
C+ = 78–79
C = 72–77
C– = 70–71
D = 60–69
F = 59 and below

CLASS PARTICIPATION GRADE

I'll assign up to 10 points for class participation. If you attend and participate regularly, you will do fine on this measure. Prepare for class. Come with questions. Engage with peers and be helpful to others in class. Have your drafts ready for review. Say something during class. Show some initiative. Pay attention.

ACADEMIC INTEGRITY/PLAGIARISM

Any work that you submit at any stage of the writing process—draft, thesis and outline, bibliography, final version—must be your own; in addition, any words, ideas, visuals, or data that you borrow from other people or places and include in your work must be properly documented. Failure to do either of these things is plagiarism. The University of Delaware protects the rights of all students by insisting that individual students act with integrity. Accordingly, the University severely penalizes plagiarism and other forms of academic dishonesty.

We will talk in class about how to document sources, including sound, video, artwork, Web sites, and printed material. If in doubt about how to credit your sources, ask in class.

Stephen A. Bernhardt, University of Delaware

TEAMWORK

It is important to learn to work with other people. Working together is a great way to learn together. We will practice peer review and sometimes collaborate on authoring texts. You will have one group through the semester, so there will be people you can rely on. You can help each other be successful if you take your group members seriously.

SUPPORT RESOURCES

Writing Center: The Writing Center provides free one-on-one instruction to students who have writing assignments in this or any course. You may make an appointment by visiting the Center's Web site: www.english.udel.edu/wc. If you work with a tutor, I get a note about what you worked on from the Writing Center. I interpret such work as showing commitment to the course and to improving your writing.

Disability accommodations: Students with disabilities should use the services the University provides: diagnosis, support, and special accommodation. See http://www.udel.edu/ADA/.

If you believe you have a disability, you should visit the ADA office. Let me know if you have a documented disability that affects your performance in this class, and we will find ways to work together, in confidence.

ASSIGNMENTS

This course is organized as a series of assignments with points attached to each.

All work should be well labeled: your name, the course, the date, with page numbers. Whenever you cite sources, you should consistently apply MLA, APA, *Chicago*, or CSE style. Choose the style appropriate to your major.

Typically, you will have a draft due on one date and a final version due later. A strong score on a draft does not necessarily mean a strong score on a final paper—you need to do a solid revision and improve on the final version to get a strong score. You will receive feedback on your drafts from me and through peer review.

Assignment	Due Date and Time	Points
Letter to Professor	Aug 30, 2013, 1:30 pm	✓
Diversity Profile Draft	Sep 6, 2013, 2:45 pm	2
Diversity Profile Final	Sep 11, 2013, 2:30 pm	8
College Finance Draft	Sep 19, 2013, 11:30 pm	2
College Finance Final	Sep 25, 2013, 2:30 pm	8
Arak Argument Structure	Oct 2, 2013, 2:30 pm	5
Arak Source Analysis	Oct 9, 2013, 1:30 pm	5
Exploratory Essay Draft	Oct 16, 2013, 1:30 pm	5
Exploratory Essay Final	Oct 21, 2013, 2:30 pm	5
Annotated Bibliography	Nov 1, 2013, 2:30 pm	10
Nutshell Your Argument	Nov 4, 2013, 1:30 pm	5
Draft Researched Argument	Nov 18, 2013, 2:30 pm	5
Fixing Your Own Problems	Nov 25, 2013, 1:30 pm	10
Final Research Paper	Nov 27, 2013, 2:30 pm	15
In-Class Essay Exam	Dec 2, 2013, 2:30 pm	5
Class Participation	Dec 4, 2013, 5:00 pm	10
Extra Credit	Nov 25, 2013, 5:00 pm	5

Stephen A. Bernhardt, University of Delaware

ASSIGNMENTS WITH DIRECTIONS

▶ Assignment 1: Letter to Professor

Complete the homework assignment on p. 23 of Ramage. Write a letter to me, introducing yourself as a reader and writer, highlighting your experiences and discussing a particular piece of writing you did that you are proud of.

I'll use this sample of your writing to get a sense of how you write, how you think about writing, and your ability to follow instructions. This won't be graded, but I'll check off whether or not you completed the assignment.

Read Ch. 1, pp. 1–23. Page through the rest of the book, looking for information you can use. Include a picture if you can, so I can start to associate names with faces.

✓ = you did what was expected
✓– = you need to do better
✓+ = you did better than I anticipated

▶ Assignment 2: Campus Diversity

For this assignment, we will take up the issue of campus diversity. What does it mean to have a diverse campus? Why should we care? What shapes our attitudes toward diversity? How do our experiences of diversity differ?

UD was recently criticized by the Middle States Accreditation report for being insufficiently diverse — too white, in other words, in terms of faculty, students, and staff. You can find a summary of the report in the list of links below. The University is responding with a number of new programs and putting more funding into diversity efforts.

Your task is to **profile an individual** who is quite different from you. You want to try to draw out the experience and perspective of someone at UD who is not like you. People can differ in many ways — race, obviously, but also in terms of citizenship, ability or disability, sexual orientation, social class, language group, political views, and so on.

How can you meet someone who is different than you? You might visit the diversity office on campus or a student group where individuals are obviously different — see the list on the President's Diversity Initiative site — there are many offices and student organizations that address diversity issues. Your roomie or a friend from your hometown is not a good subject for this paper. Part of the assignment is stepping out of your comfort zone to meet someone new and different. Take a risk.

Requirements

An effective profile will be lively and well written. It will make the subject come alive, providing sufficient background on that person as well as current information. It will use the language of the individual in direct quotation to explore attitudes and experiences. It might feature one or more pictures or some video footage. It might reflect your subject's identity or experience in some nonverbal way.

You can use yourself as a point of contrast — how you see and experience things in ways that are either similar to or different from your subject. Feel free to use first person to refer to yourself. Be sure to define diversity and what it means for UD.

Plan for 3 pages, single spaced with double spacing between paragraphs, generous margins, 10–12 point type. Sources are not required, but if you use any, follow either MLA, APA, CSE, or *Chicago* style for citation.

See Sakai for deadlines, team review schedules, posting guidelines, and due dates for both draft and final versions.

Writer's Help Tips

Some of the following search terms may point you to help for this assignment: *quotation, punctuation with quotations, first person, using visuals, citing sources, style, document design.*

Stephen A. Bernhardt, University of Delaware

Evaluation Criteria

- Good choice of subject to profile
- Lively, well-written profile that brings the subject to life
- Thoughtful definition of diversity and reflection on what it means at UD
- Good level of detail, quotes from subject, range of ideas
- Incorporation of picture, video file, or other media

Useful Links

Do some reading to familiarize yourself with what diversity means in the campus context. If you find some really good information, let the class know where it is.

President Harker's Initiative: http://www.udel.edu/diversity/
National Campus Diversity Project: http://gseacademic.harvard.edu/~ncdp/
Peter Schmidt. "Much Research on Campus Diversity Suffers from Being Only Skin Deep, New Studies
    Suggest." *Chronicle of Higher Education*, April 13, 2010. http://chronicle.com/article/Much
    -Research-on-Campus/65051/

Final Draft

Carefully consider feedback from your peers and instructors as you revise.

    Use the Add Attachments button in Sakai to submit. Include a cover note to me, identifying what you did well, what might need more work, and how you think you did on this assignment.

    Same criteria of evaluation as for your draft.

▶ Assignment 3: Financing College

For this assignment, we will work in pairs, writing an argumentative paper on student debt. Consider the difference between writing that is informative vs. argumentative. Your paper will be based on facts and present information, but it should have an argumentative edge. You should be taking a position, so be clear about your purpose. Your audience is other students like you — those in the first-year class at UD.

Requirements

Plan for 3–4 pages, single spaced with double spacing between paragraphs, generous margins, 10–12 point type, and at least two data displays (tables or charts). You will probably want to use headings to break up your major sections. You will need to cite a few sources, following MLA, APA, *Chicago*, or CSE style.

    See Sakai for deadlines. We will have team reviews of drafts before final papers are turned in.

Evaluation Criteria

- Paper presents a compelling argument based on a clearly stated thesis.
- Paper usefully introduces a few credible sources in support of positions.
- Paper follows documentation conventions for in-text and end-of-text citations.
- Paper includes two or three useful visuals (charts, tables) that help advance the argument.
- Paper meets format and length requirements.
- Paper is well written in terms of professional style and correctness.

Tips

Some of the following search terms may point you to help for this assignment: *evaluating sources, thesis statements, tentative thesis statements, using evidence, argument, using visuals, labeling visuals, headings, headers and footers, document design.*

Stephen A. Bernhardt, University of Delaware

Web Links for E110 Assignment: Student Debt

Here are a few good links to get you started. Do some reading and exploring of the topic to formulate your own thinking. You don't need to cite everything you read, just the sources you quote directly or indirectly. If a source shapes your thinking and your argument, you should cite it.

http://www.washingtonpost.com/national/higher-education/analysis-2-new-studies-on-college
-confirm-value-show-middle-class-carries-more-student-debt/2012/08/20/b73f55e2-eaf8-11e1-866f
-60a00f604425_story.html

http://projectonstudentdebt.org/

http://www.udel.edu/finaid/

http://www.nytimes.com/2011/11/03/education/average-student-loan-debt-grew-by-5-percent-in-2010
.html?adxnnl=1&adxnnlx=1345663657-cT5caVMEh+FVzseYbhcOgg

http://www.nytimes.com/2012/05/13/business/student-loans-weighing-down-a-generation-with-heavy
-debt.html?_r=1&pagewanted=all&gwh=1DFA8CEF6A3AB48AFB5B743234E52909

Final Draft

Carefully consider the feedback from your peers and instructors as you revise.

Use the Add Attachments button in Sakai to submit. Include a cover note to me, identifying what you did well, what might need more work, and how you think you did on this assignment.

Same criteria of evaluation as for your draft.

▶ Assignment 4: Fixing Your Own Problems

As a college writer, you need to understand your own strengths and weaknesses, so you can solve your own problems and get control of your writing. This assignment runs throughout the term. It has several parts. The goal is for you to document your own problems, figure out ways to fix your problems, and end the course ready to write in a variety of academic settings. You might be working to correct certain grammatical errors, to gain control over sentence structure, to improve your vocabulary, or to become a better editor. We'll concentrate in this assignment on small stuff—grammar, spelling, punctuation, sentence structure.

For this assignment, you need to document your problems and your actions to fix those problems. We'll call this your Learning List. You should begin by constructing a table of the kinds of things that give you trouble. Decide what is most important to work on. Provide examples from your own writing that you know are problems.

Then develop a plan to address your weaknesses. As you go along, document your progress, your new understanding, or your problems solved. On the due date at the end of the term, turn in a report that presents your independent work.

As you consider my marks on your papers and as you get feedback from peers, you will be identifying areas you need to work on, so pay attention to that feedback and use it to identify areas of improvement that are important to you. If I mark something in your paper and write "Learning List," that means you should work on solving the problem as part of this long-term assignment.

Let's say you don't really have a very good idea of what parallel structure is, so you set that as a learning goal. You then might use our books, do the exercises in *Writer's Help*, and go to the Writing Center to get help. You might go back to your own papers to see if you can improve the parallel structure. You would want to first define your learning goal, then your strategy for learning the skill, and then document your progress.

At another level, let's say you are totally confused about how to use a semicolon and how it is different from a colon. Set that as a goal—to learn this really well once and for all. Then figure out how. Would you do exercises? Would you read passages and look at examples in *Writer's Help*? Work with someone in class? Study style guides? Edit your own writing or that of others? Google it?

Stephen A. Bernhardt, University of Delaware

As a final example, let's say you are a double major in math and chemistry, and you know you need to be good at typing and editing formulas, but you don't have a lot of experience and nobody ever really taught you. How can you develop this skill? Are there Web materials, tutorials, or guides that you can use? Can you do what you want in Microsoft Word, or do you need some special formula editor? Does the Chem department offer any support? What's a good equation editor and can you learn to use it?

I'll assign points based on your final report, but also on my observations of how you manage this project during the term. I'll be fairly liberal, so if you approach this seriously, spread the work over the term, and help others do well on this assignment, you'll get the full points. If you don't define meaningful problems, don't post your work in the Forum, and do a last-minute job on the report, you won't get much credit.

Writer's Help Tips

As part of this assignment, use the exercises in *Writer's Help*. Assess which exercises are most valuable to you and whether they help you understand your own skills. I'll be able to see your exercise activity in *Writer's Help*.

▶ Assignment 5: *Arak* Argument Structure

You have a copy of the *Arak Anthology*, which contains award-winning student work from last year's classes. Choose one of the pieces and do an "after-the-fact" outline. How did this writer choose to structure his or her work? Show beginning, middle, and end, and describe what happens in each major section.

Show how paragraphs are working, either as independent units or as part of a series of related paragraphs. Does the writer use topic sentences to control the flow of ideas from paragraph to paragraph?

As you create the outline, consider some of the following:

- What is the structure of the argument?
- How is the argument signaled through organizing statements, thesis statements, topic sentences, or transitional devices?
- How are sources introduced, used, and documented? What kind of evidence is used to support the argument?
- Do you see places to improve on the author's work? What would you have done differently?

For this assignment, plan to turn in your outline, accompanied by your commentary on how the writer has managed the staging of the argument and supporting evidence. Include comments about what has been done particularly well or what could be improved.

You can think of yourself as making an argument about why this paper works well, why it has been judged to be excellent. Your outline will probably be about one page and your commentary about 2–3 pages.

Important chapters in Ramage for this assignment are Chs. 9 and 12. Use the terms, techniques, and reasoning in these chapters as you construct your analysis.

Writer's Help Tips

Some of the following search terms may point you to help for this assignment: *outlines, organization, prewriting, paragraph structure, evidence, transitions, topic sentences, introductions, conclusions.* Take another look at the discussions of how to construct and evaluate arguments.

This is a single-shot assignment, with no opportunity to revise.

Evaluation Criteria

- Provides a strong analysis of the argument in the *Arak* paper
- Uses the terms and methods of the Ramage text, especially Chs. 9 and 12, as well as advice in *Writer's Help*.

Stephen A. Bernhardt, University of Delaware

- Presented in a strongly designed paper
- Uses professional and correct writing

▶ Assignment 6: *Arak* Source Analysis

Working with one of the *Arak Anthology* pieces, track down at least two of the sources, investigating the source and how the author used the source to advance his or her argument. If you can, please choose at least one source that represents a study in an academic journal. Articles will work better than books for this assignment, though you could use one of each.

Check to see that the author used the source appropriately. If the source uses direct quotation, check to see that the exact wording and punctuation are correct. Check the in-text and end-of-text citation to see that it conforms to the conventions of a style guide (MLA, APA, *Chicago*, CSE).

Report on your investigation. Provide the citation, a brief summary in your own words of the content of the article, and a description of how the *Arak* author used the source. Judge whether the source was used in appropriate ways and whether all aspects of documentation were well done. Indicate whether the author was quoting, paraphrasing, or summarizing the source. Tell how you tracked down the source.

Important content to help you with this assignment can be found in Chs. 13 and 14 in Ramage. *Writer's Help* has everything you need to know on in-text and end-of-text citations in all relevant styles. Some of the following search terms may point you to help for this assignment: *citations, using sources, signal phrases, paraphrase, quoting sources.*

There is no required length. I could imagine you doing a good job in one page, if you arrange information well and design something that reports your results efficiently, but you will probably need two pages.

This assignment is worth 5 points. No revisions on this assignment, so do a good job the first time.

▶ Assignment 7: Exploratory Essay

Following suggestions in Ramage, pursue initial research toward your major research paper. Identify an important question you would like to pursue. Read an initial article and follow that with two or three more articles or a book to shape your thinking. Keep track as one question leads to a more refined question, or as one source leads to an even better source for developing your thinking and your arguments.

Write an exploratory essay, as defined on pp. 128–38 in Ramage. This essay is likely to be 2–4 pages (single spaced) and include 3 or more sources that have potential to inform your more formal research paper. This exploratory essay leads into your annotated bibliography, which in turn informs your more formal research paper. There is a good example of an exploratory essay on p. 144.

We'll review the exploratory essays on Wednesday, October 16 (so you need to have an e-copy or hard copy). You will then have the chance to revise and submit the essay during or soon after class on October 21, after we proofread.

Writer's Help Tips

Some of the following search terms may point you to help for this assignment: *evaluating sources, citing sources, analysis, tentative thesis statements, prewriting, finding sources.*

Evaluation Criteria

- Does the essay begin with (or lead to) a well-focused question or issue? Does the essay help identify and narrow the focus for a strong researched argument?
- Do you convey a clear narrative of your thinking and action as you explored the topic?
- Did you track down valuable, credible sources that are appropriate to an academic paper?
- Is each source well introduced through in-text citations and documented with end-of-text citations?
- Do you engage with the intellectual content or argument of each source? Are you able to use your skills of critical analysis?

Stephen A. Bernhardt, University of Delaware

Points = 5. The final draft is worth 5 additional points for a total of 10. That means you need to significantly develop your ideas between draft and final to gain additional points. See Sakai for deadlines.

▶ Assignment 8: Annotated Bibliography

Working with your tentative list of sources for your research paper, write an annotated bibliography, using annotations of 3–5 full sentences, packed with good information about the source. You might choose also to indicate how the source will be used in your research paper.

You can choose to follow MLA style, or another style (APA, *Chicago*, CSE) depending on your discipline and your learning goals. *Writer's Help* has up-to-date instructions on all styles. Indicate at the top of your work what style you are following.

Put a heading on your annotated bibliography. Include a title for your research paper and a brief description of your topic and argument. Then format the paper as an end-of-text reference list. Alphabetize the list by authors' last names and use a hanging indent for each entry. Use a block indent for the annotation under each citation.

For a discussion of annotated bibliographies, see Ch. 6 (pp. 139–42) in Ramage. For sample annotated bibliographies, search *Writer's Help* for *annotated bibliography*.

You need to read each article to the point where you understand the content, and then set the article aside and write a summary of the content. **Warning:** Do not copy and paste from a published abstract and then try to change the wording—that's one route to plagiarism.

Have your annotated bibliography completed by Oct. 28. We will review the citations and annotations for format. If you need time to revise following peer review, you can finish later that day.

This assignment is worth up to 10 points. There is no revision opportunity. A successful submission will include the following:

- An appropriate list of credible, well-chosen academic sources, both print and online. You may include other sources: interview or informant, expert opinion, primary sources, your own data.
- Well-written, informative annotations of 3–5 full sentences each, written in your own language, not copied from online source material.
- Perfect formatting, perfect punctuation, and complete citations.

▶ Assignment 9: Nutshell Your Argument

For this assignment, you will present a nutshell of your researched argument to the class. Use the Nutshelling document as a planning tool. These are the categories of information to organize your nutshell:

- Paper Title
- Purpose
- Audience
- Thesis Statement
- Main Lines of Argument
- Counterarguments to Be Addressed
- Types of Evidence to Be Used

Plan to give a 3-minute presentation, followed by a couple of questions from the audience.

Audience members should be prepared to ask questions, such as *What motivated you to pursue this topic?* or *What evidence would prove your thesis wrong?*

Stephen A. Bernhardt, University of Delaware

Writer's Help **Tips**

Some of the following search terms may point you to help for this assignment: *evidence, thesis statements, counterarguments, argument.*

We will get through as many presentations as we can on Friday, Nov. 1, and Monday, Nov. 4, and finish in subsequent sessions if we need more time.

Turn in your nutshell document following your presentation to the class.

▶ Assignment 10: Research Paper Drafts

This is the major paper for the course. You need to present a researched argument on a topic of your choosing. The argument should flow from your work on your exploratory paper and annotated bibliography.

The draft is not your final paper, but it should be relatively complete. If there are places where you know you need to do more work or add source material, you can indicate that in brackets. Include your bibliography, and format the draft as though it were the final (header/footer, pagination, title and date, and so on). Figure out what visuals you will be using, even if you have not incorporated them yet.

You are making an academic argument, and you are using sources to back up your position, provide authority, and increase the depth and complexity of your thinking. An argument makes a claim, stated in a thesis statement. It takes a stand on a debatable or complex issue.

You might argue for a solution to a problem or a response to a crisis or make a proposal for some action that should be taken. You might make a historical argument or a philosophical argument or an argument for a certain way of interpreting some event or text or object.

Requirements

- 5–10 pages, but no more than 10, including references
- Single-spaced, 12 pt font, with space breaks between paragraphs, ample margins, and headers or footers
- Conference with me during development or revision
- 8–10 sources, some print, some electronic, perhaps using informant interviews or collected data
- Thesis-driven argument—taking a position and using source-based evidence to build your case, attending to counterarguments or alternative views and voices
- Visuals: at least 2 tables, photos, graphs, drawings, or other visuals, appropriately labeled and sourced or created by you

Evaluation Criteria

- Strong thinking with a clear thesis and coherent argument
- Good evidence and support from credible academic sources
- Strong representation of the complexity of the issues
- Well organized from beginning to end, with a clear progression of argument
- Good design layout and use of visuals
- Well done in-text and end-of-text citations
- Strong and correct sentences, punctuation, and word usage

Draft Reviews: Everyone should get two reviews (in writing) from teammates and write two reviews. Post your drafts in the Forum. Attach written reviews with your final submission. Also submit an assessment of your own work—what is done well and what needs more work.

Completing reviews for your peers is part of your participation score. If you do an excellent job, I'll offer extra credit to the strongest, most helpful reviews.

You will document the reviews in your cover memo on the final paper.

Stephen A. Bernhardt, University of Delaware

Revised research paper: See Sakai for due dates. Attach your paper in the Assignment area of Sakai. Also attach the reviews you received from your teammates.

Write a cover memo detailing what you did well and where you need improvement. What is the strongest part of your work and what is the weakest? What help did you receive and how did you make this the best paper possible?

In-Class Essay Exam

For one of your other classes, predict 3 questions that might appear on an in-class essay exam as part of your final. Post those questions to the Forum before class on Nov. 29. Write questions that force you to synthesize lectures, readings, and class discussion. Try to find an issue that requires you to take a debatable position, rather than a question that simply forces you to regurgitate information. Write questions that would require approximately 2 typed pages of response. Figure about 400–500 words.

I will pick one of your three questions, and on Dec. 2 you will have the class period to write your essay in class. I may tweak your question or combine questions in some way. You can use your notes or your book or readings. You are expected to show command of the readings and to be able to cite information from class lectures.

The goal of this assignment is to help you review for exams, practice writing under timed conditions, become a better predictor of exam content, and get you a better grade! I also get to learn something about what you are studying, and I enjoy learning about your classes.

Your essay will be scored for a maximum of 5 points, based on the following criteria:

- Deep, rich content from the subject area that answers the question posed
- Strong use of material from lecture or readings with appropriate citation
- Tight organization and strong paragraphs
- Clear, well-constructed sentences

Stephen A. Bernhardt, University of Delaware

Assignment 1: Workshop on Revising Paragraphs

Time required: 20 to 50 minutes	Pre-workshop homework assignment: Have students bring their handbooks and a copy of their first essay to class.
Purpose: Teaching paragraph revision	

Workshop on Revising Paragraphs

As a class, begin by modeling the following steps with a sample paragraph (see handout). Then work individually, in pairs, or in small groups to complete the activity with your own paragraphs. You may want to refer to your handbook's advice on sentence structure, word choice, transitions, topic sentences, and paragraphing. If you are still lost, ask questions!

Activity

1. From your essay, choose a paragraph in need of significant revision, and explain why you think it needs to be revised.

2. Write down the first word or couple of words from each sentence in list form. If you find yourself writing the same words repeatedly, consider other ways you might begin your sentences to create variety. (Later, when you revise your entire essay, you can list the first word for each *paragraph* to check for variety.)

3. Now consider whether your sentences are varied in length. Do your paragraphs contain long sentences or short sentences, or a combination? Use a mix of long and short sentences within each paragraph to avoid monotony and choppiness. Can you combine any sentences? Should some longer sentences be broken into two or more shorter sentences?

4. Consider consistency and coherence. Look back at your thesis sentence and then reread the paragraph you are working on. Is the paragraph clearly related to your thesis? Does it effectively support your main idea? If not, talk with your partner about whether the paragraph is irrelevant and should be removed or whether it can be revised to clearly offer support.

5. In addition to supporting your thesis, each paragraph should focus on one main point. Identify the main ideas in the paragraph. Does the paragraph begin with one point or idea (usually expressed in a topic sentence) and then move on to a new one? If so, you should probably divide those ideas into separate paragraphs. If those new paragraphs are too short or choppy, you may want to add to them, keeping the focus on one main idea.

6. (If you created two paragraphs in step 5, choose only one for discussion in step 6.) Do the sentences in your paragraph proceed smoothly from one idea to the next? For example, if you begin the paragraph with a topic sentence, does your next sentence logically follow and build on that idea? If not, how might you reorganize the paragraph so that each sentence follows logically from the sentence before it?

Laura Detmering, Northern Kentucky University

Assignment 2: Textual Analysis

Time required: At least one week for students to complete a draft outside of class. Allow roughly two weeks for peer review, instructor comments, and revision.	**Purpose:** Teaching textual analysis and argument **Book in use:** *The Arlington Reader*, Second Edition (2008), by Lynn Z. Bloom and Louise Z. Smith

Due dates

Rough draft: Due by e-mail no later than by 5:00 p.m., September 16.
Final draft: Due in class (entire paper packet) on September 30.

Assignment overview

This assignment, an analysis of a text, involves writing similar to what scholars produce for book reviews in academic journals such as *Computers and Composition Online* or *Kairos*. Most published reviews are 1,000 words or less. The norm for publication is 500–800 words, and writing such a brief essay can be a challenge. Writers must decide which details are most important and which insights are pivotal. Luckily for you, this assignment gives you three to five pages to play with so that you have more room to discuss the article in detail. Here's how you start:

- Choose one of the articles below.
- In small groups, summarize key points of the article.
- Think about criteria.
  - Develop specific criteria and apply them to the text. We will brainstorm in class about different criteria and when they are most effectively used. The Source Evaluation Sheet exercise will help with analyzing article content.
- Write your draft. Get feedback. Draft again.
  - Your group's discussion and input will provide a strong foundation, but your essay will be just that—yours. The thesis, argumentative structure, and flow of ideas will be your own.
  - Submit your rough draft as an e-mail attachment. I will return your draft via e-mail with feedback in comment fields.

Articles available in your reader for the textual analysis

- "Notes of a Native Speaker" by Eric Liu; pp. 112–117
- "Blaming the Family for Economic Decline" by Stephanie Coontz; pp. 229–231
- "Every Dictator's Nightmare" by Wole Soyinka; pp. 476–479
- "Designer Genes" by Bill McKibbon; pp. 501–510
- "Life in the Lap of Luxury as Ecosystems Collapse" by William E. Rees; pp. 678–682

Elements of a textual analysis

Your textual analysis should be a fully developed argumentative essay (three pages is okay, but a thorough discussion will likely fill four or five pages) with a clear thesis, an introduction, several body paragraphs, and a conclusion. Before handing it in, check it for the following:

- **A clear introduction to the article:** Be sure that you clearly state the author's name and the article title within the first paragraph of your textual analysis.
- **A brief summary of the article:** Early in your textual analysis, you should include a very brief summary of the article and any background information that the reader might need to understand the topic. Don't assume that the only possible audience is your instructor or that she has already read the article. Your draft will also be read by your peers, who can give valuable feedback on clarity. In addition, your end-of-semester portfolio may be read and evaluated by an instructor who is unfamiliar with these articles. Keep the summary short without sacrificing clarity.

Lanette Cadle, Missouri State University

- **A discussion of the article's audience and purpose:** Whom is the author trying to reach? What information is the author trying to convey to those readers?
- **An evaluation based on relevant criteria:** You must present your own thesis (separate from the author's thesis) regarding the success of the article. Clearly state your overall judgment of the article's effectiveness and note the specific criteria that you have used in making that judgment (for example, validity, quality of research, and attention to important counterarguments).

  To be sure that your criteria are relevant, keep in mind the author's purpose; different audiences have different expectations. For example, it would be unfair to fault the author for using too many technical terms if specialists in the field or even undergraduates in that major are the intended audience. In a case like that, it would be better to simply make a point about the article's value as a research source for undergraduates without relevant scholarly background. You could note that the article uses jargon or assumes background knowledge and recommend that the undergraduate researcher keep a dictionary handy.
- **References and details to support the evaluation:** Assume that your readers do not have the article in front of them or that they have not read it. You need to provide them with specific evidence (in the form of several quotations or paraphrases) to support your conclusions. You also need to explain specifically how this evidence supports your judgment; do not assume that the connection is clear.

  When you quote or paraphrase from the text, include page numbers in parentheses. See your handbook for models.
- **Conclusion:** Offer a fully developed claim about the overall validity of the article. You may remind readers of both good and bad points of the writing. It may be useful to discuss your views concerning the effectiveness of this source for different audiences.

Please feel free to ask me for help, either during office hours (4:30–5:30 Wednesday, before class) or by appointment. I can also answer questions by e-mail. Good luck!

Lanette Cadle, Missouri State University

Assignment 3: Defining and Addressing Plagiarism

Time required: One session of 15 minutes or more for discussion of the assignment. One week is recommended for writing time outside of class. **Purpose:** Teaching the meaning of plagiarism and how to avoid it	**Resource:** This assignment assumes that students are enrolled in CompClass. The assignment can be revised to work without CompClass.

Guidelines

Your goal is to write an in-depth discussion of plagiarism in roughly 1,200 words. The key to writing this paper successfully is to choose a focus and support it with evidence. Once you have chosen your focus and done some preliminary research, create an outline. Organize your thoughts as specifically and as logically as possible.

Be sure to define terms that can have multiple or ambiguous meanings so that your reader knows what you mean. Don't assume that your reader agrees with you. As the writer, you guide the reader into a new way of thinking: your own. Be sure you don't lose the reader on the journey!

Finally, remember that a tight thesis will drive your paper (and will make it much easier to write!).

Prompts

The prompts that follow can help you brainstorm. As you think through them, choose just one direction that interests you and will allow you to write a tightly focused essay.

What does plagiarism mean?

- Think back to the first time you heard the word *plagiarism* or participated in a discussion about it. What was the context? What was the message?
- Who owns *your* ideas? What if they've been influenced by outside sources — your parents, school, church, the media?
- How well do you know how to avoid plagiarism? What are your strategies?
- What definitions of plagiarism can you find by doing a Web search? Try the same search in CompClass. What do you discover?
- If you incorporate ideas into your writing after a teacher/tutor conference or peer review, are you plagiarizing?
- A writer's understanding of plagiarism and intellectual property may be culturally defined. In some non-Western cultures, for example, writers might weave the words of others into their own without citation as a gesture of respect and with the understanding that readers recognize the source. Should accommodations be made in American universities for students from such cultures?
- Legal writing and other professional writing often depends on templates and boilerplates. Is this kind of writing plagiarism?
- Remaking movies and songs and repurposing of TV clips are common. Under what circumstances might such activities be considered plagiarism?
- Is there a difference between, say, forgetting to cite something (or not knowing how) and using another person's ideas wholesale without credit? Are both acts plagiarism?
- When people buy things, they assume ownership. When students purchase essays online, do they own those ideas? Should they be able to turn in purchased essays as their own work?

How should we deal with plagiarism?

- What do we call people who have been accused of plagiarism? What do these labels reveal about how we view these people?

Jill Dahlman, University of Hawaii at Manoa

- Punishments for academic plagiarism vary widely; look at a sampling of college handbooks (many are online). Should plagiarism punishments be standardized?
- If a first-year student has no prior knowledge of plagiarism, no knowledge of how or why to cite sources, how should the university deal with that person as a writer? Should there be some sort of entry test? A mandatory tutorial? Or a learn-as-you-go policy?

Jill Dahlman, University of Hawaii at Manoa

Assignment 4: Mechanics Workshop: Use of the Comma, Run-on Sentences, Pronoun-Antecedent Agreement, Pronoun Reference

Time required: One session of at least 50 minutes Purpose: Teaching comma usage, run-on sentences, pronoun-antecedent agreement, pronoun reference	Book in use: This assignment has been planned with *The Bedford Handbook*, Ninth Edition. It can easily be revised to work with *Rules for Writers* or *A Writer's Reference with Exercises*. Hacker handbooks without built-in exercises can draw on PDF exercises on their book's companion site. Preparation: Groups will need to be prepared to share their exercise answers with the class. They can provide handouts or project their work.

Instructions

Using *The Bedford Handbook* (*BH*) as a reference, each group should prepare a ten-minute presentation on the major rules and key terms governing one of the grammatical discussions below. Group members should complete the exercise associated with their topic ahead of time and share their corrections with the class, explaining the reason for each correction or why an already correct item needs no change.

- Each member of the group should take part in the group presentation.
- In addition to preparing their group presentations, students should complete each of the following exercises on their own. Students should raise questions about any exercise items they do not understand during the group presentation on that exercise.

Group 1: Major Uses of the Comma, *BH*, Section 32, Exercise 32–1
Group 2: Unnecessary Commas, *BH*, Section 33, Exercise 33–1
Group 3: Run-on Sentences, *BH*, Section 20, Exercise 20–2
Group 4: Pronoun-Antecedent Agreement, *BH*, Section 22, Exercise 22–1
Group 5: Pronoun Reference, *BH*, Section 23, Exercise 23–1

Bobbie Kilbane, Volunteer State University

Assignment 5: Visual Literacy and Analysis

Time required: Two sessions of at least 50 minutes for prewriting and peer review. Time for writing outside of class.	Preparation: Students should bring a draft and their handbooks for the peer review workshop.
Purpose: Teaching visual analysis	

Task overview

Drawing from the ideas generated in our class discussion, write a two-page essay that analyzes the visual text shared in class. Avoid simply describing the image. Instead, assert a position on the meaning of the image, and show your readers how the elements in the image contribute to the overall meaning of the text.

Purpose of the assignment

- To practice rhetorical analysis through writing about a visual image
- To enhance visual literacy skills
- To practice essay-writing skills

Assignment steps and due dates

1. Prewriting/idea generation: Complete in class on _____.

2. Preliminary draft for peer review workshop: DUE at the beginning of class on _____.

3. Revised drafts: Once you have received feedback from the peer review workshop, revise your draft at least once before you turn it in. I recommend that you complete at least three drafts, taking your second draft to the writing center/lab for additional feedback.

4. **Final draft: DUE on _____.**

Essay guidelines

1. **Introductory paragraph:** Your introduction should (1) engage the reader, (2) provide appropriate background information about the visual text (a brief description), and (3) assert your thesis. In this case, your thesis will be your assertion of what the intended meaning of the image is: What is the image trying to "say" to its audience?

2. **Body paragraphs (at least 3):** Each body paragraph should include a topic sentence that clearly supports the thesis. Each paragraph should (1) identify an element of the visual text that contributes to its overall meaning, (2) briefly describe the element to establish a context for your readers, and (3) explain HOW the element conveys or contributes to the central meaning of the visual text. **Answering the "HOW" part is crucial to your analysis. It is not enough to just identify the characteristics; you must also discuss how these characteristics create meaning or make a statement.**

3. **Concluding paragraph:** The concluding paragraph should (1) evaluate the effectiveness of the visual image and (2) lead the reader out of the essay.

Formatting instructions

Use MLA style for formatting your paper and citing your source (in a works cited page).

Elizabeth Canfield, Virginia Commonwealth University

Assessment guidelines

Successful papers will display the following characteristics:

- A thesis that clearly and fluidly asserts the meaning of the visual text
- Developed body paragraphs that identify, explain, and analyze the elements of the image that contribute to the visual text's overall meaning
- Organization that supports the thesis and helps readers follow your discussion
- Clear, error-free sentences in academic English
- Accurate page formatting and citations in MLA style

Extra help

If you have any specific questions about your draft, stop by my office during office hours or visit the writing center.

Elizabeth Canfield, Virginia Commonwealth University

Assignment 6: Essay 4: Writing in Your Discipline

Time required: Time for writing outside of class. One session of 30 to 50 minutes for group workshops.

Purpose: Teaching writing in the disciplines

Book in use: This assignment works best when students are using *A Writer's Reference with Writing in the Disciplines* or *Writing in the Disciplines: Advice and Models*, a Hacker Handbooks Supplement.

Preparation: Students should bring their Hacker handbook to each class session.

Discipline-specific content: 250 words

Discipline discourse analysis: 500 words

Outline due _____ for group workshops

Rough draft of 500 words for conferences due by beginning of class on _____

Assignment overview

As I stated on the first day of class, ENGL 1101 is not just an English course. It is a writing course administered by specialists in the English department. ENGL 1101 and 1102 are required in part because they prepare you to write for courses in your major. We establish principles such as assignment analysis, coherence, structure, development, and critical thinking. Once you can demonstrate proficiency in these areas, you should be able to transfer those skills to writing assignments in your history, science, philosophy, business, education, and other courses.

This assignment, Essay 4, asks you to create *discipline-specific content* (DSC)—in other words, a short piece of writing in your discipline. Find your major on the following list and see the type of assignment you should produce for the DSC. If your major is not represented on the list, or you have not declared a major, please e-mail me right away! (Note: If you choose an assignment that is NOT associated with any major in the following list, please contact me for approval of your assignment topic.)

DSC assignments by major

1. Business (includes Management, Finance, Marketing)
   You are managing a project for a major insurance company. Insurance premiums are going up across the board at the start of the next calendar year, and you oversee a group of insurance agents who must be informed of the new premiums for different policies. Generally speaking, the major medical policies will increase an average of 25 percent; the dental policies will increase an average of 15 percent; and the eye-care policies will increase an average of 30 percent. Patients covered by policies affected by these premium increases may alter their coverage (number of dependents registered under an account, type of policy, breadth of coverage) during the next open enrollment period, depending on whether they have private coverage or are enrolled under a group plan. Write a memo to the insurance agents you oversee to (a) inform them of the premium increase and (b) explain their role as insurance agents during this transition to higher premiums. Refer to your Hacker handbook for tips on writing well for a business audience.

2. Education (includes Exercise Science, Early Childhood)
   During your time at this university, you will be required to design curricula (plural of *curriculum*) for classes you might teach. Your assignment is to create a lesson plan around the theme of sharing. The concept of sharing is often emphasized as we prepare K–12 students to become part of a larger community. How will your role as a physical education teacher (Exercise Science majors) or an elementary school teacher (Early Childhood majors) dictate how you should teach your students about sharing? Be creative, and refer to your Hacker handbook for the components involved in writing a lesson plan for an audience of educators.

Molly Wright, Columbus State University

3. Art (includes Art History and other related fields)

   Whether you are an artist who creates or an art historian, you need a critical framework, a set of ideas about what art is and what makes good art. This critical framework helps you appreciate art on a higher level, and the framework also helps you explain art to others. The best way to develop a critical framework is by learning about various critical theories and practicing your skills by criticizing art. Your assignment is to choose a piece of artwork and critique it. (Provide either a picture of the artwork in the text or a URL where I can look at it online.) Begin by explaining in general terms your framework; feel free to refer to an existing critical school. Then analyze the artwork using that framework, making sure to provide detailed evidence from the work itself. I have made a photocopy from a guide to writing about art that you will receive in class.

4. Sciences (includes Biology, Chemistry, Communication, Pre-Engineering, Nursing, Psychology, Sociology, Computer Science)

   When taking science courses related to your major, you will have to know how to write a literature review. These short assignments, which consider and evaluate the findings of a number of research papers, allow students to show that they comprehend the prevailing research. Review an article that I have given you (you will receive it in class unless you request an electronic copy in advance), OR choose an article of your own with my approval. Use the description set forth in your Hacker handbook to guide you as you compose your review.

5. Theater (includes Theater Education)

   When exploring the world of theater, you will need to know how to critically assess a performance of a play. Write a review of the film *A Midsummer Night's Dream* (DVD number 3 in the library), analyzing how well the play has been adapted to the screen and discussing the acting, scenery, cinematography, and so on. For a model, see Roger Ebert's review of the film (http://rogerebert .suntimes.com/apps/pbcs.dll/article?AID=/19990514/REVIEWS/905140304/1023).

Discipline discourse analysis

After composing the discipline-specific content of 250 words, write a 500-word analysis of the discussion (or discourse) going on in your field.

Address the following questions:
- What are people writing about in your discipline, and how are they writing about it?
- What are the most common genres of writing in your field (for example, research articles, case studies, lab reports, reviews of literature, critical analyses)?
- How is ENGL 1101 preparing you to write in your discipline?
- What aspects of your writing process should you focus on now, while you are learning the basics, so that you can best prepare yourself for your major courses?

You will be graded on the following:

1. Fulfilling the prompt. (If you need clarification of these instructions, e-mail me or come talk to me about a draft.)

2. A coherent and well-placed thesis/main idea.

3. Using sound, well-developed evidence.

4. Other items as listed on the First-Year Composition rubric.

If you have any questions regarding this assignment, let me know by e-mail or in class.

Molly Wright, Columbus State University

Assignment 7: Rhetorical Analysis

Time required: At least two weeks for students to prewrite, draft, and receive feedback. Allow one week for revision.

Purpose: Teaching rhetorical analysis

Books in use: Hacker/Bernhardt/Sommers, *Writer's Help* (writershelp.com)

Purpose

Thus far you have written a draft of a "This I Believe" narrative in which you practiced some techniques of autobiographical writing and a résumé and cover letter in which you practiced a form of writing with specific generic requirements. For our third assignment, you will be returning to the narrative form but from an analytic stance. More particularly, you will be examining the construction and techniques of "This I Believe" essays to analyze how the authors employ certain generic features (tone, word choice, evidence) to create, fulfill, and/or challenge audience expectations. Being able to reverse engineer and discuss the structure of a text is important in itself, but this analysis will also give you valuable insight and techniques as we move into our next assignment.

Summary

You will write a rhetorical <u>analysis</u> comparing two of the essays assigned for weeks 4 and 5. Your 4-to-5-page analysis will examine the ways in which the respective authors use specific persuasive strategies to speak to an audience; you will use <u>close reading</u> of the texts and evidence in the form of <u>quotes</u> to support your reading.

Underlined terms are links to relevant pages in Writer's Help.

Process

Prewriting

1. **Close reading and annotations:** As you read through the essays from *This I Believe II* and *Y1 Writes*, note essays that you found to be particularly effective. Review the <u>Guidelines for active reading</u> in *Writer's Help*. With those strategies in mind, reread two or three of those essays and highlight or underline sentences, words, or passages that you thought were particularly effective.

2. **Notes:** Review the <u>Guidelines for analyzing a written text</u> in *Writer's Help*, and for each text, jot down answers to the questions.

3. **Working outline:** Review <u>Outlining a written or a visual text</u> in *Writer's Help* and create a working outline for your rhetorical analysis, remembering that your thesis will focus not on *what* the essays say but on *how* and *why* they say it in that particular way.

Keep these prewriting documents for possible use in your electronic portfolio.

For more help with prewriting, you can also search *Writer's Help* for some of the following terms: *prewriting, reading, analysis, outline, rhetorical strategies.*

Drafting

Review your notes and outline and draft your rhetorical analysis. Your paper should focus on rhetorical strategies and should use evidence from the texts in the form of quotes to support your claims. Your paper may be organized by essay (for example, *essay 1 uses the following strategies in these ways; essay 2 uses different strategies to accomplish similar goals*) or by strategy (for example, *both essays use <u>metaphor</u> and <u>emotionally charged language [pathos]</u> to appeal to audience sympathy*).

For more help with drafting, you can also search *Writer's Help* for some of the following terms: *drafting, claims, analysis.*

Due Date

September 23, 2013. The revision will be due Monday, September 30.

Eric Hoffman, Northern Illinois University

Rubric 1: Textual Analysis Assignment (with references to the course handbook)

The codes in parentheses refer to sections in *A Writer's Reference*, Seventh Edition.

CRITERIA	Exemplary 15–20 pts.	Effective 10–14 pts.	Developing 5–9 pts.	Needs work 0–4 pts.
Summary	• Highlights the main argument, important claims, and relevant context (**A1-e**) • Is concise yet comprehensive (**A1-c**) • Can be understood easily by someone who has not read the original article	• Summary highlights the main argument, important claims, and context information	• Gives basic background information about the article, but is missing information essential to a reader who has not read the article	• Leaves the reader wondering which article is discussed and what its argument is
Evaluation	• Presents a clear, debatable thesis (**C1-c, C2-a**) • States overall judgment as well as specific evaluation criteria • Demonstrates fairness and an open mind (**A2-g**)	• Includes a thesis and evaluation criteria • Shows a good-faith effort to be fair and open-minded	• Includes some evaluation of the article but thesis could use refinement • Missing important elements such as the evaluation criteria or a fair consideration of the article	• Does not express an identifiable position or judgment about the article
Audience and purpose	• Reflects thoughtfully on the specific purpose and audience of the original article (**R2-c**)	• Speaks to both the purpose and the audience in general terms	• Includes some information about either the article's purpose or its audience, but remains vague	• Does not consider the intended audience or purpose of the article

Jennifer Lin O'Brien, Washington State University

CRITERIA	Exemplary 15–20 pts.	Effective 10–14 pts.	Developing 5–9 pts.	Needs work 0–4 pts.
Support	• Uses specific evidence from the article—both quotations and paraphrases—to support the thesis (**R3-c, MLA-2**) • Always makes clear connections between the evidence and evaluation (**A2-e**) • Cites all sources correctly in MLA style (**MLA-4**)	• Uses some evidence from the article for support • Makes connections between the evidence and evaluation • Cites most sources correctly in MLA style	• Uses limited evidence from the article • Does not always connect evidence to the conclusions • Cites some sources correctly in MLA style	• Uses no specific evidence from the original article • Does not cite sources
Organization	• Introduction states the author's name, article title, and thesis (**C2-a**) • Each paragraph develops one main idea (**C4-a, C4-b**) • Transitions between paragraphs and ideas aid understanding (**C4-d**) • Conclusion comments on the article's overall effectiveness (**C2-c**)	• Includes a clear introduction with a thesis, body paragraphs that each develop an idea, and a conclusion • Includes some smooth transitions between paragraphs and ideas	• Includes an introduction, body paragraphs, and a conclusion • Paragraph organization is not always easy to follow • May be missing important elements of the introduction or conclusion	• Includes no identifiable introduction or conclusion • The organization of the paragraphs causes significant confusion

Bonus points/deductions for sentence-level concerns:

+5 points   Document demonstrates outstanding proofreading and editing

–5 points   Document has numerous and/or significant errors

–10 points   Errors in the document severely impede meaning

Jennifer Lin O'Brien, Washington State University

Rubric 2: Visual Analysis Assignment

CRITERIA	Mastering	Developing	Emerging
Analysis	• Provides key background information about the visual text that the reader will need to follow the analysis • Asserts the meaning of the text clearly and strongly with a thesis statement • Offers a thoughtful and detailed analysis of how the visual elements of the text create meaning • Expertly applies the concepts of audience, purpose, and visual rhetoric covered in class to the analysis	• Provides some background information • Includes an identifiable thesis statement • Offers some analysis of how the visual elements of the text create meaning • Shows some understanding of concepts such as audience, purpose, and visual rhetoric that were covered in class	• Provides little or no background information about the text • Includes no thesis statement or one whose connection to the visual text is unclear • Offers little to no analysis of how the visual elements of the text create meaning • Shows little understanding of concepts such as audience, purpose, and visual rhetoric
Organization and support	• Includes a strong introduction and conclusion • Uses each body paragraph to focus on one element of the visual text • Uses specific evidence to analyze how the element contributes to the central meaning of the text • Uses transitions to help readers follow the discussion	• Includes an introduction, conclusion, and a main idea for each body paragraph • Includes some evidence that provides support for the thesis • Uses some transitions to move readers through the discussion	• Missing important organizational elements such as an introduction, conclusion, transitions, or a main idea for each body paragraph • Includes little or no evidence that provides support for the thesis
Revision	• Includes evidence of significant revision following peer review	• Includes some evidence of revision following peer review	• Includes little to no evidence of revision following peer review

Elizabeth Canfield, Virginia Commonwealth University

CRITERIA	Mastering	Developing	Emerging
Format and citation	• Uses MLA style consistently and accurately throughout for page format and citation	• Uses MLA style for page formatting and citation, with some inaccuracies or inconsistencies	• Does not use MLA style for page format or citation
Editing	• Demonstrates outstanding evidence of proofreading and editing	• Includes some sentence-level errors	• Includes sentence-level errors that are significant, numerous, and/or impede meaning

Elizabeth Canfield, Virginia Commonwealth University

Rubric 3: Multimodal Composition Assignment

This rubric is a tool for evaluating the final version of your multimodal composition. The criteria in each of the categories—purpose, focus and information, textual elements, integration, arrangement, and polish—let you know what I'll be looking for as I grade your work. The rubric allows me to mark your final product on a scale from "developing" to "mastering" under each criteria category. Your score on the scale will let you know which areas you are excelling in or mastering and in which areas you are still developing and can use improvement. While planning, creating, and revising your project, use this rubric as a checklist to determine if your work is meeting the goals of the assignment.

PURPOSE

- There is a clear purpose to the composition. It is obvious what the composition is meant to do (teach, persuade, warn, or entertain, for example).
- The thesis or central idea is easy to identify and relevant to the intended audience.

5	4	3	2	1
Mastering		Proficient		Developing

FOCUS AND INFORMATION

- The topic selected is interesting and focused.
- The composition provides conclusions supported by the introduction and body of the project.
- The examples and evidence are credible, reliable, and timely.

5	4	3	2	1
Mastering		Proficient		Developing

TEXTUAL ELEMENTS

- Textual elements—examples, descriptions, explanations, quotations—are appropriate for the text's intended purpose, audience, and genre.
- The modes of the textual elements—words, static images, audio, video—are appropriate for the text's intended purpose, audience, and genre.
- Each element contributes to the text's purpose.
- The quality of video, audio, and photographic content meets audience expectations for the genre.

5	4	3	2	1
Mastering		Proficient		Developing

INTEGRATION

- The modes used in the composition work well together to serve the composer's purpose and to address the composer's intended audience.
- Design elements connect related information.
- When appropriate, captions, transcriptions, and descriptions guide audience understanding.

5	4	3	2	1
Mastering		Proficient		Developing

Dànielle Nicole DeVoss, Michigan State University

ARRANGEMENT

- Design elements organize the textual element and are consistent with genre expectations.
- The composer uses transitional devices to effectively guide the audience between and across ideas.
- The composition includes a starting point that serves to establish a context for the audience and to introduce the audience to the purpose and focus of the composition.
- The composer uses graphic elements consistently and appropriately.
- Design elements provide emphasis and establish a hierarchy of information.

POLISH

- The composition is relatively free of grammatical, technical, typographic, and spelling errors.
- The technical craft is excellent and detail-oriented.
- Sources are cited consistently and in a way that is fitting for the modes and genre of the text.

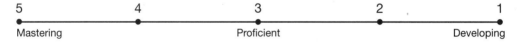

Dànielle Nicole DeVoss, Michigan State University

Rubric 4: Literary Analysis Assignment

The codes in parentheses refer to sections in *Rules for Writers*, Seventh Edition.

CRITERIA	Mastering	Meeting	Developing	Beginning	Missing
FOCUS, UNITY, & ORGANIZATION					
Addresses the specific requirements of the assignment (**1a**)					
Provides a developed introduction with thesis (**2a**)					
Paragraphs focused on a main point (**4a**)					
Organizes paragraphs logically, using transitions within and between paragraphs (**4c, 6c**)					
Reaffirms and extends the thesis in the conclusion (**See example in 5e**)					
DEVELOPMENT OF CONTENT					
Analysis					
Uses relevant literary terminology correctly					
Focuses on analysis, using summary only as needed (**5c, 5d**)					
Includes specific details and examples from the text, quoted or paraphrased as appropriate (**6e**)					
Interpretation					
Demonstrates accurate comprehension of the text as well an understanding of historical and cultural contexts					
Includes textual evidence relevant to the topic (**6d**)					
Integrates discussion of form and content, techniques and themes					
Includes writer's own insights beyond what was said in class					

Anne Ramirez, Neumann University

CRITERIA	Mastering	Meeting	Developing	Beginning	Missing
SENTENCE SKILLS					
Employs varied and sophisticated sentence structure (**15a–15c**)					
Maintains an appropriate and consistent level of formality (**17d**)					
Uses standard grammar, spelling, and punctuation (**19–27, 32–39**)					
Uses precise and appropriate vocabulary (**18a–18e**)					
RESEARCH SKILLS (if required)					
Selects appropriate academic sources (**54c**)					
Avoids citing or copying common knowledge (**57a**)					
Demonstrates a clear understanding of source material; competently integrates material into essay (**58a–58c**)					
Balances use of sources and own thoughts					
Follows MLA format correctly (**59–60**)					
Includes all cited sources in works cited list and all listed sources in parenthetical citations (**See example on p. 532**)					

Anne Ramirez, Neumann University

Rubric 5: Analysis and Synthesis Essay Assignment

CONTENT (Total possible points = 72)

Content develops and enhances thinking in the following categories:

Your finished essay presents a clearly identifiable thesis that addresses the assignment prompt in a significant and relevant manner.

4   3   2   1   0   (x3)

Your summary of each assigned reading is accurate, fair, succinct, and clear for an audience unfamiliar with the work.

4   3   2   1   0   (x3)

Analytical section of your essay clearly compares and contrasts in a comprehensive manner each author's rhetorical strategies including target audience, purpose, values, assumptions, angle of vision, and claims.

4   3   2   1   0   (x3)

Appropriate and accurate textual evidence is presented to support claims about each author's rhetorical strategies.

4   3   2   1   0   (x3)

Synthesis section of your essay demonstrates your thoughtful, independent interaction with and thinking about the assigned articles.

4   3   2   1   0   (x3)

Conclusion reiterates the values and limitations of the analyzed essays, pulls together your new insights, and leaves readers thinking about your views.

4   3   2   1   0   (x3)

DOCUMENTATION (Total possible points = 16)

Complete and correct MLA works cited page is included.

4   3   2   1   0   (x2)

Paraphrases, summaries, and direct quotations are presented with appropriate signal phrases and complete reference information throughout the essay.

4   3   2   1   0   (x2)

Deirdre Mahoney, Northwestern Michigan College

STYLE AND USAGE (Total possible points = 12)

Readability is enhanced in the following categories:

Sentence structure is clear, fluid, and effectively engages the reader. Your sentences are clear, concise, coherent, and complete. Sentence fragments, comma splices, run-on sentences, and mixed constructions are rare.

4   3   2   1   0

Your word choice and vocabulary develop the reader's thinking and communicate ideas clearly.

4   3   2   1   0

Your essay follows academic conventions for grammar, mechanics, and usage. These include proper capitalization, punctuation, spelling, subject/verb agreement, verb forms/tense, and pronoun/antecedent agreement.

4   3   2   1   0

Subtotal _____

FORMATTING

Points deducted from subtotal above for any lack of the following:

Required formatting is presented: This includes standard margins; appropriate font; double-spacing; descriptive title; name, date, assignment # in right-hand corner of first page; staple top left; page numbers centered on bottom of pages (beginning after page 1).

_____ Yes   _____ No

Word count is met and documented: 1,800 words minimum.

_____ Yes   _____ No

Required rough draft material is included.

_____ Yes   _____ No

Total _____

Instructor's additional comments:

Essay Grade _____

Deirdre Mahoney, Northwestern Michigan College

Rubric 6: Research Paper Assignment

CRITERIA	Superior	Strong	Satisfactory	Unsatisfactory
1. Clear Thesis	Thesis and purpose are clear to the reader and respond to the writing task.	Thesis and purpose are fairly clear and respond to the writing task.	Thesis and purpose are vague OR only loosely related to the writing task.	Reader cannot determine thesis and purpose OR thesis has no relation to the writing task.
2. Original Thesis	Thesis offers a fresh insight that challenges the reader's thinking.	Thesis shows some original thinking.	Thesis may be obvious or unimaginative.	Thesis is missing.
3. Audience Awareness	Stance is that of an expert who consistently and skillfully anticipates reader's needs; writing is rhetorically sophisticated.	Stance is somewhat tentative; the writing meets reader's needs with some skill.	Stance is that of a novice attempting to please an expert.	Little or no awareness of audience or of the assignment's requirements.
4. Organization	Clear logic used to support the thesis and fulfill the purpose; sequence of ideas is effective; transitions add coherence.	Logic is evident; transitions are mostly appropriate; sequence of ideas could be improved.	Some signs of logical organization; some abrupt or illogical shifts; ineffective flow of ideas.	Unclear organization OR organizational plan is inappropriate to thesis; no transitions.
5. Support/ Evidence	Substantial and concrete development of ideas; assumptions are made explicit; evidence is relevant and convincingly interpreted.	Assumptions are usually made explicit; contains some appropriate details or examples.	Offers some obvious support that may be too broad; details are too general or not interpreted; offers solid reasoning, but not original.	Offers simplistic or undeveloped support for the ideas; off-topic generalizations, faulty assumptions, or errors of fact.

Jennifer Lin O'Brien, Washington State University

CRITERIA	Superior	Strong	Satisfactory	Unsatisfactory
6. Use of Sources/ Documentation	Uses sources to support, extend, and inform, but not substitute for writer's own development of ideas; combines material from a variety of sources; doesn't overuse quotations.	Uses sources to support, extend, and inform, but not substitute for writer's own development of ideas; doesn't overuse quotations, but may not always conform to required style manual.	Uses relevant sources but lacks in variety of sources or the skillful combination of sources; quotations and paraphrases may be too long or inconsistently referenced.	Neglects important sources; overuse of quotations or paraphrase to substitute writer's own ideas; possibly uses source material without acknowledgment.
7. Style: Sentences, Diction, and Tone	Sentences are varied and complex; diction is precise, appropriate, and sophisticated; tone is suitable for the audience.	Sentences show some variety and complexity; uneven control; diction is generally appropriate, yet less advanced; tone is usually appropriate.	Sentences are simplistic and show little variety; diction is somewhat immature; relies on clichés; tone is inconsistent.	Superficial and simplistic language; oral rather than written language patterns predominate; tone is inappropriate.
8. Writing Conventions: Grammar, Spelling, Usage, and Punctuation	Error-free; evidence of superior word usage.	Mechanical and usage errors that do not interfere with meaning.	Repeated weaknesses in mechanics and usage; pattern of flaws or wrong words.	Mechanical and usage errors so severe that writer's ideas are hidden.
9. Presentation	Essay looks neat, crisp, and professional.	Essay looks neat but violates one or two formatting rules (type size, font, margins, spacing).	Essay looks untidy and violates two or more formatting rules.	Essay looks untidy and does not follow any basic formatting rules.

Jennifer Lin O'Brien, Washington State University

Index